# WHERE HAVE ALL THE COWBOYS GONE!

CAROLYN MCGIVERN

Reel Publishing

35 Anders Corner
Bracknell
Berkshire
RG42 1PU
England


123456789


Copyright © McGivern 2006


ISBN 0-9540031-2-8

Cover Design: Scott Wilson © 2006

To all the family and friends who have been patient through difficult times ...

... and you know who you are.

*Author McGivern at Lone Ranger Rock, Chatsworth, California.*

In Chatsworth, California, near Iverson's Ranch, a craggy rock formation looks oddly familiar. American kids who grew up in the 1950's and 60's would immediately recognize that this is Lone Ranger Rock. They watched Silver rear up before it in the title sequence of every episode of *The Lone Ranger.* Today the formation still stands, straight, tall, imposing, but things have changed and kids have changed. The rock is now surrounded by modern buildings and new roads, and children are less quick to worship heroes, less ready to accept absolute good, absolute bad.

# CONTENTS

# FOREWORD

## by Michael Coyne

Author of
*The Crowded Prairie: American National Identity in the Hollywood Western*
(I. B. Tauris, 1997)

**OVER** 1958–9, eight of the top ten shows on American television were Westerns. Film was the great art form of the 20th century, America the supreme purveyor of celluloid dreams, and the Western was the most uniquely, classically, indigenously American genre of them all. The fact that the Western had come to dominate prime-time TV schedules by the late 1950's illustrated the breadth and depth of the genre's appeal even on the most everyday domestic basis. In the living-room as well as cinemas, the Western was a crucial component of mid-20th-century American society, identity and culture.

I was born in 1960 – the very year that old frontier values were eulogized on the big screen in John Wayne's *The Alamo*, and the year that America readied itself for the New Frontier with the election of John Fitzgerald Kennedy. I've often remarked, *vis-à-vis* my love for the Western, that I was born on the 'edge of the cusp' – near the end of a long line of Western devotees. Had I been born a couple of years later, I might instead have grown up a huge fan of sci-fi, which fired the imagination of a new generation of youngsters.

But no – the Western was my cinematic and televisual first love. Part of my roseate recollection of childhood is that, when I was very small, Westerns were shown on television most evenings – especially on Saturdays. It could scarcely have been Saturday *without* a Western! Looking back, how appropriate that the day of the week most identified with personal freedom should be integrally associated with the genre which championed and celebrated individualism and liberty. I must admit, this insight didn't occur to me as a little boy. I was far more interested in the make-believe world of cowboys and Indians. I remember once aiming my toy six-shooter at the television and pulling the trigger at precisely the moment one of the villains bit the dust. So impressed was I by my own marksmanship that I even carved a notch on the handle of my gun!

A fistful of laconic, iconic, resonant one-name titles – *Gunsmoke, Bonanza, Rawhide, Cheyenne, Maverick, Laramie, Sugarfoot, Bronco* – were branded into the hide of US popular cultural consciousness; and mine. I knew the characters from TV Westerns as well as I knew friends and acquaintances in my own village: *Gunsmoke's* Matt Dillon and Chester; the Cartwright boys of the Ponderosa; *Wagon Train's* Major Adams and Flint McCullough; the Cannon clan of *The High Chaparral;* and the list could go winding on. I recall my shock at age six on learning that Eric Fleming, *Rawhide's* Gil Favor, had drowned in a canoeing accident; happily, the tall lanky fellow who played his sidekick Rowdy Yates was born under a luckier star.

As I grew up and hung up my six-guns, enthusiasm for television Western series was tapering off significantly. Certainly, by the early 1970's, the seemingly interminable conflict in Vietnam had ravaged the twin conceits of righteousness and invincibility. Suddenly, the Western hero as two-fisted dispenser of right and justice seemed more than a little *passé*. Both the era and the ethos of the Vietnam War shattered many of America's Manichaean moral certitudes and, consequently, the cowboy hero was a cultural casualty on screens big and small. Formulaic hero *vs.* villain narratives thus tended to be recast in the genre of cops and robbers rather than cowboys and Indians. The moral backdrop to the titanic televisual battle for the soul of America shifted from endless prairies and cactus-crowned canyons to mean streets, crowded sidewalks and alleyways of sprawling urban centres, in which law enforcement officers and private eyes (latter-day hired guns) fought for good against the bad, the ugly, and sometimes just the downright greedy. Ironically, by the time Ronald Reagan (former host of the Western series *Death Valley Days*) was elected President in 1980, the first-run Western series had all but disappeared from American television's prime-time schedules.

A few weeks after Reagan's election, I bought my first VCR; and, from the very first, the Western *film* formed the heart of my collection. I've remained a devotee of Westerns through all the years since. Yet for my money, two of the greatest Westerns I saw in that decade – two of the greatest I've *ever* seen – were *television* epics: the 21-hour saga *Centennial* (1978), based on the book by James A. Michener and long-overdue for release on DVD; and the wonderful *Lonesome Dove* (1989), based on the Pulitzer Prize-winning novel by Larry McMurtry. My love affair with the Western culminated in my book *The Crowded Prairie: American National Identity in the Hollywood Western* (I. B. Tauris, 1997), in which I advanced my own opinion that *Lonesome Dove* may have a respectable claim to the title of 'greatest Western of all time'.

One consequence of *The Crowded Prairie* was that shortly after its publication I was contacted by a lady who was writing a book on John Wayne. That lady was Carolyn McGivern; the result of her labours, *John Wayne: A Giant Shadow*, is a particularly fine biography of the greatest of all American screen icons.

# FOREWORD

I'm very pleased and honoured to be asked to write the Foreword for *Where Have All the Cowboys Gone?*, which has all the hallmarks of Carolyn's earlier excellent work, in its ambition, awesome scope and infectious enthusiasm. It harks back to a mythic past in which courage, integrity and virtue triumphed – and in which, for those of us transfixed by the flickering screen, the best of life was just one big Saturday night.

© MICHAEL COYNE

26 September 2006

# PART ONE

'As far as I'm concerned, Americans don't have any original art except Western movies and jazz.'

Clint Eastwood

# INTRODUCTION

**IN** seeking to understand the life and death of the television Western an analysis of the interrelationship between popular culture, television and socio-political development in the USA is needed. And more than that, the shows themselves need the examination they must now be entitled to.

For anyone like me, who grew up in the 50's and 60's and remain nostalgic for those comfy-Cadillac times, ***Where Have All The Cowboys Gone?*** is a vivid tribute to American 20th century art as it celebrates the largely unsung glory that was the television Western. The cowboy stars of those towering shows were our clean cut heroes and perhaps, (although we would never dare admit it now we are all so politically correct – almost to the point of extinction,) they still are. Their daring-do was embellished and their historic as well as physical stature stretched to incredible lengths. Who cared? We didn't need accuracy. We wanted justice and action and we wanted it fast and with a predictable outcome.

As soon as the chance came along to write this book I grabbed the opportunity to reminiscence about the way things used to be in the good old days, when they all first rode into our living rooms, because it provided me with the perfect chance to re-acquaint myself with so many of my old favorites who now sat drinking rot gut in the tumbleweed dust of my distant memory.

It came as an unexpected shock to find not only my old maverick heroes, but so many undiscovered gold nuggets that I'd never even heard of before. Although many of these gems are turning up, crisp, clear and vibrant again, on DVD and on an abundance of cable and satellite channels as the major companies come to realize the commercial potential in the old black and white productions, I found the greatest pleasure trawling through old video stores in Southern California, particularly Eddie Brandt's Saturday Matinee where I was treated like Queen Elizabeth (I think it was the accent that did it!) and encouraged to dig out boxed copies of *Have Gun – Will Travel, Cheyenne* and *The Rifleman*. My favourite find was The Collector's Edition of *Wagon Train*, which included the *Colter Craven Story*, which had first aired on 23 November, 1960. The episode had been directed by crusty old John Ford and starred Michael Morris (better known as John Wayne!) as General Sherman.

It was such a joy to be transported back to my youth as I sat and watched the popularized myth, falsehood and exaggeration again and again. How wonderful to see those cowboy heroes stride out into the blinding light of desert frontier lands again, gun belt slung loose and low, well worn, rugged and fighting to uphold their image and it would be nice to think that, after reading about and re-living the wild shenanigans in Dodge City, some readers rode out themselves to find some of the rare magic of *Gunsmoke* or any of the other 200 or so shows investigated here.

Between 1926 and 1966 Westerns had accounted for a quarter of all the motion pictures made in Hollywood. Generally they were an un-acclaimed bunch, and although some were indeed run of the mill oaters, even the immensely popular and huge box office earners, often made by the most highly regarded producers and directors and starring the greatest talent of the day, tended to be ignored when Oscar time rolled around. No self respecting writer of a column of an Eastern newspaper would stoop to pass comment on a mere Western. And when it inevitably made its transition to television just as the gunslingers of the Saturday morning shoot 'em up faded into the sunset, the new shows were considered to be purely Boot Hill fodder. The television cowboy was the poorest relation and he was kicked around and consistently treated with disdain and scorn when it came to historical and critical inquiry.

It is a curious anomaly that whilst the television trail, initially blazed by juvenile and sanitized cowboy heroes and later by the more brooding and dangerous loners, has long since grown cold, we are now once again in need of uncomplicated honest-to-goodness heroes like Gene Autry, Roy Rogers, Hopalong Cassidy, The Lone Ranger, Matt Dillon or even Rin Tin Tin. Perhaps the time has come to award them all some long over due retrospective acclaim.

# THE BIRTH OF THE TELEVISION WESTERN

**THE** early 50's saw the beginning of the end of the Hollywood budget or 'B' Western. In 1940 almost 30 Western stars were active, but 1950 offered only Roy Rogers, Allan Lane, Monte Hall, Rex Allen, Johnny Mack Brown, Whip Wilson, Gene Autry, Charles Starrett and Tim Holt; all men well into their 50's and ageing rapidly. Between 1950 and 1954 every 'B' Western series had been eliminated from the big screen and Randolph Scott maintained a lonely stance with an average of two minor 'A' productions a year for Columbia and Warner Bros. For the first time since Broncho Billy Anderson first made the genre popular in 1908, the industry launched no new Western stars.

Several factors had contributed to the sudden demise of the small scale horse opera, including rapidly escalating production costs. A western that may have cost $15,000 in the mid 30's was coming in at over $60,000 by the 50's and even these budgets could only be maintained by severely cutting corners, keeping mobile camera work to a minimum, slashing casts and even livestock to skeleton forces and making maximum use of stock footage. Only RKO's Tim Holt made any attempt to maintain worthwhile standards. His films cost up to $90,000 apiece and even these didn't make money. Every gimmick was tried in vain; there were no longer any quick, easy profits to be made.

But if the death knell sounded for the 'B' Western, the gate was thrown unexpectedly wide open for the stars of those old movies to walk through. With the advent of television, new executives had schedules to fill and a lack of ready packaged material to use; whilst established stars found their thrones threatened on the big screen, they were quick to scent opportunities to reinvent themselves for the new medium. Old film titles were being snapped up and although the major studios were reluctant to release their A films and saw television as a threat to their business, poorer studios such as Mascot, Monogram, Republic, and Columbia appreciated the new profitable development. By leasing their old films to TV they gained unexpected revenue from pictures that were anachronisms in post war theatres without having to make any investment in new production. Even old Western serials such as John Wayne's *Three Mesquiteers* were dug up from the archives for reincarnation on TV. They were dusted down and showcased in *Six-Gun Playhouse*, *Sagebrush Theater*, and *Trail Blazers' Theater*. Whilst using feature films required editing, the old serials were tailor-made for TV with each serial comprising 12 to 15 instalments which fitted comfortably into quarter hour time slots. The cliff hanger endings that had brought patrons back to the cinemas were now equally successful in alluring TV viewers back to see if the hero had survived.

Although the early TV Western was perhaps an unlikely phenomenon, with most of the low budget movies made back in the 1930's, the emergence of TV successfully revived the careers of many of the old stars and it wasn't long before the TV westerns caught the imagination of those first viewers with the old-timers helping to ensure that television would be a financial and cultural success.

New stations could now expand their hours on air and sell space to more sponsors. Everything took off and the unexpected popularity of the genre even enticed some consumers to go out and buy their first television set. They had a choice about viewing and when that was between paying to go out to see a cheap new western or view a high quality oldie on the television for nothing, audiences increasingly stayed at home.

Perhaps the most successful of the early TV Westerns actually derived directly from radio. *The Lone Ranger*, based on the popular radio show which featured William Conrad as the masked hero, debuted in 1949 on ABC and was an immediate hit. Naturally the show's success saw other juvenile series swiftly follow in its wake and many of the stars of these shows were the veterans of the 'B' Western. The first of the old stars to ride in on the back of these changes was Gene Autry. He made his play whilst still producing his own theatrical westerns for Columbia. In the face of hostile reactions from exhibitors he argued that his television films would stimulate extra business for his theatrical ones. He was a shrewd business man and he set up Flying A Productions to develop several TV series including the *Range Rider* group with Jack Mahoney, *The Adventures of Champion, Buffalo Bill Jr* starring Dick Jones and *Annie Oakley* with Gail Davis.

He found that requirements for television were far more rigid than they ever were for theatrical releases and everything his new company made had to pass the inspection of sponsors and advertising agencies long before they were broadcast. Each story had to be told in a running time of 26 minutes, providing a half hour show with time for commercials. In addition, it must be constructed so that the dramatic or action highlight immediately preceding the break for the commercial was strong enough to hold the viewer's attention. He was under pressure but recognized that to facilitate quick and economical productions he had to build up a stock company of top technicians and actors and he had soon put together an efficient unit where he pooled talent and applied the same energy that marked all of his activities.

Mass production inevitably meant that quantity was more important than quality and the early television Westerns were certainly no better than the downgraded theatrical westerns they replaced, but since their stories were told in only three reels, they were faster, slicker and more suited to a juvenile audience. They concentrated on action and simple comedy, avoiding all sexual elements, strong drama and brutality. They had to be completely safe and Autry was forced to make anaemic films and what would have been a mere plot element in one of his theatrical films was now strung out into the full plot line. Nevertheless, he and his Cowboy Code were immensely popular and as TV Westerns developed through the following years, they ultimately adhered to its essence and the rules he laid down:

1  A cowboy never takes unfair advantage, even of an enemy.
2  A cowboy never betrays a trust.
3  A cowboy always tells the truth.
4  A cowboy is kind to small children, to old folks and to animals.
5  A cowboy is free from racial and religious prejudice.
6  A cowboy is always helpful, and when anyone's in trouble he lends a hand.
7  A cowboy is a good worker.
8  A cowboy is clean about his person, and in thought, word and deed.
9  A cowboy respects womanhood, his parents and the laws of his country.
10  A cowboy is a patriot.

The small screen required the maximum of close up work and a minimum of fast intercutting. The necessity for close up work had distinct disadvantages for Autry and some of his colleagues who were ageing so quickly; the use of doubles in action scenes also became that much more obvious, as were the tacky studio sets. A blank white backdrop with a couple of false trees planted in front of it could never look like a real exterior. Cheaply made series such as *The Lone Ranger* staged almost all their action, interior and exterior, within these cramped stages. A few chases, for use throughout the entire series, would be shot in genuine exteriors and these were intercut with all the patently artificial studio footage.

Above all else, the shows had to be completed on schedule to meet their air time deadlines and so the earliest television Westerns were necessarily simple, factory made products. With so many limitations placed upon them, it is perhaps surprising that so many emerged as well as they did. One reason that they did was maybe because they were not made by television personnel, but by the same veterans who had been making theatrical westerns for years. Television did not invent new techniques of its own, it borrowed the very best from the movie establishment.

In the wake of Autry's success, the trend grew to exploit both old Western stars and actual historical figures. In the former category Autry's number one rival was William Boyd. His black-clad Hopalong Cassidy character became the most successful packaging of a vintage 'B' Western star. Boyd was all business, and by 1948 he had already acquired the TV rights to his western features and taken up the option to produce more Hoppy films for TV. His show began running in New York and Los Angeles, but by 1949 it was brought by NBC and given national exposure. Hopalong Cassidy was soon a phenomenon and for a 16 month period reached over four million homes per weekly show.

The success allowed Boyd to market his endorsement, including peripheral products like Hoppy roller-skates and lamps. One million Hoppy jackknives were sold in the first ten days of availability. He even managed to sell black shirts to children. Boyd understood the impact the show had and the market he reached, 'Hopalong is a simple man, friendly and informal. He's very intimate. I didn't treat kids as kids – they don't like that – I play the adults. That pleases everybody. Then there was the idea that maybe Westerns, which kids have always loved, might be used to teach them things like fair play and having respect for themselves and one another. I even had a hunch that if I could make the right sort of Westerns, never forgetting they had to be action pictures and good entertainment, I might even do my bit to reduce crime among kids and juvenile delinquents.'

The carefully marketed product was a commercial exercise concerned with ratings, residuals, advertising rates and profits. Yet it had a broader significance, and as a popular cultural phenomenon it embodied many relevant social issues. Hoppy's character communicated more than a simple story of cowboys fighting the outlaws. For a whole generation of children, many born into Depression or World War, some having lost fathers, the paternal guidance of Hopalong Cassidy became crucial. To Autry's Cowboy Code, Boyd now added discipline, devotion to others, and bravery. He completed difficult tasks, was strong, compassionate; a warrior who longed for social harmony. In a time of Cold War tension and atomic bomb potential, Hoppy fought for simple, decent families.

Boyd had been on the verge of bankruptcy when television arrived to save the day, but in setting himself up as a producer and securing the rights to his apparently worthless Hopalong Cassidy films, he found himself a national hero within two years. In 1950 he drew the largest circus attendance ever at the Chicago stadium and headed the Macy's Thanksgiving Parade. This accomplished he was able to start a completely new series of Hoppy westerns specifically for television use. Boyd's tenure as a television cowboy was brief but for a while he was its brightest star and he

continued to reap subsidiary benefits which far exceeded the mere grosses from film rental.

After quitting theatrical film production a little later, Roy Rogers was also soon seen in his own television series. His shows were less successful than Autry's or Boyd's and it soon became clear that new gimmicks were going to be needed if the television western was going to endure. Rogers allowed more violence to creep into his morality plays and he justified this by referring to history, 'The Westerns I make come right out of the history books.'

# RIDING HIGH

'We are a nation of hero-worshippers and the cowboy can be anybody's hero.'

Clint Walker

**HOPALONG CASSIDY** and the Lone Ranger entertained youngsters all over the world but a revolution was about to burst the floodgates as several new television Westerns got set to make their debuts. They had been produced to provide prime-time cowboy action for grown-ups and for the first time the central characters would not be flawlessly moral, they would remain tough but would now also have deeper and more complex sides, be altogether more believable, more adult in tone. The 'adult' Westerns differed from the earlier series with their focus more on character development and interaction than on plot or action.

It is difficult to say exactly when the concept for the first adult Western was developed but the best starting point lies around 1952 when the radio show, *Gunsmoke* and the movie *High Noon* both debuted. Their success led to the new type of television programing which hit the small screen with a bang in the 1953–4 season with *Last Notch*, a teleplay about a gunfighter who didn't care for gun fighting, which aired as part of The Steel Hour. The first four Western TV series were launched hot on its heels during the following season with the premieres of *The Life and Legend of Wyatt Earp* on ABC, television's version of *Gunsmoke* on CBS, *Cheyenne* on ABC and *Frontier* on NBC.

In September 1955 *The Life and Legend of Wyatt Earp* was the first to debut. It featured Hugh O'Brien as the legendary marshal in a series that involved character development and politics as often as it did action. *Gunsmoke* followed it just four days later. It stands as the most successful Western TV show of all time, running longer than any other entertainment series with continuing characters. It carried the structure of the radio show to television and centred on the exploits of the Marshal of Dodge City, Matt Dillon. Dillon was surrounded by a group of close friends including his loyal deputy, Chester, the bluff, kind-hearted Doc Addams, and the owner of the Longbranch Saloon, Miss Kitty. Much like *The Life and Legend of Wyatt Earp*, the emphasis of *Gunsmoke* lay in relationships as it examined the lives of Dodge City's inhabitants, and, in the show's later days, it tackled various serious social issues such as rape and racial injustice.

*Gunsmoke* had been introduced to television viewers by John Wayne who directly addressed the camera and stated that *Gunsmoke* was the first TV western in which he would have felt comfortable appearing. His endorsement was a self-conscious attempt by CBS to set *Gunsmoke* apart from juvenile fare.

*Cheyenne,* produced by Warner Brothers with all the lavishness of their movies, featured Clint Walker as wanderer Cheyenne Bodie, a man who travelled the West taking a variety of jobs.

*Frontier* was the fourth to arrive. It starred Walter Coy as the narrator of one of the screen's earliest anthologies which featured a different actor each week.

Each show was enthusiastically met. *Cheyenne* ranked in the top twenty programmes from 1956 to 1959, while *The Life and Legend of Wyatt Earp* ranked in the Top ten for several years. *Gunsmoke* of course had the most lasting success, ranking number one from 1957 to 1960, and sitting in the Top ten through much of the 60's. It ran a record 20 years. *Frontier* was less triumphant than the other three shows and it has rarely been seen since going off the air in September 1956.

The popularity of the bland and monotonous early TV Westerns declined just as the 'Bs' had done before them, fading away not least because the continued transmission of well made old movies exposed their inferiority, and the path was clear for the rapid emergence of the grittier new style of Western.

The viewing figures of the groundbreaking four shows were high enough to precipitate the Western boom that followed hard on their heels. While the 1956–7 season saw three new Western series premiere, by 1958–9 there were 28 Westerns on the air each week, with seven of them showing in America's top ten shows. By 1959 TV Western film footage represented the equivalent of 400 feature films per year, more than was ever produced in Hollywood during the golden age of the 'B' western.

This period produced many of television's all-time best loved and most successful series, including *Maverick, Have Gun-Will Travel, Rawhide, Wagon Train, Bonanza* and *The Rifleman.*

These were not the only remarkable series to emerge out of the 50's, but unfortunately a lot of the others were more mundane and are consequently less well remembered. A huge number of them dealt with either gunslingers or lawmen; there were so many in fact, that it was often hard to tell one series from another. Some producers felt the need to give their hero a gimmick in order to differentiate him from the cowboys of other shows. Sundance, the hero of *Hotel de Paree*, wore a black Stetson with a row of polished silver discs with which he could blind opponents, while Bat Masterson, in the series of the same name, used his cane to disarm opponents more often than his specially designed gun. The lack of any real variation between the Western TV series is probably the reason most of them lasted only one or

WHERE HAVE ALL THE COWBOYS GONE?

two seasons, and some not even that. They didn't all have a gimmick, but with so much Old West programming filling the weekly schedules, writers were hard-pressed to develop innovative and attractive new characters, resulting in a number of regular heroic guises cropping up; the peace officer, military officer, the mercenary, gambler, gunfighter, railroad builder, newspaperman, circus owner, rodeo performer, detective. They ran chronologically from the late 18th century to modern times. Some were town-based others were set on sprawling ranches. Some were loners, some rode with pals.

Offering two to three dozen shows per season was creatively exhausting, and many shows were necessarily imitations of what had gone before. Writers devised entire series by melding other genres into the Old West, as in *The Wild, Wild West*, a Western and a spy fantasy reminiscent of contemporary James Bond films.

Frank Gruber, a long-time western writer and co producer of *Tales of Wells Fargo* said that there were only seven basic types of Western:

1   The Union Pacific story-tales of railway, telegraph or stagecoach lines.
2   The Ranch story-tales of cattlemen, rustlers and rivalries.
3   The Empire story-focusing on the large ranches or powerful western families.
4   The Revenge story-the righting of wrongs.
5   Custer's Last Stand-the story of conflict between Indians and the cavalry.
6   The Outlaw story-usually a sympathetic focus on the bandit's struggle against society.
7   The Marshal story-looking at the dedicated lawman.

Still, the new heroes were unprecedented on TV, mature and human; some could be seen in saloons drinking hard liquor for the first time, chatting to bar girls and playing poker. They may all have similarities but at least they broke the early stereotypes. Occasionally they got angry, they made mistakes and paid the price. The adult Western also created a batch of new stars including James Garner, James Arness, Robert Culp and Steve McQueen who all quickly became national celebrities. Older leading men from motion pictures, like Rory Calhoun, John Payne and Ward Bond also found renewed popularity on television.

The television Western nurtured new talented personnel behind the scenes with many prominent film directors plying their trade first in TV with newer crews making their names here before going on to work in feature films. Top directors such as Andrew V. McLaglen and Sam Peckinpah worked together on shows like *Gunsmoke*.

The motion picture industry finally began to see the lucrative possibilities in TV and began to withdraw its initial hostility toward it. Many new series sprang increasingly from the big film companies long famous for their quality westerns. Among those studios were Warner Bros, who made *Maverick, Colt .45, Bronco, Cheyenne* and various other new programs, 20th Century Fox produced *Broken Arrow, Lancer, Daniel Boone* and *Custer.* United Artists made *Bat Masterson, Stoney Burke* and *MacKenzie's Raiders*, Metro-Goldwyn-Mayer made *Northwest Passage, A Man Called Shenandoah, Hondo* and *How the West was Won.*

Each company saw that the adult Western offered a sound genre in which to blend dramatic conflict, human insight, outdoor beauty and subtle moralizing. Some felt the Freudian overtones of such Westerns overshadowed and ruined the simplicity of the cowboy story but the emergence of the adult Western did not signify the erosion of heroism. Clint Walker believed the new format supplied champions for everyone to enjoy, 'We are a nation of hero-worshippers and the cowboy can be anybody's hero.'

Undoubtedly the new Westerns had great appeal and during their first decade more than 60 million viewers nightly were entertained by them. There was so much confidence in the genre that networks believed they were sure fire winners and adult Westerns could be recognized immediately by their sponsors; where Sugar Pops and Cheerios were connected to *Wild Bill Hickok* and *The Lone Ranger*, the newer dramas were underwritten by expensive and obviously adult products. Greyhound Bus sponsored *Cimarron City* and *Sugarfoot.* The persuasive adult sales alignment can best be summarized in the flourishing Marlboro Man. Marlboro ads appeared on *Rawhide* and *Tombstone Territory.* Sponsors quickly recognized that the adult Western was attracting sizeable audiences. And the acceptance of the genre, although it had happened rapidly, was no passing fad.

Although the 1960–1 season marked the end of the first boom of adult Western TV series, with just seven rather short-lived series premiering, and the 1964–5 season saw no new Westerns appear, the drought proved short-lived, and in 1965–6 eight new shows premiered. Five more debuted during the 1966–7 season, to be followed by seven more in the 1967–8 season. The 60's Western TV series boom may have been smaller than that of the 50's, but it produced some well remembered shows that noticeably distanced themselves from their more violent cousins.

This new boom was probably created in part by the success of *Bonanza*, the pioneering domestic Western (which was the number one show in the 1964–5 season) and *The Virginian,* both of which revolved around family and a central patriarchal figure.

Although the third period saw some Western comedies emerging, the best of which included *Alias Smith and Jones* and *F Troop* which focused on the incompetent cavalry unit at Fort Courage somewhere in the West, the most significant indicator of the change in popular taste was seen in the domestication of the genre and in its modified product. The new shows often focused on large cattle empires or other enterprises maintained by rugged individuals. Typically, in the *High Chaparral*, the Cannon family and its employees, fight to keep their large ranch viable in the Arizona desert. Rugged country became the setting for the domestic Western which spoke of land, home and close relationships; themes more readily understood by modern viewers than the violent justice of the Old West. When the adult Western was under fire from all sides for its violent content, the domestic Western offered a soothing antidote.

# PART TWO

## The shows A-Z

*Rugged country was often the backdrop for the domestic Western.*

# THE SHOWS A—Z

| | | | |
|---|---|---|---|
| Cowboy in Africa | 09.11.1967 | Chuck Connors | 120 |
| Cowboy Theatre | 1956–57 | Anthology | 121 |
| Cowboys, The | 02.06.1974 | Jim Davis/Moses Gunn | 121 |
| Custer | 09.06.1967 | Wayne Maunder | 122 |
| Dakotas, The | 01.07.1963 | Jack Elam/Michael Greene | 124 |
| Daniel Boone | 09.24.1964 | Fess Parker/Patricia Blair | 126 |
| Daniel Boone-Walt Disney | 12.04.1960 | Dewey Martin | 127 |
| Davy Crockett | 12.15.1954 | Fess Parker/Buddy Ebsen | 129 |
| Deadwood | 03.21.2004 | Ian McShane | 130 |
| Death Valley Days | 12.10.1952 | Stanley Andrews | 135 |
| Deputy, The | 09.12.1959 | Henry Fonda/Allen Case | 136 |
| Destry | 02.14.1964 | John Gavin | 137 |
| Dirty Sally | 01.11.1974 | Jeannette Nolan | 137 |
| Dr.Quinn, Medicine Woman | 01.01.1993 | Jane Seymour/Joe Lando | 138 |
| Dundee and The Culhane | 09.06.1967 | John Mills/ Sean Garrison | 139 |
| Dusty's Trail | 09.11.1973 | Bob Denver | 140 |
| Empire | 09.25.1962 | Ryan O'Neal/Terry Moore/Richard Egan | 141 |
| F Troop | 09.14.1965 | Forrest Tucker/Ken Berry | 142 |
| Father Murphy | 11.30.1981 | Merlin Olsen | 144 |
| Frontier | 09.25.1955 | Walter Coy | 145 |
| Frontier Circus | 10.05.1961 | Chill Wills/Richard Jaeckel/John Derek | 145 |
| Frontier Doctor | 09.26.1958 | Rex Allen | 146 |
| Frontier Justice | 1958-61 | Guest hosts | 146 |
| Fury | 10.15.1955 | Bobby Diamond/Peter Graves | 147 |
| Gabby Hayes Show, The | 12.11.1950 | George "Gabby" Hayes | 150 |
| Gene Autry Show, The | 07.23.1950 | Gene Autry | 151 |
| Gray Ghost, The | 10.15.1957 | Tod Andrews | 156 |
| Gun Shy | 03.15.1983 | Barry Van Dyke | 158 |
| Guns of Will Sonnett | 09.08.1967 | Walter Brennan/Dack Rambo | 158 |
| Gunslinger | 02.09.1961 | Tony Young | 160 |
| Gunsmoke | 09.10.1955 | James Arness | 161 |
| Have Gun Will Travel | 09.14.1957 | Richard Boone | 173 |
| Hawkeye | 09.18.1994 | Lee Horsley/Linda Carter | 177 |
| Hawkeye and the Last of the Mohicans | 04.03.1957 | John Hart/Lon Chaney Jr. | 178 |
| Hec Ramsey | 10.08.1972 | Richard Boone | 179 |
| Here Comes the Brides | 09.25.1968 | Joan Blondell/David Soul/Robert Brown | 179 |
| High Chaparral, The | 09.10.1967 | Cameron Mitchell/Leif Erickson | 181 |
| Hondo | 09.08.1967 | Ralph Taeger | 190 |
| Hopalong Cassidy | 09.19.1952 | William Boyd | 191 |
| Hotel De Paree | 10.02.1959 | Earl Holliman | 192 |
| How The West Was Won | 02.12.1978 | Bruce Boxleitner/James Arness | 193 |
| Into the West | 10.06.2005 | Matthew Settle | 195 |
| Iron Horse | 09.12.1966 | Dale Robertson | 197 |
| Jefferson Drum | 04.29.1958 | Jeff Richards | 197 |

| | | | |
|---|---|---|---|
| Outlaws, The | 09.29.1960 | Jock Gaynor/Barton MacLane/Don Collier | 257 |
| Overland Trail | 09.07.1960 | William Bendix/Doug McClure | 259 |
| Paradise | 10.27.1988 | Lee Horsley | 260 |
| Peacemakers | 07.30.2003 | Tom Berenger | 262 |
| Pistols 'N' Petticoats | 09.17.1966 | Ann Sheridan | 263 |
| Pony Express | 04.06.1959 | Earle Hodgins/Grant Sullivan/Don Dorrell | 264 |
| Quest, The | 04.22.1976 | Kurt Russell/Tim Matheson | 264 |
| Range Rider, The | 04.05.1951 | Jock Mahoney/Dick Jones | 265 |
| Rango | 01.17.1967 | Tim Conway | 266 |
| Rawhide | 01.09.1959 | Eric Fleming/Clint Eastwood | 267 |
| Rebel, The | 10.14.1959 | Nick Adams | 270 |
| Redigo | 1963- | Richard Egan | 271 |
| Restless Gun, The | 10.23.1957 | John Payne | 271 |
| Rifleman, The | 09.30.1958 | Chuck Connors/Johnny Crawford | 272 |
| Riverboat | 09.13.1959 | Burt Reynolds/Darren McGavin | 274 |
| Road West, The | 09.12.1966 | Andrew Prine/Barry Sullivan/Glenn Corbett | 274 |
| Rough Riders | 10.02.1958 | Kent Taylor/Jan Merlin/Peter Whitney | 275 |
| Rounders, The | 09.16.1966 | Chill Wills/Ron Hays/Pat Wayne | 275 |
| Roy Rogers Show, The | 12.31.1951 | Dale Evans/Roy Rogers | 276 |
| Saga of Andy Burnett | 10.02.1957 | Jerome Courtland | 277 |
| Sara | 02.13.1976 | Brenda Vaccaro | 277 |
| Saturday Roundup | 1951- | Anthology – Guest Stars | 277 |
| Sgt. Preston of the Yukon | 09.29.1955 | Richard Simmons | 278 |
| Shane | 09.10.1966 | David Carradine | 278 |
| Sheriff of Cochise | 09.21.1956 | John Bromfield | 279 |
| Shotgun Slade | 09.11.1959 | Scott Brady | 279 |
| Sky King | 09.16.1951 | Gloria Winters/Kirby Grant | 280 |
| Spin and Marty | 1955- | Tim Considine/David Stollery | 281 |
| Stagecoach West | 10.04.1960 | Wayne Rogers/Robert Bray/Richard Eyer | 282 |
| State Trooper | 09.25.1956 | Rod Cameron | 283 |
| Steve Donovan, Western Marshal | 08.30.1955 | Douglas Kennedy | 283 |
| Stoney Burke | 10.01.1962 | Jack Lord | 284 |
| Stories of the Century | 01.23.1954 | Jim Davis | 285 |
| Sugarfoot | 09.17.1957 | Will Hutchins | 286 |
| Swamp Fox, The | 10.23.1959 | Leslie Nielsen | 287 |
| Tales of the Texas Rangers | 09.22.1955 | Harry Lauter/WillardParker | 288 |
| Tales of Wells Fargo | 03.03.1957 | Dale Robertson | 289 |
| Tall Man, The | 09.10.1960 | Barry Sullivan/Clu Gulager | 291 |
| Tate | 06.08.1960 | David McLean | 291 |
| Temple Houston | 09.19.1963 | Jack Elam/Jeff Hunter | 292 |
| Texan, The | 09.29.1958 | Rory Calhoun | 292 |
| Texas John Slaughter | 10.31.1958 | Harry Carey Jr./Tom Tryon | 293 |
| Tomahawk | 1957- | Jaques Godin | 294 |
| Tombstone Territory | 10.16.1957 | Pat Conway | 295 |

# ACTION IN THE AFTERNOON
## 2 FEBRUARY 1953

**THE** first airing of *Action in the Afternoon* was 2 February 1953 with the last show going out on 29 January 1954. The show aired on CBS-TV for a half-hour, Monday thru Friday. It was filmed in black and white.

Charlie Vanda, the President of WCAU created the show. One day when he was in New York pitching shows to CBS-TV he came up with his Western idea set in a town called Huberle, Montana in 1884. The town's name was made up from CBS executives Hubbell Robinson and Harry Ommerlee. WCAU had only a few weeks to get a pilot together with a budget under $7,000. And that was for five shows.

Episodes were produced live on the back lot of WCAU-TV, Channel 10 in Philadelphia. It was television's only live daily network Western, going out at a time before CBS owned the station. Then, it was owned by the Philadelphia Evening Bulletin. The station was on City Line Avenue at Monument Road, located in Bala Cynwyd. The area, which wasn't particularly built up, had a natural creek running through it which was dammed up when they wanted to film water fights. The interior shots were done in the studios and exterior shots outside on the back lot, which was also the parking lot for the station's employees.

Mockups of different Western buildings were put up and as it was low budget, there were only three to five buildings; the Copper Cup Saloon, which was the best known watering hole in town, the *Huberle Record* newspaper office and the sheriff's office/jail. The false-front Main Street also had a Wells Fargo office which blew down and had to quickly be rebuilt just before the first broadcast. There was a blacksmith's stable and a totem pole, which in reality was the bottom part of a post that held the television lights and which also served to hide a telephone pole.

The station leased horses from the riding academy in Fairmount Park. The chase scenes were all done live. The backlot was over 300 feet long and as the horses rode off into the sunset, every once in a while it was possible to hear a motorcycle drive by or to see the top of a truck or a plane fly past.

An advertisement from June of 1953 referred to it as 'A spectacular experiment in outdoor television. Adventurous as the West! Alive as America! First live Western on TV.'

A review in June of 1953 called the show '... an adventure series of roaring six-shooters and two-fisted brawls... one of the most novel TV ideas ever originated. ...'

Each segment featured the same cast each day starring Jack Valentine, Mary Elaine Watts (she played Red Cotten, the belle of the saloon) and Barry Cassell (shady character Ace Bancroft). The narrator was Blake Ritter. Sam Kressen starred as Sheriff Sam Mitchell and Jean Corbett as the lawman's wife, Amy Jean.

During the year that *Action in the Afternoon* was on air Corbett also portrayed 'Aunt Molly' on a WCAU-TV cooking and homemakers show, *Home Highlights*. John Zacherle was an extra who worked up to a co-starring part as the undertaker, Grimy James. Nate Friedman, fresh out of Temple University, played many bit parts. He went on to become an attorney.

CBS (and later ABC) Sportscaster Jack Whitaker also had a bit part. Philadelphia Eagles player from 1948 to 1951 Walter 'Piggy' Barnes had a recurring role. Director Bill Bode said that Piggy was 'huge, and we used him because he could fight... because we had people fighting all the time.' Initially, he played bad guys, but once they found out he could act, he became a good guy. Barnes, who died in 1998, played in other Westerns and shared credits with Clint Eastwood, among others.

Just like in the early days of radio, actors were expected to play more than one role, one with a beard and one without, or put on a bandanna to become part of a gang robbing the bank.

When the station made *Shock Theater* later in 1957, Zacherle was chosen to star in it and in fact wore the same costume as Roland he had used as the undertaker in *Action*.

If the show's producer didn't like the acting job being done by anyone, he would simply re-write the script for the next day and the character was speedily killed off.

Filming began at eight am and usually lasted until midnight with many rewrites, rehearsals and planning for the next week's shows. It could take 60 seconds to go from the exterior shots to interior action. To fill the time, sometimes the Tommy Ferguson Trio would play Western songs. Bill Bode who directed the show and wrote some of it, once said that he simply rewrote Macbeth and it worked fine. Bode said that for the first half of the show's run, they really weren't that good but they were terrific for the second half of the season.

Valentine, who sang country and western songs on a local radio station before winning his part had been performing a night club act in Forth Worth when Stan Lee Broza's father- in-law first saw him. He was hired by the station as a staffer (doing whatever needed to be done). He replaced Ed McMahon who was in the US Marine Corp serving in Korea. He is best known for his work on *Action in the Afternoon*.

After the show was cancelled by CBS-TV, Valentine got hosting duties on a daily film strip of old shorts that ran in the five pm time period. He also starred in *Valentine's Day*. He went on to perform in local night clubs and made several records with the Tommy Ferguson Trio (of *Action in the Afternoon* fame) backing him up.

For most of its run, the show had four writers, each writing a week's worth of programming. Then the next writer would do the next week. Sometimes changes were done shortly before airtime and occasionally while the show was actually going out live on the air.

Hugh Best who was part of the crew said that the show was about violence. It

## TRIVIA

An article about the star of the show stated, *'Jack Valentine can do almost anything. His talents can best be summed up by saying that he's an entertainer's entertainer.'*

Valentine was born in Washington, DC, and raised in Boston, New England. His idols were 'The Sons of the Pioneers.'

Barry Cassell (who read the news on WCAU-TV at the weekends) would every so often go home dressed as Ace, wearing his prop six gun shooters to amuse his kids.

regularly featured drownings, hangings, shootings, burnings, tramplings, etc. and was aptly titled.

Microphones were hidden all over the place; in different hitching posts, on buildings, tree stumps and in rocks. Each scene had to be shot close to one of those places. If a mike went dead, the action was moved so a working mike could pick the sound up. One time, a horrible sound was heard over the air. No one could figure out what had happened until the camera panned and revealed a horse trying to eat the microphone.

The horses could indeed be very moody and once when Valentine was getting ready to rush out of Huberle to head-off some stagecoach bandits, he mounted his horse which stubbornly refused to budge. He prodded the horse to no avail. Valentine, in a frantic moment, created his own choice ad lib, 'Ben, I'll catch up with ya!' Fortunately, Director Jim Herschfeld had punched in the camera that followed Ben racing out of town.

Creighton Stewart was also on the show for a while, as Banker Grimes. On Radio he had a smooth voice and British accent. Unfortunately, when his old radio listeners saw him on TV they clamored for him to be dropped. The producers quickly agreed to write him out by being shot. They couldn't afford to alienate viewers, even if Creighton was upset about it. When his last scene was being filmed he didn't take the assistant director's cue when it was time to drop dead. He was inside and the shooters were outside. Apparently he didn't hear the cue. So they had to quick cue the outside robbers to shoot again. Finally Creighton dropped dead.

The rousing theme for the show was Aaron Copeland's 'Billy the Kid.'

Dick Lester was the show's Music Director.

Bode once said that Dick had to select music to not just fit the emotion of the scene, but pick melodies that would cover the noise from buses, trucks and airplanes. Lester later went on to direct two Beatles movies, *A Hard Day's Night* and *Help*, along with other critically acclaimed motion pictures.

John Ullrich was the original director along with Les Urbach, the veteran from Hollywood and senior Director who gave each performance his glossy finishing touch. Ullrich passed away shortly after *Action in the Afternoon* went off the air.

Bill Bode said, 'The opening of *Action in the Afternoon* was a 'freeze' with the live cast in frozen positions. ... When the Billy the Kid music was over, plus Barry Cassell's voice introing the show, there was then a gunshot which set everything in motion and started the people moving. Then we added a stage coach and, as I recall, a buckboard, riding thru. It was a complicated opening.'

Scripts were handed out just the day before shooting. The lines and cues had to

be memorized in time for rehearsal on set the next morning. Mornings were set for blocking, one run through, then a 'dry run' with cameras. A short break, and then air time.

# THE ADVENTURES OF BRISCO COUNTY, JR.

## 27 August 1993

'Smile. You're about to meet your new hero.'

**EPISODES** of The Adventures of Brisco County, Jr., ran 60 minutes each from the premiere on the Fox Network on August 27, 1993 through to May 20, 1994. Twenty seven color segments were made by executive producers Jeffrey Boam and Carlton Cuse.

*Christian Clemenson,*
*Julius Curry,*
*John Astin,*
*Bruce Campbell*
and
*Kelly Rutherford*

Spoof *The Adventures of Brisco County* was a short lived tongue-in-cheek, action-packed Western with a science fiction element. It premiered the same night as *X-Files*, and although it proved popular and won critical acclaim, the show was not picked up for a second season; perhaps the runaway success of its competitor was the major reason for its premature demise.

Overseen by executive producers Carlton Cuse and Jeffrey Boam (the latter was the screenwriter for *Lethal Weapon 2* and *3)*, the show followed the late 19th century adventures of Harvard law graduate, Brisco County, who rides through the West searching for his father's killers. He is hired by robber barons to search for members of the infamous John Bly gang, the same men who had murdered the famous marshal and Western legend, Brisco County Sr.

The evil John Bly (played to slithery perfection by Billy Drago), mysteriously happens to be from the year 2506 and he was on a quest of his own, searching for a mysterious orb.

Bruce Campbell starred as Brisco, Kelly Rutherford played his manipulative girlfriend, Dixie Cousins. John Astin was Professor Wickwire, an inventor of rockets and other gadgets. Julius Curry was Lord Bowler, (whose real name is revealed in an early episode as James Lonefeather) a bounty hunter who continually crosses the path of Brisco. Christian Clemenson is Socrates Poole, a loyal side-kick of Brisco. R Lee Ermey played Brsico Sr. John Pyper-Ferguson starred as Peter Hutter who had an obsession with his gun, which he nicknamed Pete's piece.

Accompanied by his one-time rival and fellow bounty hunter Lord Bowler, Brisco encountered the mysterious golden orbs with strange abilities and many colorful characters who help or hinder his mission as he hunts down the gang one by one.

Throughout the quest, County falls in and out of love, deals with bad guys such as the Swill Brothers, gets the help of goodhearted lawyer Poole and also has glimpses of the future through the eyes of the mad scientist, (there was wonderful interplay between all the actors involved in the series). On top of that there was always Randy Edelman's booming theme song.

## TRIVIA

The pilot, screened on 8.27.1993, featured many top Western stars including James Drury (Ethan Emerson), Paul Brinegar (Francis Killbridge), Stuart Whitman (Granville Thorogood), Robert Fuller (Kenyon Drummond), John Astin (Professor Wickwire) and Carlton Cuse (Owen)

Brisco's horse was billed in the credits as Comet the Wonder Horse, and called Comet in each segment. It was implied throughout that he was the smartest character on the show. In fact, Comet was portrayed by four separate horses, with the horse used in any particular scene being chosen according to the type of action he was expected to perform.

Plot points in the series were rarely important; what mattered more was the sense of reckless fun; when Harvard botanist Dr. Milo (Timothy Leary) was asked to give the eulogy at an impromptu funeral of a stagecoach passenger he recited a crazy quilt of Beatles lyrics: 'When I find myself in times of trouble, I say, 'Boy, you gotta carry that weight. I am he, you are, you are me. We're all together, speaking words of wisdom. Come together, right now. Amen'.'

While the humor may have been more 1990's than 1890's, the show's underlying depiction of the West may have been closer to reality than in some more serious Westerns. While Lord Bowler, who's black, falls into the stereotypical role of the sidekick to the white hero who gets the girls, this was a West full of mixed races; a fact that is never even remarked upon in the series but may be more truthful than in other depictions. According to William Loren Katz's 1971 book, *The Black West*, a large number of black cowboys populated the West (the first man shot in notorious Dodge was a black cowboy named Tex) and 'found less discrimination out on the trail than in town, more equality back on the ranch than in the frontier communities. Oddly enough, clashes between black and white cowboys themselves were rare.'

Frustratingly Fox television might as well have been broadcasting to the far side of the sun, and today it languishes in relative historical obscurity. Perhaps the fantasy elements, especially involving the orb, veered out of control at times, and this probably contributed to viewer confusion and sinking ratings during its original run.

It is a shame because it stood out from the rest of the broadcast pack of its era. It may have fallen into the Western category and therefore been seen as part of what was considered to be a dead genre, but it was also a crazy, multiracial Western that tempered fisticuffs with fantasy, innocence with irony, and its romantic vision of the Old West with an abiding New World faith in the future's infinite possibilities. Its direction was certainly closer to Quentin Tarantino than John Ford or Howard Hawks. Indeed *The Adventures of Brisco County* has made something of a comeback recently with the 27 episodes being aired again by TNT on Saturday mornings. Evidence that the cult following is growing may also be seen on the two unofficial *Brisco* home pages on the Internet and recent release of the series to DVD.

# THE ADVENTURES OF CHAMPION
## 30 SEPTEMBER 1955

'Like a streak of lightning flashing across the sky, like a mighty cannonball he seems to fly; soon everyone will know the name of Champion, the Wonder Horse.'

THE half-hour black and white program was set in America's Southwest during the 1880's. The show premiered on CBS on 30 September 1955 and ran just one season before closing on February 1956 after only 26 episodes.

Gene Autry produced the show through his Flying A Productions and his own chestnut Tennessee walking horse, Champion The Wonder Horse, was the star. (Champion had also appeared on *The Gene Autry Show*/CBS/1950–56.)

*The Adventures of Champion,* an outgrowth of a 1950's comic book series, starred Jim Bannon as Sandy North, owner of a ranch near where the wild stallion, Champion roamed free. Young Ricky North (Barry Curtis) is the only human that Champion trusts because the boy had saved the life of one of the herd's foals. Although Ricky, who lived on his Uncle Sandy's ranch, had a magnetic attraction for trouble, he was always speedily rescued by the horse, aided by his other bosom companion, German Shepherd, Rebel.

Jim Bannon was born in Kansas City, Missouri on 9 April 1911 and died 28 July 1984 from the effects of emphysema. He had a successful radio

---

# TRIVIA

Although Frankie Laine made a recording of the 'Champion the Wonder Horse' theme, it was Norman Luboff, the writer of the music, who sang the theme for the introduction and over the credits of the series, due to Frankie Laine's unavailability for the recording session.

---

career in Kansas City through the 1930's. He had a superb voice and took work announcing and narrating on a variety of radio programs, including: *The Joe Penner Show* (1939–40), *Stars Over Hollywood* (early 1940's), *The Great Gildersleeve* (1941–2), *The Adventures of Nero Wolfe* (1943–4), and *The Eddie Bracken Show* (1945–6). He went on to do various screen tests and eventually became a contract player at Columbia Pictures in the mid 1940's before finding fame in *The Adventures of Champion.*

# THE ADVENTURES OF JIM BOWIE

## 7 SEPTEMBER 1956

**THE** knife-wielding hero, Jim Bowie was played by Scott Forbes. Bowie cut'em from 7 September 1956 until 29 August 1958 on the ABC Network. The 76 episodes, half-hour black and white series was based loosely on the real life of James Bowie and was set in the Louisiana Territory of the 1830's.

Produced by Louis Edelman, the series was adapted from the book *The Tempered Blade* by Monte Barrett. Robert Cornthwaite played John James Audubon, in some episodes Peter Hanson starred as Rezin Bowie, Jim's brother, and Minerva Urecal as Ma Bowie.

The real life adventurer gave his name to the knife he supposedly invented after his regular one broke in a fight with a grizzly. However, critics often complained about the excessive violence and knife use on the show. Bowie was a rich planter who ran across many interesting characters such as Johnny Appleseed, Jean LaFitte, Sam Houston and President Andrew Jackson, all set against the backdrop of New Orleans. This is the period in Bowie's life before he left for Texas and was killed at the Alamo.

Minerva Urecal died in 1996 of a heart attack.

Scott Forbes, born 11 September 1920 in High Wycombe, England, died on 25 February 1997 in Wiltshire, England.

*The Adventures of Jim Bowie* theme song was recorded by The Prairie Chiefs.

*'Jim Bowie! Jim Bowie!*
*He was a fighter, a fearless and mighty*
*    adventurin' man!*
*He roamed the wilderness unafraid*
*From Natchez to Rio Grande*
*With all the might of his gleaming blade*
*    flashing from either hand.*
*Jim Bowie! Jim Bowie!*
*He was a fighter, a fearless and mighty*
*    adventurin' man!"*

# THE ADVENTURES OF KIT CARSON

## 1951

**ONE** hundred and four half-hour black and white episodes of this fast-moving TV series from Revue Studios (later sold to Universal) were made between 1951 and 1955.

The show was very loosely based on the exploits of real-life mountain man and explorer, Kit Carson, who was part of the Fremont Expedition into Wyoming, Colorado and California before 1850. The show had little to do with history however and this show pretty much stole Carson's name and invented a character to appeal to the children's market.

Kit Carson and El Toro, his Mexican sidekick, roamed the Wild West, traveling from Wyoming to Texas during the 1880's, chasing desperadoes, tracking wild game, drinking coffee by their campfire, and delighting youngsters everywhere. In fact the real Kit Carson died in 1868 aged 59. At the time he was an Indian agent at Fort Lyon, Colorado.

Bill Williams starred as Kit and Don Diamond played his partner, El Toro.

William's real name was Herman Katt. He was married to Barbara Hale, who played Della Street on *Perry Mason*, and was the father of actor William Katt *Greatest American Hero*.

He died 21 September 1992 of a brain tumor, in Burbank, California. Don Diamond now often guests at Western memorabilia shows around America.

---

## TRIVIA

Williams made over 58 guest-starring appearances in other TV series including *77 Sunset Strip, Laramie, Daniel Boone, Gunsmoke* and many more. Diamond's credits included a career highlight in *The Old Man and The Sea*.

# THE ADVENTURES OF RIN TIN TIN
## 15 OCTOBER 1954

**HERBERT** B Leonard Productions, in association with Screen Gems produced 164, half hour black and white episodes of the show which aired on Sunday nights at 8 pm, on the ABC Network from 15 October 1954. The program ended 28 August 1959, although reruns could still be seen until 1964. The show, largely filmed at the Corriganville Movie Ranch, was always one of the most popular on television, with consistently high ratings.

*James Brown, Rand Brooks, Rin Tin Tin, Lee Aaker and Joe Sawyer*

Boys and their faithful dogs had long been a staple of Hollywood, but *Rin Tin Tin*, was one of television's earliest canine heroes.

Rusty, played by Lee Aaker, was orphaned and the only survivor of an Indian raid on the wagon train he had been traveling with in the first episode. He and his trusty German Shepherd were adopted by the troopers at Fort Apache. Lt. Ripley 'Rip' Masters became Rusty's father figure and Sergeant Biff O'Hara and Corporal Boon, his best friends. Major Swanson, the fort commander, only went along with the arrangement reluctantly after Masters made Rusty a Corporal.

Masters was played by Jim L. Brown. Joe Sawyer was Sergeant O'Hara, Rand Brooks was Corporal Randy 'Kit' Boone, Major Swanson was played by William Forrest. Tommy Farrell played Corporal Thad Carson. Rin Tin Tin was a descendant of the original Rin Tin Tin who had starred in films from 1922. Lee Duncan, his owner and trainer said, 'He was very close to his great grandfather,' who had at one time been the highest paid performer in the film industry! Television's Rinty was the only dog in Los Angeles to be listed in the telephone directory.

Jim Brown died of cancer on 12 April 1992, aged 72.

Joe Sawyer died of liver cancer on 21 April 1982 in Oregon, USA.

Lee Aaker lives in Mammoth Lakes, California.

Rand Brooks died of cancer on 1 September 2003.

# TRIVIA

According to Hollywood legend, the original Rin Tin Tin died in the arms of actress Jean Harlow. His owner, Lee Duncan, arranged to have the dog returned to his country of birth for burial in the Cimetière des Chiens, the renowned pet cemetery in the Parisian suburb of Asnières-sur-Seine. Rin Tin Tin was honored with a star on the Hollywood Walk of Fame at 1623 Vine St.

Duncan's Rin Tin Tin IV featured as the lead dog in the TV series, although much of the work actually was performed by Rin Tin Tin II and several other dogs.

# THE ADVENTURES OF WILD BILL HICKOK

## 1951

*'Hey, Wild Bill, Wait For Me!'*

**THE half-hour series was action packed throughout its run on the CBS Network between 1951 and 1958. There were 113 black and white, and later color, episodes filmed at such locations as Big Bear, Vasuez Rocks and also at Corriganville, California.**

James Butler 'Wild Bill' Hickok was a real life gunfighter and part-time lawman of dubious reputation. Guy Madison, who starred as Hickok, bore absolutely no resemblance to him in this highly fictionalised series. Andy Devine starred as his partner, Jingles P. Jones. Devine will be remembered for his cry of 'Hey, Wild Bill, wait for me.'

Madison said, 'We made a half hour show in two and a half days. That included dialogue, action, everything. At one point we knocked out seven films in 17 days. We never had any problems on set, because we worked too damned hard. I'd loose ten to 15 pounds every production season wearing the heavy leather pants, jacket and guns. Sometimes we didn't get a chance to sit down. We were so busy that in the entire time we were in production I think I only saw three or four episodes.'

*The Adventures of Wild Bill Hickok* was filmed by units experienced in making cowboy dramas for Monogram Pictures, and true to Monogram budgets, each episode was made at a basement cost of just $12,000. Guy Madison said, 'We couldn't afford to waste any time in TV.'

Madison rode a magnificent Appaloosa named Buckshot and 300 pound Devine's long suffering mount was named Joker.

Jingles described Hickok as 'The bravest, strongest, fightingest US Marshal in the whole West.' And that's about it: he beat up all the bad guys and somehow kept his good looks.

Madison died of emphysema on 6 February 1996, in Palm Springs.

Devine died on 18 February 1977 from leukaemia.

# THE ALASKANS

## 4 OCTOBER 1959

**EACH black and white episode was an hour long. The show, produced by Louis Edelman, debuted on Sunday 9.30–10.30 on the ABC Network on 4 October 1959.**

This Warner Bros series, set in the Skagway of the Gold Rush of Alaska during the 1890's, featured the adventures of Silky Harris (Roger Moore) and Reno McKee (Jeff York), accompanied by beautiful singer, Rocky Shaw (Dorothy Provine).

When gold was discovered in the Yukon in the 1890's, thousands of hopeful prospectors headed north for a chance at becoming rich. The easiest passage to the Yukon was through the small Alaskan port town of Skagway, which quickly exploded into a sprawling boom town, offering almost everything a miner could want, for a price. The Gold Rush brought Silky, Reno and Rocky to Skagway in search of riches.

*Roger Moore*
*Dorothy Provine*
*Jeff York*

Since hunting for gold proved too strenuous for them, they found other ways of making a living. Silky and Reno would rather gamble than dig and sometimes only Rocky's singing jobs fed them all. Rocky sang in the saloon of bad guy Nifty Cronin, (Ray Danton). Silky and Reno were a shade shy of honest, but they never did any serious harm.

*The Alaskans* often used scripts recycled from *Maverick*, another Warner Bros. Western series also on ABC-TV at the time, and Roger Moore later moved across to *Maverick* to play Bret Maverick's cousin Beau Maverick through the following season, after the cancellation of *The Alaskans*. It was reported that all cast members were unhappy with the scripts, and none were apparently sad to see the show end on 25 September 1960 after just 36 episodes had been filmed.

Ray Danton died of kidney disease on 11 February 1991, aged 60. Jeff York died in 1995 at the Motion Picture Home in Calabasas and DeKova in 1981. Roger Moore went on to become James Bond and now spends most of his time in the South of France. Dorothy Provine lives in Seattle.

# ALIAS SMITH AND JONES

## 21 JANUARY 1971

THE first color, hour-long show produced by Universal Studios aired on the ABC Network 21 January 1971. Each show featured a top guest star and was filmed mainly at expensive locations around Moab, Utah. *Smith and Jones* was an attempt by ABC to capitalize on the movie success of *Butch Cassidy and the Sundance Kid.*

Hannibal Hayes (Pete Duel) and Kid Curry (Ben Murphy) alias Joshua Smith and Thaddeus Jones were two gallant and amiable outlaws trying to go straight in this light-hearted, fast-paced show. The governor of the territory where they roamed had offered them both pardons if they could manage to stay out of trouble for a year.

Recurring guest stars included Burl Ives, JD Cannon and Slim Pickens. The show also attracted the talents of top writers and directors including Roy Huggins and Harry Falk. Huggins was Executive Producer with the story by Gene Roddenberry, Robert Guy Barrows and Huggins.

The show was fun-packed, but behind the scenes all was not well. Pete Duel suffered mental health problems and he eventually shot himself to death on 31 December 1971.

Universal quickly hired Roger Davis to stand in as Smith and the series continued for a further 17 episodes before closing on 13 January 1973. Davis had been doing the show's opening and closing narrations, now he had to re-shoot segments that Duel had already completed. Roy Huggins had originally wanted Davis for the star part when Universal had forced him to take Duel. Many of the people working on the show were horrified at the speed with which Davis moved into Duel's place; they had assumed that as there were only four more shows to be filmed for the season, it would simply be scrapped.

John Russell played semi-regular Sheriff Lom Trevors, the man Smith and Jones had to report in to at regular intervals.

Murphy's acting career had taken off in 1968, with a regular role on *The Name of the Game* and appearances in *It Takes a Thief* and *The Virginian*, and in 1970 he was cast as Kid Curry in the *Alias Smith and Jones* pilot. The pilot was picked up as a mid-season replacement in early 1971 and did well enough to be renewed for the next year.

After Duel's death, Murphy continued in his role for the remainder of the season and for the following season, until the show was cancelled in mid-season.

Murphy's later series included *Griff* (1973–4), *Gemini Man* (1976), *The Chisholms*

## TRIVIA

As of 2006, Alias Smith and Jones could be found airing on Encore's Western channel.

Burl Ives and Cesar Romero had recurring roles as Patrick McCreedy and Señor Armendariz, two ranchers waging a feud with Heyes and Curry stuck in the middle.

(1979–80), *Berrenger's* (1985), and *Dirty Dozen: The Series* (1988). He guest starred in such series as *Kojak, Marcus Welby, The Love Boat, Murder, She Wrote* and *Scarecrow and Mrs. King,* and appeared in the miniseries *The Winds of War.*

He still acts occasionally, and in the 1990's has shown up in guest spots on such shows as *In the Heat of the Night, Baywatch Nights, Silk Stalkings,* and in the recurring role of Ethan Cooper on *Dr. Quinn, Medicine Woman.*

He is divorced and lives in Malibu.

Peter Ellstrom Deuel had been considering medicine as a possible career, but after deciding that his real love was acting he withdrew from college after two years to study with the American Theater Wing in New York City. His younger brother Geoffrey followed in his footsteps as an actor, and his sister Pamela became a nightclub singer, later switching to contemporary Christian music.

After touring with the national company with *Take Her, She's Mine,* Duel settled in Hollywood, where he landed a number of guest spots in various television programs. His first recurring role was in 1965–6, as the brother-in-law of the title character in *Gidget* starring Sally Field. This was followed by a leading role as a young married architect in the sitcom *Love on a Rooftop* (1966–7), in which he co-starred with Judy Carne. After *Love on a Rooftop* was cancelled, Duel settled down to some film work and a large number of TV guest spots. He appeared in many of the most memorable shows of the era, including *The FBI, The Fugitive, The Virginian, Ironside, Marcus Welby, The Name of the Game,* and *The Bold Ones.* His films included *A Cannon for Cordoba Generation,* and the TV movie *The Young Country,* in which he played the villain, to Roger Davis' hero.

In 1970, he co-starred with Ben Murphy in the pilot for *Alias Smith and Jones.* Despite stiff competition from the top-rated show on television, *The Flip Wilson Show,* it did well enough to be renewed for a second season. The show continued to do fairly well and had been developing a large following.

Early on 31 December 1971, Duel died of a gunshot wound to the head in an apparent suicide. He was discovered by his girlfriend,

Diane Ray, who reported to police that she had been sleeping in another room and had been awakened by the sound of a gunshot. Duel had long struggled with depression and was apparently despondent over a number of things, including a failed relationship, an alcohol problem which had led to the loss of his driver's license, the shooting schedule of the series which left him with little time for other work or for his favorite pastime of wilderness camping, and an overwhelming sense of pessimism about the future of the world, and particularly the environment.

Both Murphy and Davis live in Southern California.

# THE AMERICANS
## 23 JANUARY 1961

**THE** Americans had its first airing on 23 January 1961 and was produced in color by MGM TV. Only 17 episodes were shot, but when its original run was over it stayed on air in reruns until 11 September 1961.

Brother against brother is the basic premise of this hour long NBC Network series. Darryl Hickman starred as Union soldier, Ben Canfield and Richard Davalos co-starred as his brother Jeff, who fought for the Confederacy.

Just as the Civil War was a period of fury so too were the ratings wars when *The Americans* aired. Another Western, *Cheyenne*, screening at the same time as *The Americans*, was more successful and helped push it toward an early demise.

Neither Hickman nor Davalos act much anymore.

# ANNIE OAKLEY

## APRIL 1953

**GENE** Autry's Flying a Productions produced this fun series of 83, black and white episodes for syndication from April 1953 to December 1956.

Gail Davis starred as Annie and along with Brad Johnson as Deputy Lofty Craig and Jimmy Hawkins as her little brother, Tagg, tried to keep law and order around the town of Diablo. Fess Parker starred as Tom Conrad and Shelley Fabares as Trudy.

Her uncle Luke MacTavish is the town sheriff, but he is never seen. Annie's horses were named Target, Tagg's Pixie, and Lofty's Forest.

Most of the location filming was done near Pioneertown, California and many of the familiar western faces of the time appeared on the show which set out to promote wholesome moral values.

Jimmy Hawkins eventually went into film production. Brad Johnson died in 1981.

Gail Davis died on 15 March 1997 from cancer. She was one of televisions first female heroines, giving the girls someone to root for, she was a gun-toting, hard ridin' rancher and during her time on *Annie Oakley*, she was voted Best Western Performer for two

consecutive years by Billboard Magazine. She was awarded a Golden Boot Award for her work in Westerns.

The show was aimed at children and it worked well and garnered a large following. 'Grandmas' around the world recall Annie Oakley as a model for what women can achieve.

Gail Davis was a crack shot and skilled rider and she did most of her own stunts on the series.

# BARBARY COAST

## 8 September 1975

**BARBARY** Coast was shot in color and the hour-long show debuted on the ABC Network on 8 September 1975. All filming was completed at Universal Studios until the show went off the air on 9 January 1976 after just 13 episodes.

*William Shatner* and *Doug McClure*

William Shatner played Jeff Cable an undercover man secretly working for the governor of California around San Francisco's Barbary Coast during the 1870's.

Working from The Golden Gate Casino as his cover, he takes down criminals and enemy agents with style and flair. His ally was gambler Cash Conover played by Doug McClure. Both men wanted the area cleaned up.

The show was reminiscent of *The Wild Wild West* and tried to emulate the James West/Artemis Gordon partnership, with limited success. It also tried to emulate the elaborate cons and machinations of *Mission: Impossible* (going so far as to use a number of writers from that show), but again with less then satisfactory results.

Overall the show was entertaining but just never quite sparked its audience.

Doug McClure died of cancer on 4 February 1995 at the age of 59. McClure, educated at UCLA, had a long career of apparent agelessness, playing one young sidekick after another through numerous movies and one TV series after another, playing twentiesh roles well into his late 40's.

Although he made more than 500 appearances in his career (counting TV episodes separately), he is undoubtedly best remembered as Trampas in the series *The Virginian* and *The Men from Shiloh* and the movie *Backtrack!*

McClure was fighting cancer the last couple of years before his death; despite this, he continued working, appearing in the *Maverick* movie as one of the gamblers, as well as in *Riders in the Storm* and episodes of *Burke's Law* and *Kung Fu: The Legend Continues,* which didn't appear until after his death. McClure won a star on Hollywood's Walk of Fame shortly before his death.

# TRIVIA

Whilst William Shatner gained fame playing James Tiberius Kirk of the USS Enterprise in the television show *Star Trek* from 1966 to 1969 and in seven of the subsequent movies, he has had more recent acclaim as attorney Denny Crane on the television drama *Boston Legal,* for which he has won an Emmy and a Golden Globe Award.

# BAT MASTERSON

## 8 OCTOBER 1958

**THIS series was loosely based on the exploits of real-life western figure William Barclay 'Bat' Masterson. Produced by ZIV TV Productions, the show starring Gene Barry as Masterson, ran on the NBC Network from 1958 to 1961. One hundred and eight episodes of the black and white, half-an-hour show were made.**

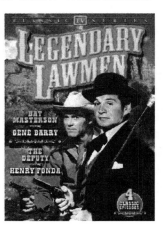

Bill Baldwin was the announcer and Stardust was Bat's horse. Masterson hired out as a sheriff, drover, guide and bodyguard, but was more at home in a card game. He was a smooth talking, dapper enforcer of the law in the 1880's, carrying a gold-tipped cane which hid a sword. He also carried a gun, one that was custom built for him by the people of Dodge City during his service as sheriff.

However, the TV Bat Masterson would rather talk his way out of a fight than resort to violence.

In real life, Masterson was a deputy of Wyatt Earp's.

### BAT MASTERSON THEME SONG

**by Havens Wray**

Back when the west was very young,
There lived a man named Masterson.
He wore a cane and derby hat,
They called him Bat, Bat Masterson.
The trail that he traveled is still there,
No one has come yet to replace his name.
And those with too handy a trigger, forgot to figger
On his fighting cane.
A man of steel the stories say,
But women's eyes all glanced his way.
A gambler's game he always won,
They called him Bat, Bat Masterson.
Now in the legend of the west,
One name stands out of all the rest.
The man who had the fastest gun,
His name was Bat, Bat Masterson.

# BEARCATS
## 16 SEPTEMBER 1971

**BEARCATS** was an hour long color series which debuted on the CBS Network on 16 September 1971. Only 13 episodes were made and the series went off air on 30 December 1971.

The show was set in the American Southwest around 1914 and the time frame gave the series an unusual flavor, being something other than a traditional Western. Two soldiers of fortune, Hank Brackett and Johnny Reach travel to their assignments in a Stutz-Bearcat automobile. Rod Taylor and Dennis Cole starred in the title roles and made a good team.

Location work was mainly shot around Tuscon and Santa Fe.

*Bearcats* was Rod Taylor's second attempt at a weekly television series. The show's concept had appealed to Taylor when it was presented by series creator, veteran Hollywood writer/producer Douglas Heyes (who had also worked with Taylor on a *Twilight Zone* episode).

Taylor's character, Hank Brackett, is a former Army captain, a veteran of the Spanish-American War campaign in the Philippines. He had left the Army and settled in the Southwest, where he acquired a reputation as a troubleshooter.

Brackett had saved the young Johnny Reach (Dennis Cole) from being unjustly lynched as a cattle rustler. Together they cleaned up a couple of border towns and eventually people flocked to them for help with their problems. Brackett was responsible for the clever plans the pair came up with to defeat their well-organized foes. Reach often did the more athletic stunts. Any conflict in their relationship resulted from the good-natured competition for some of the inevitably beautiful and available women they met during their adventures.

They were mercenary about the jobs they took and set their fee as a signed blank check. They would fill in the amount only after successfully completing their job, the amount being determined by the degree of difficulty encountered. Their rationale was simple: If you could put a dollar amount on your trouble, then you didn't need their help badly enough.

The soldier-of-fortune business must have paid well, as Brackett and Reach traveled in the new Stutz Bearcat – then a $2,000 sports car that would be the equivalent of a Corvette, Ferrari, or Mercedes SL today. The Stutz Bearcat was the most famous American sports car of its era. Production continued well into the 1920's, when it entered folklore as part of the 'Jazz Age.'

For the series, Hollywood custom car builder George Barris was commissioned to make two authentic replicas of a 1914 Bearcat. (Barris also made a third car to display at car shows.) For safety and reliability, the replicas had modern engines and running gear. The pair of replicas used in the show reportedly cost $25,000; this at a time when a new Corvette sold for $5,000 and the most expensive American car sold for $8,000.

Typically the two worked for railroads, landowners or the government. As private citizens they were able to cross the Mexican border where normal lawmen or the military could not go.

The period during which *Bearcats* was set allowed for the use of unexpected props, including machine guns and airplanes.

In the first episode, they fought a bandit who stole an Army tank to rob banks. Another episode saw them fighting a group of Germans who were attacking Mexican villages dressed as US soldiers, in an attempt to get Mexico to attack the United States, thus preventing America from joining the war against Germany.

Taylor played Brackett with his usual light touch and charm. Off-screen, Taylor often was less than charming in the much publicized fights with CBS testified. He was adamant about making the show different, as he told a 1971 TV Guide article,

'The one thing we've got going for us is the era. It was an interesting and funny era, with old-fashioned melodrama and hissing the villain… Let's play this partly for laughs, with the broad gesture and even maybe the girl tied to the railroad tracks… The show should have the feeling of looking at daguerreotypes.'

He also fought to take the characters away from the Southwest occasionally and capitalize upon the onset of World War I. And there were fights over censorship, too, with Taylor moaning, 'What do you mean I can't look euphoric after that night with the beautiful Mexican broad?'

Whilst Taylor won the battles with CBS, the show lost out the ratings war.

## TRIVIA

*Bearcats*, despite its large promotional campaign prior to its premiere, was a huge disappointment in the Nielsen ratings, losing badly to both *The Flip Wilson Show* on NBC and the more traditional Western, *Alias Smith and Jones*, on ABC. It was ignominiously cancelled at midseason. (This marked the last time that two Westerns broadcast by major US networks competed in the same time slot for viewers, marking a milestone in the decline of the Western era in US network television programming.)

# BEST OF THE WEST
## 10 SEPTEMBER 1981

**THE show was shot in color, ran half-an-hour and debuted on the ABC Network on 10 September 1981. It went off the air on 23 August 1982.**

*The Best of the West* was a comedy series about Marshal Sam Best of Copper Creek. Sam was a Civil War veteran from Philadelphia who had journeyed west in 1865 with his smart 10-year-old son, Daniel, and new wife, Elvira.

Sam had run off a gunslinger named The Calico Kid by accident, and then, by default, became town marshal.

Joel Higgins starred as Sam Best, Carlene Watkins was Elvira and Meeno Peluce was the precocious Daniel.

The evil saloon owner was played by Leonard Frey and his slow henchman, Frog, was Tracey Walter. Veteran Western stars such

as Chuck Connors and Slim Pickens starred in occasional episodes during the run.

Leonard Frey died of Aids on 24 August 1988.

# THE BIG VALLEY
## 15 September 1965

**THE** show debuted in color, at an hour length, on the ABC Network on 15 September 1965, and ran 112 episodes, leaving the air after four years on 19 May 1969; cancelled from the producer's choice, for once not because of poor ratings.

*Lee Majors,*
*Richard Long,*
*Peter Breck,*
*Linda Evans*
and
*Barbara Stanwyck*

*The Big Valley* portrayed the adventures of a wealthy ranch family in the 1870's and starred major motion picture actress Barbara Stanwyck as Victoria Barkley, widow of Tom and matriarch of the massive Barkley Ranch. She ran the holding near Stockton, California, all 30,000 acres of it, including mines, vineyards, orchards, cattle, together with further property in Mexico with the help of her four offspring. She was nobody's fool.

Oldest son, Jarrod was a lawyer and was played to perfection by Richard Long. He split his time between Barkley interests and his other legal cases.

Peter Breck starred as quick-fire Nick, second oldest son. He ran the ranch with his mother and his persona was a sharply drawn contrast to his older brother's smooth urbanity.

He had performed in regional theaters until Robert Mitchum plucked him from obscurity, selecting him for a role in *Thunder Road* (1958). He then made several further appearances in television shows including *Have Gun; Will Travel* with Richard Boone. In 1959 he starred in his own Western series, *Black Saddle*, in which he played gunslinger-turned-lawyer Clay Culhane. That show lasted only one season.

In 1965 he had been the first actor signed for *The Big Valley*. When he accepted the role he asked his wife, 'How in the world can I understand such a complex character?'

She told him, 'Just look in the mirror.'

Breck acknowledged, 'Nick was the loud mouth. He really was a redneck. He had a horrible scene where he beats up a gypsy because of grapes. It was really awful of him. He didn't apologize.'

For the episode *Night of the Wolf*, his most memorable segment, he was nominated for an Emmy in 1966.

Whenever he talks about the series it is always with much fondness, 'We all adored and loved each other. We had a great family, a wonderful relationship with one another.' And although it is the role of Nick Barkley that he is most often identified with, he has no complaints, 'I don't mind it. He bought my house. Nick's been very good to me. I'm very happy to say that I'm proud I was Nick Barkley or that I am Nick Barkley.'

In 1986 he moved to North Vancouver in British Columbia, Canada and started up the Breck Academy for the Performing Arts there.

He is working to get a *Big Valley* reunion movie off the ground.

## TRIVIA

Both Richard Long and Peter Breck had been regulars for a short time on another classic Western series, *Maverick*, although in different seasons; Long played 'Gentleman Jack Darby' to pick up the slack when Efrem Zimbalist, Jr., began *77 Sunset Strip* and could no longer play 'Dandy Jim Buckley,' while Breck assumed the role of 'Doc Holliday' when Gerald Mohr was unavailable.

Lee Majors later recounted on *The Tonight Show* how he was justly taken to task by Barbara Stanwyck after he developed a star complex that threatened to adversely affect the series.

Recently he was awarded the Buck Jones Film Festival Award.

Third son, Heath was played by Lee Majors. Heath was the illegitimate son of Victoria's late husband. While away on business, injured Tom had been nursed back to health by Leah Simmons. When he left to return to his family she never told him she was pregnant. Eventually a grown Heath seeks to discover his roots and Victoria welcomes him in warmly as one of her own clan. He shows up in the pilot episode, *Palms of Glory* as an angry young man, but eventually mellows into the strong silent type and an effective foil to Nick's wild outbursts. His life experiences, which contrasted so sharply from the other family members became the source of many interesting alternative story lines.

In 1963 Majors had moved to Los Angeles with his young family and started work with the Los Angeles Park and Recreation Department as the Recreation Director for North Hollywood Park. While working at the park, he met many people in the entertainment business, including agent Dick Clayton. Clayton enrolled him at MGM's drama school, and he started studying with Estelle Harmon, a highly respected drama coach. His audition for the role of Heath Barkley in *The Big Valley*, was his first big break. Hundreds of experienced actors with long lists of credits had tried for the part, 'They asked for my credits,' remembers Majors, 'and I didn't have any.'

Even after securing the role of Heath, he continued working at the park right up to the time shooting began, and even stayed on their inactive list for another two years just in case the series didn't work out.

Barbara Stanwyck took him under her wing and became his mentor. Majors credits her with teaching him how to be a professional actor.

After *The Big Valley* closed and following only his second movie, *The Liberation of L.B. Jones*, co-starring Lee J. Cobb and Roscoe Lee Browne, Majors won the role of Roy Tate in *The Men from Shiloh,* the revised version of the *Virginian*. It lasted only one year and he was then out again looking for work.

In 1973 he received a script for a movie of the week called *The Six Million Dollar Man*. When the show became a regular on the schedule Majors said, 'I started out as fourth or fifth banana in *The Big Valley*, third banana in *The Men from Shiloh* and second banana in *Owen Marshall*. Now I'm the top banana in my own series, and I couldn't be happier.'

The series quickly became a big hit until its last airing on 6 March 1978. Eventually three reunion movies were made, one each in 1987, 1989 and 1994.

After the show ended, Majors decided to give movies another try. He made *The Norsemen, Steel, Killer Fish, Agency* and *The Last Chase* all in the next three years. None fared well at the box office and his marriage was also on shaky ground.

In July of 1979, six years after they married, Farrah Fawcett announced they had separated. During the separation she began dating Major's best friend Ryan O'Neal.

In 1981 he began filming his next series, *The Fall Guy*. The story about a Hollywood stuntman and bounty hunter named Colt Seavers, was an immediate success and once again Major's career was on a roll. He asked many of his friends and former co-stars from other shows to do guest spots or cameos. This list included Richard Burton, Peter Breck, Lindsay Wagner, Linda Evans, Roy Rogers, Milton Berle, Doug McClure, Robert Wagner, James Drury and Richard Anderson. The show had a very successful run and eventually ended in 1986.

After *The Fall Guy* ended he made three series pilots, *Harris Down Under* in 1988, *Roadshow* in 1989 and *Daytona Beach* in 1996.

In 1991–2 he starred with Jeffrey Meek in *Raven* as Herman Jablonski 'Ski.' That show lasted only one year. He also appeared in episodes of *Tour of Duty, Lonesome Dove, Promised Land, The War Next Door* and *Walker, Texas Ranger*. Majors has also done some TV and theatrical movies in recent years, including *The Lost Treasure of Dos Santos, Musketeers Forever, New Jersey Turnpikes* and *Trojan War*.

Linda Evans starred in *The Big Valley* as the only daughter, Audra. In the first year she was full of energy, but her character became less well-defined as the show went on.

Napoleon Whiting played Silas, the Barkleys hard-working butler. Charles Briles starred as Eugene Barkley, youngest, college-aged son who appeared in the first half year of the series, then disappeared (the 1965 the draft board actually had something

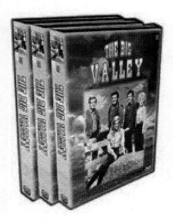

to do with this). Sheriff Fred Madden was played by Douglas Kennedy. He appeared frequently during the last two years.

Barbara Stanwyck later appeared in four episodes of *Wagon Train* and Richard Long appeared in one too.

Stanwyck died of congestive heart failure on 20 January 1990, aged 82. Richard Long died in 1974 of heart problems. Douglas Kennedy died in 1973 of cancer. Napolean Whiting died in 1984.

Misty Girl was Victoria's horse and Coco was Nick's. Eventually Breck bought Coco. He was riding the horse on the set when it suddenly died underneath him from a burst heart.

*The Big Valley Theme* song was by George Duning, Joseph Mullendore and Elmer Bernstein.

# BLACK SADDLE

## 10 JANUARY 1960

**BLACK Saddle debuted on NBC TV on 10 January 1959 and ran for 44, half-hour black and white episodes until 30 September 1960.**

*Black Saddle* tells the story of gunfighter turned lawyer, Clay Culhane, strongly played by Peter Breck. After Clay's brothers are killed in a shootout he gives up his violent ways to become a circuit lawyer. He carries his law books in his saddlebags as he travels through post Civil war New Mexico helping people who need his legal assistance.

Russell Johnson played Marshal Gib Scott, who isn't convinced about Culhane changing his ways and he keeps a wary eye on him.

Settling in Latigo, New Mexico, Clay lodges at The Marathon Hotel, run by Nora Travers, played by Anna-Lisa.

Russell Johnson later starred in *Gilligan's Island*.

The series was produced by Four Star-Zane Grey Productions. *Black Saddle Theme* was by Hershel Burke Gilbert.

## TRIVIA

Russell Johnson had no intention of acting until Paul Henreid 'spotted' him and cast him in *For Men's Only*, a 1952 movie. He used the G.I. Bill to pay for his acting studies and subsequently won many great roles. He starred in many movie and TV roles, but when he auditioned the part of Roy 'the Professor' Hinkley for *Gilligan's Island*, his life changed forever.

# BONANZA

## 12 SEPTEMBER 1959

THE show, conceived and created by David Dortort, premiered on 12 September 1959 and ran for 260 episodes. It was the first network series to be photographed in color from the outset. Much of it was shot 7,000 feet above sea level at Lake Tahoe. Although NBC began calling itself, 'the rainbow network,' there is no truth behind the rumor that *Bonanza* was created to help sell color television sets for its parent company RCA.

Second only in longevity to *Gunsmoke,* this hour-long series was a standout on the NBC Network for 14 years, reaching as high as number one in the ratings in some seasons and from 1959 through to 1973, *Bonanza* rode television Western's biggest wave of popularity. The flagship Sunday night slot at 9.00 pm had been purchased for the show by sponsors General Motors and the Chevrolet division.

Jay Livingston and Ray Evans penned the theme for *Bonanza*, but David Rose scored each episode, without incorporating the theme. Rose wrote original music for each episode and used a thirty piece orchestra to record it. This lent a cinematic effect which contributed to the show's reputation. Landon used Rose on every program he later made, calling him a genius.

David Dortort, the show's creator, said he wanted *Bonanza* to shed the image of the gunfighter; he didn't want to focus on a loner, who solved problems and then rode off into the sunset, saying that character 'had little, if anything, to do with the actual life of a flesh-and-blood human being.' Instead he wanted something that focused on family values and a sense of deep humanity.

He wrote the parts of Little Joe and Hoss specifically for Michael Landon and Dan Blocker, and although Lorne Greene (Ben Cartwright) and Pernell Roberts (Adam) completed the cast, NBC were not initially happy with his choices. They were particularly opposed to Blocker, saying no audience would accept a large, fat man as a hero. But Dortort argued he had assembled a cast that could handle drama, comedy and tragedy with ease, sometimes within one episode, 'I told the network I knew my people, I had written the parts with them in mind.'

To emphasize contemporary issues such as racism, violence, mental illness, political and religious corruption, social injustice and the generation gap, Dortort placed his production facility at Paramount Studios. He said there he could give his series a sense of timelessness. Paramount was the only studio left in Hollywood that still had a set that didn't look like a generic cow-town. NBC had to pay a heavy price for the facility which included Stages 16 and 17 as well. The interior sets for *Bonanza*, including the Ponderosa, were filmed on those sound stages. The sets were designed by Paramount's Hal Pereira, Earl Hedrick and Dortort himself.

Many assume that all the exteriors were shot at Lake Tahoe's Incline Village, but in fact location work was done over numerous sites in California, including Iverson's Movie Location Ranch, Corriganville, Golden Oak ranch and throughout the Simi Valley. In 1959 an expensive residential area had been constructed around Incline Village and possibilities for filming up there had been significantly reduced.

Through its 14 seasons, *Bonanza* used more than 75 directors including Robert Altman and Michael Landon himself. Through 1960 to 61 at the time Altman was endeavoring to carve out his movie foothold at Warners he was also helping to establish *Bonanza's* reputation, and despite the fact that he later rarely mentioned his time on the show, his role in it was far from marginal. Dortort had a fiery relationship with the temperamental director but also heaped credit on him, 'In some respects he was my best director… a giant among pygmies. He had a large share in the strength and the popularity of the show.'

Dortort would only work with Altman on the proviso that he promised to abstain from drinking, stay on budget and on time and honor the script he was given. He says the director always kept his word and added, 'There was a quality to his work immediately. First of all his camerawork, or let's say the way he uses his cameraman, was consistently brilliant, and I think that the show under him always had an extremely professional look. His setups were immaculate. He gave the show a wonderful look. Also, because of his savage wit... he made his shows stronger than most directors. Not in terms of the action, but the impact. Very strong. Altman was happier in a situation where cruelty was part of the story. He wasn't terribly patient with soft, gentle stories, he needed something with bite.'

*Bonanza* became a hit despite the formidable competition it faced during its first months; it was a thinking-person's Western, and it always tried hard to be meaningful. Its stories focused on the life of Ben Cartwright, the patriarchal owner of the Ponderosa Ranch, a 1,000-square-mile ranch nestled on the shore of Lake Tahoe, close to nearby Virginia City, Nevada. When Dortort was establishing the background for *Bonanza*, he was careful about getting historical facts right, even though his characters were of course entirely fictional.

The discovery of the richest silver strikes on the Comstock Lode at the eve of the Civil War had led to a great migration west toward Virginia City, and played a decisive role in the establishment of some of America's great dynastic fortunes. This set the scene for the arrival of the Cartwrights to the area.

Dortort always believed the creation of the great Ponderosa Ranch was his crowning achievement, saying it became something of a mythical place along the lines of Shangri-La and Camelot, 'The Ponderosa's message was universal.' The name Ponderosa, comes from the many ponderosa pines growing on the ranch.

Widower Ben had three sons, all from different mothers (his wives had all died tragically; Adam, Hoss, and wild Little Joe. That original cast is the most familiar one, although changes were made later. After running 14 seasons the audience accepted the cast as family.

## BEN

Choosing the actor to play Ben had been critical to Dortort's original plan to have the father as the authority figure. He said he chose Greene after seeing him argue with Ward Bond, the blustery star of *Wagon Train*, 'Lorne not only dominated Bond, he made him look, by contrast, a weak, indecisive man.'

Greene said he accepted the part because Dortort had created 'a love story of four men. A true story of mankind.'

Ben had led an action-packed life before settling down on the Ponderosa. He had been a sea captain, an officer in the military and had also worked in a foundry.

Born in Ottawa, Ontario, Canada, on 12 February 1915, Greene was a well known celebrity long before Americans came to know his work on *Bonanza*. In Canada he was often referred to as 'The Voice of Doom,' an epithet he acquired during his days as the chief radio announcer on CBC radio from 1939 to 1942.

His interest in acting and media had begun when he joined a drama club while studying engineering at Queen's University in Kingston, Ontario. Always seeking a challenge, he joined the CBC radio where his distinctive voice soon propelled him into newscasting.

In 1953, like many of his contemporaries, Greene migrated south to pursue his acting career. He made numerous appearances on various US telecasts such as *Studio One, Climax* and *Playhouse 90*. He also made two movies, *The Silver Chalice* and *Tight Spot*. After a role in the Broadway production of *The Prescott Proposals*, he was offered the part in the Western movie *The Hard Man* in 1957.

In spite of his friends' concerns that getting involved in a Western would limit his appeal, he accepted the role by way of exploring the genre. He quickly followed it up with a part in *The Last of the Fast Guns* and eventually he arrived on the small screen in an episode of *Wagon Train*. It was after seeing him in *Wagon Train* that Dortort selected him.

Over time, Greene came to have great influence over the scripts he was involved in. He was a committed pacifist, so the show's level of rough action decreased as his power increased. As a consequence, *Bonanza* was always less violent than other Westerns. Ben preferred to talk first, shoot second.

After *Bonanza* ended with the collapse of the Western's television popularity, Greene starred briefly in 1978 in the ill-fated *Battlestar Galactica*, a science fiction television series about a flotilla of human refugees voyaging to Earth while hunted by evil subhuman Cylons.

He died of pneumonia in Santa Monica, California, 11 September 1987.

## ADAM

Adam was the oldest, best educated and the most logical of Ben's sons. His mother had died in childbirth, when Ben was a sea captain. Adam was philosophical, loved to read, played the guitar, and was usually around to tell his younger brothers, 'I told you so'. However, he occasionally got involved with or even instigated some of the shenanigans the Cartwright boys were known for.

Pernell Roberts always seemed to consider the show beneath his dignity and he scornfully voiced his concern about the 'psychological motives' of people who developed a fanatical devotion to actors.

Dortort said that casting Adam had proven difficult because it had been the least appealing of the four roles. Adam was the most independent-minded of the brothers, and in that respect Roberts was well suited to the part. He was critical of scripts, refused to socialize during filming and was unwilling to make personal appearances after the first season.

He generally resented authority and later became an outspoken proponent for civil rights. Although he risked his career by vigorously demonstrating against discrimination, he continued to speak his mind and didn't seem to care much about the effect his actions had on the show. Although *Bonanza's* sponsor, Chevrolet, was deluged by hate mail, Dortort, who personally shared Robert's views, said that he couldn't tell a grown man what to do when he was off the show. He did however admit, 'I had difficulties with Pernell right from the beginning. On the second day of shooting, he came to my office and said he didn't want to wear his hairpiece. I didn't even know he was bald… I told him, 'when you and I shook hands on the deal, you had that on. You're going to keep it on as long as you're on the show'.'

Roberts turned on Dortort and commented, '*Bonanza* could be really good if the

> # TRIVIA
>
> In 1979 Roberts was back in a series of his own, *Trapper John, MD* which ran for several years and won him his only Emmy nomination to date

powers-that-be cared enough to make it that way.' He wanted less sentimentality and family togetherness and didn't like the fact that the show's stories were inevitably written for all four characters, saying, 'We need time to develop individuality.'

Roberts eventually left *Bonanza* hoping to join a repertory group in Minneapolis, but when that didn't work out he rejected Dortort's offer of a return and instead took parts in other TV shows like *The Virginian* and *Gunsmoke*. His departure was regrettable, but the seventh series in 1965 soon became another *Bonanza* triumph. The show remained at number one in the year-end ratings without Adam.

**Michael Landon said, 'I never stopped seeing Lorne as my Dad. Lorne was a solid pillar for both me and Dan Blocker.'**

## Hoss

Dortort had created the part of Hoss specifically for Dan Blocker, and he obstinately refused to consider anybody else. Altman too seemed to find Hoss the character he empathized with most and he became great friends with Blocker. The director was always at his best in the episodes that featured the gentle giant.

Blocker was enormously gifted as an actor and he **was** Hoss, the intelligent, even-tempered middle son. His ready capacity for love and forgiveness made him popular with the rest of the cast and Dortort said, 'Over the years, he gave me the least amount of trouble.'

Hoss' mother was Inger, whom Ben had married when Adam was a baby. Inger had swiftly fallen victim to an Indian attack and was killed when Hoss was still a baby. Inger was Scandinavian and Hoss means 'good luck' in Norwegian. Hoss was always good for a laugh or for back-up in fights that his other brothers, particularly Joe started. Hoss was periodically talked into wild schemes by his younger brother.

As the show grew in popularity, Blocker found his own status becoming a problem saying, 'A man never appreciates his privacy until he's lost it. I still can't believe that people are that interested in me.'

In June 1967 Blocker confessed that he didn't want to renew his contract, 'I will have been with the show 12 years. I am tired.' He also felt that his $11,000 salary was too little, 'Considering what the show does, our salary is comparatively small.' (Chuck Conners was then taking home $25,000 for *Cowboy In Africa*) He argued, 'We're bringing in our show under budget, and have been for seven years. We get $165,000 a show, but have brought it in under $100,000. This show has been in the black since its second year.'

Blocker was also disgruntled that NBC-TV had refused to allow him to take the role of Lennie in ABCs production of *Of Mice and Men*.

He did renew his contract and continued to work on the show but continued to bemoan the constant pressure of working on the series, 'You have to fight continually to keep fresh. I've got two or three things working for me that a lot of guys don't have. I have a happy home life and can completely divorce myself from the show the minute I leave the stage. Every morning I am totally re-created. I keep myself away from the business as much as possible when I'm not working.'

Blocker, like Roberts became involved with the Civil Rights Movement. He did more work away from *Bonanza* than the rest of the other Cartwrights, including making films such as *Come Blow Your Horn* and *Lady in Cement* with Frank Sinatra.

# LITTLE JOE

When Dortort selected Michael Landon to play the part of the youngest son, Little Joe, he said, 'It seemed to me that Mike had depth, certainly more than anybody the network wanted me to cast, and a great potential for growth.' Dortort proved to be correct when Landon went on to co-write five *Bonanza* scripts between 1962 and 1967, followed by a further 14 of his own. He also directed 14 episodes between 1968 and 1973. Landon said that the show had been a better training ground than any film school he might have gone to.

Landon took his work seriously and even performed many of his own stunts (for which he was paid extra). Throughout *Bonanza* Landon used his athletic ability in full measure, leaping over card tables, flying backward over chairs, bursting through windows, and head-butting his rivals. By such means he instilled his own electric personality into the part. He was so agile and ambidextrous that he also became efficient with gun and knife in either hand. He became one of the Hollywood elite fighters, horsemen and stuntmen.

When called upon, he could also be rugged and strong, and in fact was an ideal man of the West. But in an era inundated with Westerns, when he eventually outgrew his TV saddle he went on to become one of the most popular Hollywood stars. TV success as a cowboy rarely translated into a long career and Landon could easily have disappeared along with so many others and he said, 'When *Bonanza* ended it was painful for everybody, it really was.' For Landon this was only the beginning.

Ted Voigtlander, one of the show's directors of photography, taught Landon the art of cinematography and said, 'Many writers can 'see' things that maybe you can't photograph, well after getting to know the camera and the lenses, Mike can write things that you can actually do.'

To repay the compliment, Landon always used Voigtlander on his post *Bonanza* projects. In fact most of the *Bonanza* crew later went with him into *The Little House on the Prairie*.

Little Joe was the son of French Creole, Marie, whom Ben met and married in New Orleans. She died after falling from a horse. Little Joe was the best loved brother by the audience and was acknowledged as the heart and soul of *Bonanza*. He was regularly involved in pranks and frequently falling madly in love. He was looked on by his father and brothers with affection, and was usually at the center of the most humorous episodes. Little Joe was hot-tempered, quick-to-fight and quick to forgive. He was shot, stabbed, beaten up, kidnapped, arrested, thrown in jail, had broken limbs, was thrown from horses, wounded by an Indian arrow, and had his heart broken more times than any other Cartwrights put together. He frequently got

himself and Hoss into trouble and Landon possessed an uncanny knack for comedy which he expressed in several of the lighter episodes of *Bonanza*.

Not the tallest in the saddle, Landon was however larger than life. He confessed in TV Guide, 6 May 1989, 'Before the start of *Bonanza* we were all taken to wardrobe. When we walked in Dan was by far the tallest. Lorne and I were the same height and Pernell was probably two inches taller. When we came out of the dressing rooms Lorne was taller than everyone but he was kinda leaning forward. So we realized he had these marvelous boots on and we all went back into wardrobe. When we came out I was the same height as Lorne, but Dan had gotten taller. Before we were done we all had these huge lifts – and that's how we played it.'

In the summer of 1962, during the start of the fourth season, Kent McCray was assigned to the series as its new production manager. McCray had been working at NBC since 1954, as a live-unit production manager.

The first time he met Landon was on location at the Iverson Ranch that summer. It was a hot, dry day and he was first introduced to Landon. 'Better get a car ready for me at one o'clock,' the star told the new production manager, 'because I'm leaving for the day.'

McCray checked the schedule and saw that Landon had to film every scene that afternoon and had to remain at the site.

McCray bluntly answered, 'There's no car and there isn't going to be one. Furthermore, it's a goddamn long walk back to Los Angeles. And if you leave before I tell you to, I'm going to sue the pants off you. You won't even get paid for your work this week.'

Landon complained, 'I don't like it.'

'What are you going to do about it?'

'I guess I'll get back to work,' Landon replied. 'I was just testing you.' Years later, McCray laughed, 'They all tested me!'

## THE HORSES

When *Bonanza* first aired in 1959 it was the first color Western on television. Along with the spectacular scenery of the location shots around Lake Tahoe and other parts of the west, the horses that the stars rode were also chosen specifically for their color. Most horses in TV Westerns of the time were brown or dark; they didn't call attention to themselves, leaving the cowboy actors to shine. The only time a horse stood out was when he was part of a unique team such as the lovely Trigger with his golden color and flowing blonde mane of course. Another outstanding horse in the color department of course was Silver for the Lone Ranger, a pure white horse who had a Pinto sidekick in Tonto's horse, Scout.

The Cartwrights however had to have colorful horses to feature in the new show. They were all rented from Fat Jones, owner of a North Hollywood ranch that regularly supplied the film industry. Little Joe rode a flashy pinto called Cochise, Adam a carrot red spirited chestnut, Hoss rode a rich black horse with white socks and a blaze, appropriately named Chub and Ben rode an all-American Quarter Horse with unique coloring; a blonde body color with dark legs, mane and tail.

Landon said Chub had a look of terror in its eye when it saw Blocker walk toward it, but in fact Blocker was probably the best rider of them all.

Cast in 1959 as a mount for Lorne Greene because of his gentle temperament and smooth, easy gait Buck stayed with the show until it ended in 1972. Greene was not a keen horseman and Landon frequently entertained audiences with tales of his expletives whenever he and Buck had to work together. Although it seems unlikely, it has been reported Lorne Green eventually bought the horse after the show ended and kept him as a pet.

Buck had begun his TV career on *Gunsmoke* as the mount for Marshal Dillon. The horses' real name was Dunny Waggoner.

## THE SHOW

Some other cast members through the years included Victor Sen Young as Hop Sing, the ranch cook, David Canary as Candy, a ranch hand, Ray Teal as Sheriff Roy Coffee, Mitch Vogel as Jamie Hunter, an orphan the Cartwrights take in and Tim Matheson as Griff King, another ranch hand, Dusty Rhoades was played by Lou Frizzel, Griff King by Tim Matheson and Deputy Clem Foster by Bing Russell.

Each week the family and their friends defended the Ponderosa against Indians or rustlers or defended some helpless person against unscrupulous outsiders. The formula was common in television Westerns but *Bonanza* differed from all its competitors. Indeed, many critics considered the series to be more of a soap opera than a Western since it downplayed the violent action and moral ambiguity which characterized other adult Westerns such as *Gunsmoke* or *Cheyenne*.

The show also always had a large female following unlike most other Westerns. Perhaps among the Cartwrights there was a man to appeal to every girl. In February 1964 Betty Friedan wrote in TV Guide, 'If housewives control the dial, why, with no women at all, are Westerns perennially so popular? 'Beefcake' of course. *Bonanza* for instance, really gives the panting woman a choice of sizes and ages — four unmarried men…' Ben was a tough yet wise father who exuded a balance between ruggedness

and compassion. Adam was a suave lady's man. Hoss was lovable and Little Joe was hot headed. It was a successful pattern that outdrew audiences for dozens of competing shows. Its family-oriented themes also made it popular when the medium was under criticism during congressional hearings on TV violence.

Initial ratings for the show however had not been overly encouraging. In 1959 the Western was at the height of its cinematic appeal with such films as *Rio Bravo* and *Warlock* proving huge box-office smashes. Television Westerns were also doing well but *Bonanza's* first reviews were less than promising. One paper even reported the show was in danger of being canceled and maybe if today's 'hit hunger' had prevailed back then, 1959 would have seen the last of *Bonanza*.

The show just about managed to hang on and Greene said, 'The problem was that the scripts had to be improved.' Changes were needed and he went on, 'There are times when I think we almost manage to transcend our constant lack of good scripts, proper rehearsal and all the other things that bug a man in this business.'

By Fall 1961 things had improved after a change of its time slot on Sunday nights and the show started its ten-season run in the top ten when it became the number two show, behind *Wagon Train*, but ahead of *Gunsmoke*. In 1962 Paramount even considered making blueprints of the Poderosa ranch house as so many people were writing in requesting them. Things were really taking off and librarians reported increased interest in the history of the Comstock and more than 450 Bonanza Booster Clubs were established, and then, in its sixth year, when most shows have outworn their welcome, *Bonanza* finally made it to the number one spot. This achievement seems all the more remarkable when considering that by then Westerns were no longer the viewing public's favorite fare. *The Virginian,* lying at number 22, was the only other Western in the Top 25.

President Lyndon Johnson admitted that he avoided *Bonanza's* time slot when he had announcements to make.

Then, in 1967 the show's ratings faltered. In July it was announced that the Cartwrights would be taking on a regular hired hand, presumably to fill Pernell Robert's place, and also to inject some new life. Dortort noticed obscure young actor, David Canary, in the Paul Newman feature, *Hombre,* and said, 'I realized immediately I had found the new foreman of the Ponderosa.'

Prior to playing Candy on *Bonanza*, he had worked in segments of the CBS show, *Cimarron Strip*. Candy played a more traditional cowboy; he was a loner, bound by no family ties and he didn't have Ben to fall back on when things went wrong. He was really thrown in to shake the program up. Blocker said, 'The kid is great. The show needs him.'

All that was ever revealed about him is that his name is short for Canaday and that he had an undisclosed shady past; Joe refers to him as Candy Canaday, but his first name is never actually revealed.

Canary left the show in 1970 after complaining that he had wanted to try his hand at writing and directing but wasn't getting his opportunity on *Bonanza*.

When he left the show it marked the beginning of the end. Television Westerns were in serious decline anyway by then but the executives were still trying desperately hard and when the show opened for its twelfth season, it had new credits, a new theme song and a new Virginia City. Production of *Bonanza* had moved from Paramount Studios to a cheaper facility at Warner Bros. in Burbank. In the opening story Virginia City had been burnt to the ground by an arsonist. New regular, fourteen year old Mitch Vogel as Jamie Hunter was introduced to inject some of the warmth that Dortort felt the show had started to miss as the Cartwright boys got older. Dusty Rhoades, played by Lou Frizzel was also included. These final episodes never received the same critical recognition that the earlier ones did, partly because they were only broadcast once and were not seen again until 1988 when they went out on The Family Channel.

On 13 February 1972, NBC broadcast a show in which Hoss was wounded and almost died. Exactly 12 weeks later on 13 May, Dan Blocker died at the age of 43. Official reports stated his death was due to complications following routine gall bladder surgery. A blood clot had formed in his lung and it burst suddenly after he left hospital. Nothing could be done to save him.

Millions of *Bonanza* fans were stunned. Lorne Greene admitted, 'After Dan's death, I didn't see how the show could continue.'

But Blocker's death wasn't the only difficulty facing the show which was then just 19 days before entering its 14th season. Both Landon and Greene remained under contract for the coming series and now found themselves having to cope with hastily re-written episodes. Chevrolet suddenly pulled its backing and NBC, disappointed by the previous season's ratings, had already pushed the show to Tuesday night. One of the producers of the show, Richard Collins also felt that the non-violence issue threatened the show, 'We can't do conventional Westerns any longer; since NBC owns the show, they apply the non-violence thing especially strictly, and we're not interested in doing shows like that anyway. So we have to move further afield, into unexplored areas.'

He and Dortort felt they actually had a chance to win new viewers, but found it especially hard to face the absence of Hoss, 'Dan is irreplaceable,' Dortort explained, 'How could a man with his enormous talent and humanity be replaced?'

He felt it was vital to grab the audience right away at the start of the fourteenth year. He asked Landon to write the episode, *Forever,* in the only two-hour segment of *Bonanza* to be broadcast on a single night. In it Joe became the only Cartwright son to marry. Although his joy was short lived when Mrs Carwright and their unborn son were both murdered, Landon said, 'I wanted to make it a catharsis for everyone. We mention Hoss's death very simply, in passing, the way it happens in real life… I'm sure that some people would rather have a whole hour memorial to Dan, but we just couldn't do that.'

Dortort circled the wagons but it wouldn't have mattered what he tried, the fact was that nothing could ever be the same again on the Ponderosa. The last fifteen episodes are set apart from the others by a somber, heavy mood. Another new character, Griff King, played by Tim Matheson was added and Candy was brought back.

By the time the last episode, *The Hunter* aired on 16 January 1973, *Bonanza* had been out of production for over two months. Although the first episodes of the season had finished in the Top 15, the interest of the viewer went into a rapid decline through October and when the show sank to number 52 in November, a victim of *Hawaii Five-O* and *Maude*, NBC ruthlessly swung the axe.

NBC had apparently considered moving the show back to a more traditional time on Saturday, but instead they pulled the plug with no warning. The stunned cast was given two days notice that filming would stop on 8 November.

Lorne Greene was deeply offended, 'They told us on Monday that we would quit shooting on Wednesday. After you've been on the air for 14 years, even if you're a caretaker, you should get a month's notice. They felt they didn't have to do that because our contract said we got paid for that year, whether we did any shows or not. But that wasn't the point. There was a lack of dignity.'

Landon agreed, 'When it ended it was very painful for everybody.' Years later he said that the way NBC had behaved was the main reason he determined to retain close control over any project he worked on in the future. He personally decided the fate of every other series he did.

Dortort of course was particularly bitter, 'I was suddenly called over to Burbank one day and given the news… needless to say, I was shocked.' He felt that many other shows were given a better chance than *Bonanza* was given at the end, but the fact was Westerns were a rarity on prime time television by 1972. When it left, only *Gunsmoke* and *Alias Smith and Jones* were reflections of a dying breed.

Dortort himself believed that the fact was *Bonanza* simply couldn't carry on without Blocker, and that he wasn't given sufficient time to try to find a replacement anyway.

Green said, 'Do you realize that *Bonanza* will be on air for the rest of our lives?' meaning there were so many years of re-runs available that somewhere in the world it would always be screening. The show had been dubbed into Chinese and sold in Hong Kong, 'I have mixed feelings about *Bonanza* ending, but I would like it to end on a high note. And let's face it, I've had lots of offers and some I'd like to do… I'll tell you what I'd really like, a Broadway musical.' By November he bitterly told *LA Times* reporter Gregg Kildan, 'If we'd known, we would have gone out with a bang, not a whimper.' The final episode shown did not even star Greene, but he admitted, 'With Dan gone, we lost the ability to do certain kinds of stories. I was surprised NBC renewed the show after Dan died.'

And maybe he also felt some relief, 'We spent more time with the crew than our families.'

Landon had more at stake; he had written and directed a number of episodes of *Bonanza,* including the story about the Cartwrights getting framed for robbery and murder, *The Gamble* in February 1962. That segment garnered rave reviews. In the 1966–67 season, he was working on rewrites for four teleplays and by December 1967 he had written his first full script *A Dream to Dream*, made the same month.

He had been allowed to direct his second written script, entitled *To Die in Darkness*, made in February 1968. By May of 1968, he had written his third script, *Kingdom of Fear.* In the 1968–1969 season he directed *The Wish*, which he had also written.

Landon took great pride in his authoring of the episode, which starred black actor Ossie Davis and aired on 9 March 1969.

He had learned his craft on the show. He had the most to loose but when it went off air he was more than ready to spread his wings.

None of the Cartwrights ever received an Emmy nomination.

## LEGACY

Landon went on to make such shows as *The Little House on the Prairie* and *Highway to Heaven.*

Immediately after *Highway to Heaven* went off air in 1989 he began developing a new project, *Us*, a series about an absent father struggling to reconnect with his family. Whilst working on this Landon began to suffer stomach pain. He feared an ulcer. In 1991 he was diagnosed with pancreatic cancer. He commented openly in the Santa Monica Outlook, 9 April 1991, 'Every moment gets a little more important. The best thing I can do is gather everyone who loves me around and make the most of life from now on.

'Playing *Highway to Heaven* will help since I was dead on that anyway.' He also said he wanted people to 'Remember me with smiles and laughter. If you can only remember me with tears, then don't remember me at all.'

He immediately established two cancer research foundations which still run today. Landon died three months after diagnosis on 1 July 1991. His ashes were interred next to those of Lorne Greene.

Greene hadn't fared as well as Landon, but within a week of *Bonanza's* cancellation he had signed to play a private detective for a new ABC series, *Griff*. His most significant role was as slave owner John Reynolds in the historic mini-series, *Roots*. In 1978 he made *Battlestar Galactica*, which he described as a Ponderosa in outer space.

Although millions yearned to see a *Bonanza* reunion, it has never happened.

Dortort went on to work on a 13 week series based on the John Wayne film, *The Cowboys* and later, *The Chisholms*. But in 1987 he announced he had finally written a reunion movie. Rumors circulated that both Landon and Greene would be in the cast.

On 19 August Greene underwent surgery for a perforated ulcer. Within two weeks he was suffering from pneumonia; recovery was slow. He was deluged by cards and 'Get Well' wishes. On 5 September both Leslie Nielsen and George Peppard visited him as he slipped away. On Friday afternoon, 11 September he succumbed to respiratory and cardiac arrest.

In October filming of *Bonanza: The Next Generation*, began in Lake Tahoe.

John Ireland starred as Ben's brother, Aaron. Also in the cast were Robert Fuller as the foreman of the Ponderosa, John Amos as the cook and Barbara Anderson as Joe Cartwright's wife, Annabelle. Michael Landon Jr., was introduced as Joe's son, Benjamin. Gillian Geene, Lorne's daughter, had a small part as the granddaughter of Virginia City's banker.

Some viewers were offended to hear about Hoss's bastard son, Josh. Also confusing was the character of Aaron, when all through the series, Ben had talked about his brother John.

On 1 July 1991 Michael Landon died at home of cancer. His ashes were interred at Hillside Memorial Park in Los Angeles, about 50 yard's from Lorne Greene's resting place.

It seemed that all hope of reviving *Bonanza* were finally dead, until in early 1992, a syndicated series based on *Bonanza: The Next Generation* was announced. Ben Johnson was scheduled to replace John Ireland as Aaron, but his role was changed at the last minute to Bronc Evans, a seasoned Ponderosa wrangler.

*Bonanza: Legends of the Ponderosa* never got off the ground, but in February 1993

NBC had a change of heart and were suddenly willing to test the water again, heartened many believed by the success of *Dr Quinn, Medicine Woman*.

On 28 November Dirk Blocker and Michael Landon Jr hosted *Back to Bonanza*, a series of clips from the original show and finally *Bonanza: The Return* was launched.

Alistair MacDougall played Adam's son, A.C., and Brian Leckner played Hoss' son Josh. Dirk Blocker was given a small part, but was too old to play Josh. Landon Jr., reprised his role as Benj and the cast was rounded off by Richard Roundtree, Linda Gray and Jack Elam. When Ben Johnson died in 1996, *Bonanza: The Next Generation* was put in limbo.

Mitch Vogel has left acting.

*David Canary starred as Candy, a ranch hand, after the departure of Pernell Roberts*

David Canary landed a part in the soap *All My Children*.

Tim Matheson starred in such films as *National Lampoon's Animal House*.

Bing Russell retired. Victor Sen Yung was wounded in an airline hijacking in California, but returned to work in various films and television roles, including *Kung Fu* and *How the West was Won*. On 9 November 1980 a neighbour smelled leaking gas from Yung's home and when police broke in they found Yung had already been dead from accidental causes for at least ten days.

Ray Teal died 2 April 1976. Lou Frizzel died, aged 59, on 17 June 1979. Guy Williams, best known as Zorro or Professor John Robinson on *Lost In Space*, retired to Buenos Aires where he died of a heart attack in May 1989.

Of the Cartwrights, only Pernell Roberts survives. He continues to work in the industry.

# THE BONANZA CREDO

## By David Dortort

**IN the Old West, it meant a lot to be a Cartwright. Being a family, loving the land, being honest and fair. Giving every man and every woman a second chance.**

More than most television shows, *Bonanza* has a heart and soul. To protect that heart and soul and to preserve the basic integrity of the show, the following are the essential values that must be maintained.

1   The Cartwright family, the good father and the good, loyal sons, are the center of gravity around which the movie revolves. They may disagree on any number of issues, but always, in the end, they are a family again, all for one, and one for all.

2   They stand for tolerance, compassion and concern for all endangered species, and that includes the stranger in need of sanctuary, the battered mother, the abandoned child, the wounded animal, as well as the forests, the mountain streams, the lakes and ponds. No woman, no child, no animal can be abused without swift and full-bore punishment for the abuser.

3   The Ponderosa, the home of the Cartwright family, should be treated as a

special kind of place, a sort of mythical kingdom on the glistening crown of the Sierra. Good people, role models, are in charge here. People slow to anger, but tread lightly or suffer the consequences. Stern, formidable, when faced with injustice, but loose, relaxed, fun-loving, a family that can laugh at itself as easily as it can challenge a swindler, a bounty hunter, a slave master, or a robber baron, no matter how high the odds are stacked against them.

It's a whole new world today, but some things never change. Such as the high standards maintained by America's most-loved family, the Cartwrights of the great Ponderosa Ranch.

# BOOTS AND SADDLES
## SEPTEMBER 1957 – MAY 1958

**THE black and white show ran 39 half-hour episodes through 1957 and into 1958.**

The series was set in the Arizona Territory of the 1870's, although it was actually shot entirely on location at Fort Kanab in Utah. The fort still stands today and was seen in the opening credits of *Branded*. It also featured extensively in *Duel At Diablo* (1966).

This series was an adult Western, told from a cavalryman's point of view, and targeted young adults who were already tuning in each week to *Gunsmoke* and the like. The show is unique in that it portrayed life from the point of view of the Fifth Cavalry as they attempted to co-exist with the Apache. It followed their story as they deal with gunrunners, renegade Apaches, crooked agents, whiskey peddlers and all kinds of outlaws in the area around Fort Lowell.

The main characters were well cast with John Pickard the lead as Capt. Shank Adams. Pickard had been considered for the lead on *Gunsmoke* after John Wayne initially turned down the role and prior to James Arness being cast.

Michael Hinn starred as Scout Luke Cummings, John Alderson as Sergeant Bullock and Patrick McVey as Commander Colonel Wesley Hays.

John Pickard was killed by a bull at a family farm in 1993. McVey died in 1973, Hinn in 1988 and Willock in 1990 after a stroke.

John Alderson and Johnny Western (another cast member) survive as does, Gardner McKay, who went on to do *Adventures in Paradise*.

# BORDER TOWN

## 1 JANUARY 1989

**BORDERTOWN** was a weekly, half-hour show which quickly became the Family Channel's highest rated original series when it debuted in 1989.

The series, produced by CTV Productions of Canada, was set in the 1880's, and centered around two lawmen, US Marshal Jack Craddock, played by Richard Comar and Canadian Mounted Policeman, Corporal Clive Bennett (John H Brennan) who share jurisdiction of a small town that straddles the US/Canadian border. Both were romantically interested in Marie Dumont, played by Sophie Barjac, the French widow of the town doctor, who took over her late husband's practice.

The syndicated series was filmed in color entirely on Canadian locations and the rain soaked and bitterly cold conditions added realistic atmosphere to the show.

# BRANDED

## 24 JANUARY 1965

'... what do you do when you're BRANDED?'

*'All but one man died*
*There at Bitter Creek*
*And they say he ran away.*

*Branded, marked with a coward's shame,*
*What do you do when you're branded,*
*Will you fight for your name?'*

**THE** show premiered on the CBS Network as a mid-season program on 24 January 1965. Originally shot in black and white it was soon filmed in color to take best advantage of the Kanab locations around Utah. Forty Eight episodes were made before it finally left the air on 24 September 1966.

*Branded* was Chuck Connor's second major series, following on the long term success he had earlier enjoyed in the *The Rifleman*. He starred as Captain Jason McCord, a West Point graduate and Civil War officer who is the lone white survivor of the Little Big Horn-like massacre at the Battle of Bitter Creek, a defeat brought on by the mental deterioration of the General in command. It is commonly believed that McCord's survival was due to cowardice, and after his court-martial, he is stripped of his rank and forced to leave the army in disgrace.

The *Branded* premise was recounted during the program's introduction, in the theme song by Dominic Frontiere (lyrics by Alan Alch). The song plays over the ceremony in which McCord's commander rips the decorations from his uniform and breaks his saber in half, tossing the bottom half out of the fort gate. McCord stoically exits the fort and as the gates close behind him, he picks up the broken saber and examines it closely, pondering his fate.

The exile travels the South-west moving from job to job, putting to use his army training as an engineer, searching for the man who had framed him. Throughout, McCord runs from his undeserved reputation as a coward, but wherever he goes, he finds it has preceded him. He suffers the outrage and attacks in silence, refusing to tell the story that would redeem him in the eyes of the public. Over the course of the series, many who start out hating McCord end up admiring him, or at least giving him the benefit of the doubt, as they witness his demonstrations of courage and determination in the face of taunts and other more deadly threats.

Often McCord encounters individuals who are themselves facing situations that require courage and ultimately it is his actions that inspire them to do the right thing. From time to time McCord encounters old friends who have kept faith in him.

In the episode *The Mission*, Colonel Snow (Jon Lormer) who refused to believe the accusations surrounding Bitter Creek, introduces McCord to President Ulysses S. Grant (William Bryant). Grant later calls upon McCord several times to work undercover for him, usually putting his reputation and dismissal from the army as a means to gain admission to groups who are at odds with the government.

In *The Coward Steps Aside*, Johnny Crawford (who played Conner's son in *The Rifleman*) appears as a young deputy who is unwilling to take lessons in courage from McCord when his town is threatened. Johnny Crawford recalls the experience, 'We were very fond of each other. He was the reason I was doing the show. He saw an episode that I could do and he said, 'I want Johnny to play that part'. It was just fun playing a different role with him'.

The creator of the show, Larry Cohen stated, 'Chuck Connors wanted to give

## TRIVIA

Connors played major league baseball for the Chicago Cubs through 1951 and also played professional basketball with the Boston Celtics.

He was probably the only guest commentator on Monday Night Baseball to use the 'F'–word.

himself an entirely different look from *The Rifleman*, which I agreed was a good idea. Connors said 'We've got to come up with something like the rifle. A weapon that I can play with.' So I came up with the broken saber, which was cut down so he'd be able to throw his saber, use that in fights, and give us something that would be symbolic for the show".

*Branded* was still a Top 20 show when it was cancelled.

Chuck Connors, one of TV's biggest stars lost his battle with lung cancer on 10 November 1992, aged 71.

William Bryant died in 2001 of cancer.

# BRAVE EAGLE

## 28 SEPTEMBER 1955

**BRAVE EAGLE was shot in black and white and each episode, produced by Roy Rogers Frontiers Inc, ran weekly for half an hour on the CBS Network. The first of 26 episodes aired on 28 September 1955. The series was filmed on Roy Rogers' 130-acre ranch in Chatsworth, California and the Corriganville Ranch in Simi Valley. It went off the air on 6 June 1956.**

Keith Larson played the noble chief of a peaceful Cheyenne tribe, Brave Eagle. He faced the challenges of daily life with neighboring tribes in the Southwest of the 19th century and strove to achieve harmony with an ever-encroaching white man. (Larson is himself part Cheyenne). *Brave Eagle* was an unusual example of an early TV series siding with the Indian point of view and the first to feature an American Indian as a lead character.

## TRIVIA

The real name of the actor who played Brave Eagle's son, Keena is Anthony Earl Numkena. The change came about as a result of Michael North, the executive producer changing the name to Keena to fit the part in the series. He also felt the name Numkena (a Hopi name) looked too oriental and changed it to Nomkena. In the later episodes it was changed to Numkena. The name Keena remained.

Usually grouped together in the 1960's with Hollywood's 'Beach Boy' set, Keith Larsen was actually more the tennis-playing type and was in fact a tennis pro at the time he was tapped by a talent scout to play a small role in 1951's *Operation Pacific*. While Larsen's film career was negligible, he prospered as a television star.

Morning Star, the lovely Indian maiden and Brave Eagle's love interest, was played by Kim Winona, a full-blooded Sioux. Keena Nomkeena was Keena, a full-blooded Indian boy of Hopi and Klamath descent, who was Brave Eagle's adopted son. Comedian Bert Wheeler starred as the tribe's wise man and scout, Smokey Joe.

Bert Wheeler died in 1968 from emphysema.

Kim Winona died from a self inflicted gun shot to the head in June 1978.

Larsen, who resides in southern California, went on to other roles and a directing career.

# BRET MAVERICK

## 1 December 1981

**EACH** one hour episode was shot in color, and the run debuted on 1 December 1981. Despite the very popular Maverick persona, and a dedicated cast and crew, the show lasted only one season and left the air on 24 August 1982, after just 22 episodes.

*James Garner
and
Darleen Carr*

Some 20 years after the original *Maverick* left the air, Warner Bros. and James Garner attempted to revive the popular series. Garner predicted the new series would be better than the original.

Initially *Maverick* had told the story of rogue card shark, Bret Maverick. It was a straightforward tale of the Old West that evolved when the writers began adding comedy into the scripts.

Bret soon found himself television Western's first mercenary, a character who helped the forces of justice only if he stood to profit from doing so. When he used a gun, he wasn't much of a marksman, and he was much more likely to slip out the backdoor when trouble began instead of sticking around for the fight.

Maverick, who had owned a ranch just out of town and was also part owner of the Red Ox Saloon in town, was now settled in Sweetwater in the 1880's, and although he still has a twinkle in the eye, his old spirit of adventure was sadly missing. He is older and wiser.

Cast members included Darleen Carr as Mary Lou Springer, owner of the town's newspaper, Stuart Margolin as a small time con-man, Philo Sandine and Ed Bruce as Sheriff Tom Guthrie. Garner had insisted on featuring a larger cast saying, 'We're going to have plenty of characters in *Bret Maverick* because I'm just not physically able to be on screen one hour every week. *Rockford* really fixed that for me.'

Garner had always had a prickly relationship with Warner Bros and had left the original series after a contract dispute, but by 1980 he told an interviewer from Playboy, 'I couldn't find anything else that interested me. I mean, I've done a detective series – so has everyone else – and doctors are dead and lawyers have been run into the ground. I started thinking what Bret Maverick would be like 20 years later and what the series would look like updated from the 1860's to the 1880's.'

He believed the show would be fun after all the time that had elapsed since he first left, 'As long as the writing is good, it really doesn't matter what the format is. And the scripts I've read for the new series are better than the originals. There hasn't been a successful Western series for a long time. For one thing they are too expensive to make. For another the public got burned out. But I think it's time to bring it back... I think that in the eighties people are wanting to get back to something we have lost. They are going back to basics. Things have gotten a little too hot and heavy, and people don't know how to handle it. So they want to get back to something they can feel. There was a code in the West that people don't even understand anymore. A way of dealing with their fellow men. A code of right and wrong.'

Unfortunately, the experiment failed and *Bret Maverick* came across as nice and easy, but outdated.

# BROKEN ARROW
## 25 SEPTEMBER 1956

**ABC** Television commissioned the half hour show from 20th Century Fox Television. Seventy eight black and white episodes were made which ran for three seasons from 25 September 1956 to 18 September 1958. During the fourth season in 1960, it was telecast in reruns.

The series was based on Elliott Arnold's novel, *Blood Brother,* and the feature film of the same name, starring James Stewart and Jeff Chandler.

In 1950, Hollywood executives had come up with the idea to do an authentic and sympathetic study of the famed Apache leader, Cochise. With the success of the movie version, it followed that it could also prove a successful concept on television and in 1956 ABC launched what is now considered one of the legends in television Western history. *Broken Arrow* presented the Indian view of white encroachment on television.

It featured Michael Ansara as Cochise and John Lupton as Indian Agent, Captain Tom Jeffords.

The first episode, *The Mail Riders*, gave the background of the unique friendship which existed between these two extraordinary men. Jeffords had been commissioned by the Army to get the mail through Chiricahua Apache lands in the Tuscon Arizona area in the 1870's, but when his coaches were shot up and his drivers ended up dead or wounded at the hands of the Apache, he decided to go alone to Cochise to seek a peaceful solution. His

bravery so impressed Cochise that the two became blood brothers. The friendship they forged was symbolized by a broken arrow. Cochise only agreed to a reservation way of life if Jeffords, whom he called Taglito in real life, would be the Indian agent.

Together Jefford and Cochise fought those who violated the peace, regardless of their race.

John Lupton died in 1993, but Ansara still lives in Calabasas in California.

# BRONCO

## 23 September 1958

**THIS** hour long series was produced by Warner Bros. and was shot in black and white for ABC Television. Sixty eight action packed features were made and a fast gun and hard fists kept Bronco on air from 23 September 1958 to 13 September 1962.

The show starred Ty Hardin as Bronco Layne, an ex-Confederate Army captain, who returned to Texas after the Civil War and didn't like what he found. Stripped of his honor and with his home confiscated, he became a loner, who preferred to avoid trouble, but as he roamed the frontier fighting injustice and outlaws, he stood firm and looked it square in the eye whenever it got in his way. He traveled Texas helping people in distress

and working at assorted jobs including running secret missions for the federal government, acting as a deputy sheriff and a ranch hand amongst other things. He chased not only bad guys and Indians, but a few charming ladies as well.

*Bronco* owed its existence to the premature demise of *Cheyenne,* and it was born from the fall out caused when Clint Walker stalked away from Warner Brothers Studios in 1958. The executives at Warner Brothers wanted to keep the hugely successful *Cheyenne* series alive... without its star Clint

Walker and when the call went out for new talent, newcomer Ty Hardin was chosen for the part of Bronco Layne, Cheyenne Bodie's country cousin.

Originally, the show still went under the title *Cheyenne*.

By the time Walker and Warner Brothers made their peace in 1959, Hardin had made such a great impression with both audience and studio (during the run of the series, he had become an adept horseman and gun handler, and he did a lot of his own stunts) that it was decided to give him a Western series of his own. *Bronco* was a huge success and it continued under its own banner for another three years.

During its first season, 1958–9, it alternated with *Sugarfoot,* which starred Will Hutchins, as part of the *Cheyenne Show*. When Clint Walker returned, it then aired with *Cheyenne* for its second season. During the third season, it alternated with *Sugarfoot* and *Cheyenne*, and for the fourth season, it alternated with *Cheyenne* once again. *Sugarfoot* was finally dropped from the group in 1961.

After *Bronco* ended Hardin found plenty of work in features and also made some European Westerns.

Hardin, who was a deeply religious man, eventually left the industry and, in the 1980's retired to Prescott, Arizona where he became a preacher. He reportedly spent some time living in South America, and although he eventually returned to Southern California, he never resurrected his career.

---

# TRIVIA

Orison Whipple Hungerford, Jr walked into Western Costume Co. on Santa Monica Blvd., to rent a costume for a Halloween party. The visit changed his life, as fate would have it, and he was 'discovered' there by Milton Lewis, a talent scout for Paramount Pictures. He was interviewed by Bill Micheljohn, the president of Paramount, given a screen test and offered a seven-year contract.

After appearing in six films at Paramount, Hungerford Jr went to see John Wayne at Batjac about a film he was doing named *Rio Bravo*. The part he was interested in had already been handed to Ricky Nelson, but The Duke was instrumental in getting him in to see Howard Hawks and Bill Orr at Warner Bros. It was Bill Orr, son-in-law to Jack Warner, who bought his contract from Paramount and changed his name to Ty Hardin after the notorious outlaw John Wesley Hardin.

# BUCKSKIN
## 3 JULY 1958

**THE half hour show was made in black and white. It debuted on 3 July 1958 and went off air after 39 episodes in January 1959.**

*Buckskin* was a summer replacement series on NBC television for *The Tennessee Ernie Ford Show.*

Widow Annie O'Connell, played by Sallie Brophy, runs a boarding house in the town of Buckskin, Montana in the 1880's. Her inquisitive, ten-year old son, Jody was played by Tommy Nolan. Because the house is the social center for the whole town, young Jody gets to interact with the townspeople and with all the guests passing through the frontier town.

Jody's surrogate fathers are the town sheriff, Tom Sellers and schoolteacher, Ben Newcomb. The Sheriff was played by Mike Road and Michael Lipton was Newcomb.

All cast members are alive and well.

Tommy Nolan retired and became a writer.

One of this show's problems was that it got moved around on the schedule four times. It was rerun in the summer of 1965.

# BUFFALO BILL JR.
## 1 MARCH 1955—6

**FIFTY two action packed episodes, full of wild stunts performed by the likes of Bob Woodward and Fred Crone, were filmed by Gene Autry's Flying A Productions in 1955 for syndication and they were originally aired on CBS. The series still runs on The Western Channel.**

Buffalo Bill Jr., was an orphan, who along with his little sister, Calamity, was adopted by Judge Ben Wiley, founder of Wileyville, Texas in the 1890's. Bill worked for the judge as an unofficial deputy and was eventually appointed marshal.

Dick Jones starred as Bill, Nancy Gilbert was Calamity and the late Harry Cheshire Judge Wiley. Dick Jones is a popular guest at many of America's western festivals. He lives in Northridge, California.

Dick's horse was called Chief Passings.

Nancy Gilbert lives in St David, Arizona.

Harry Cheshire died in 1968.

# CADE'S COUNTY

## 19 SEPTEMBER 1971

**THE** fast-paced show ran for 24 hour-long episodes in color, airing from 19 September 1971 until 4 September 1972. It was made by 29th Century Fox TV for the CBS Network.

*Edgar Buchanan*
and
*Glenn Ford*

After a string of hit movies (mostly Westerns), legendary Hollywood big screen actor, Glenn Ford gave TV a try with this weekly series, playing the tough but sensitive lawman, Sheriff Sam Cade of Madrid County, California.

Ford's first foray into television had been *Brotherhood of the Bell* and in 1970 he had agreed to work on a series for CBS. Many potential projects were discussed including a police show where Ford would counsel youngsters before he finally chose *Cade's County* saying, 'Everyone liked the idea of *Cade's County* because it had the feel of the West and yet it was modern.' He went on, 'I always preferred working in Westerns because they were so easy to make, so with the more rigorous shooting schedules that TV required, I felt that a Western-themed show would work best.'

Ford had specifically asked that Edgar Buchanan and his son, Peter, were asked to join the show, 'Even my daughter-in-law, Lynda, was in most of the episodes. It was like having my family at work with me. Producer, David Gerber kindly hired

## TRIVIA

Edgar Buchanan (20 March 1903 – 4 April 1979), the character actor with a long career in both film and television, is best remembered as Uncle Joe Carson from the *Petticoat Junction and Green Acres* television sitcoms of the 1960's. As Uncle Joe 'who is moving kinda slow', he took over as proprietor of the Shady Rest Hotel following the death of Bea Benaderet, who had played Kate Bradley.

Buchanan was originally a successful dentist before he became interested in acting.

many of the directors and fellow actors I had worked with throughout the years. Sean Penn's father, Leo, directed one of the episodes. I had worked with him in *The Undercover Man* back in 1949.' Richard Donner also directed a number of segments before going on to *Superman* fame and fortune.

The show was part contemporary western and part crime drama, and it attempted to tackle relevant issues of the day like the plight of the American Indian, and the overall discrimination of the Mexican American and other minorities. Ford himself was a strong advocate for Indian issues and he worked hard to obtain work in films and television for Native American Indians. He often joined up with Jay Silverheels who had founded the Indian Actor's Workshop. Many Native Americans from the Workshop worked with Ford on *Cade's County*.

The opening sequence saw Ford going through the mountain landscape in a Jeep, rather than on a horse and many fans claim it was one of the best TV shows from the early 1970's.

Deputy J. J. Jackson, played by veteran actor, Edgar Buchanan, assisted him, Taylor Lacher played Deputy Arlo Pritchard and Victor Campos played Deputy Rudy Danillo. Other regulars included the dispatcher in the office, Betty Ann Sundown, played by Betty Ann Carr and Deputy Pete, played by Peter Ford.

Edgar Buchanan died 4 April 1979 in Palm Desert, California, from a stroke complicated by pneumonia.

The theme music was written by composer Henry Mancini.

Glenn Ford died 30 August 2006 after a series of strokes. He had worked with many of the Hollywood greats and had an impressive list of credits to his name including *Blackboard Jungle, Midway* and *The Big Heat*.

# THE CALIFORNIANS

## 24 September 1957

**CALIFORNIA National Productions made the half hour long, black and white show for the NBC Network and it debuted on 24 September 1957 and ran for two seasons and 69 episodes before going off air on 27 August 1959.**

This show told the story of a few honest men who attempted to keep law and order in San Francisco during the Gold Rush of the 1850's.

*Richard Coogan*

The show had a complete upheaval in casting after just a few episodes had screened and originally Adam Kennedy played two-fisted Irish newspaper reporter, Dion Patrick, but Richard Coogan replaced him as Matthew Wayne. Sean McClory played mine owner and vigilante leader, Jack McGivern with Nan Leslie as his wife, Martha. Carole Matthews starred as saloon owner, Wilma Fansler. Art Fleming was Jeremy Pitt.

Coogan beefed up the show, standing at 6'3" in the role of Marshal Matt Wayne.

Nan Leslie died in 2000.

Kennedy died in 1997.

Caine in 1993.

Fleming died in 1995.

None of the rest of the cast are still active in the industry.

*The Californians* theme, '(I've Come To) California' was by Harry Warren and Harold Adamson.

# CASEY JONES

## (1957)

**SCREEN Gems produced 78 half-hour, black and white episodes of this series through 1957. Most were shot on location around Sonora, California, and they continue to be seen in syndication today.**

The warm-hearted series was loosely based on the life and exploits of John Luther 'Casey' Jones, a real-life train engineer hero who saved a town by crashing the runaway locomotive he was driving before disaster struck, but who in fact lost his life in the process of that heroic deed.

The Midwest and Central Railroad line during the late 1800's ran from Chicago to New Orleans and Jones' famous steam train, The Cannonball Express, which ran from Chicago to New Orleans, carried everyone from Geronimo to the United States President in the series.

The programs elaborated on and stretched the adventures of Jones and it turned out to be more of a Western than a realistic railroad series.

The show starred Alan Hale Jr., as Casey, Mary Lawrence as his wife and Bobby Clark as their son. Dub Taylor played the conductor on the train.

Alan Hale Jr., died of cancer on 2 January 1990 after also starring as Skipper on *Gilligan's Island*.

Neither Mary Lawrence nor Bobby Clark is still active in the film industry. Dub Taylor died in 1994 of congestive heart failure.

*Alan Hale Jr* and *Bobby Clark*

# CENTENNIAL

## 10 JANUARY 1978

**BASED** on James A Michener's novel and made by Universal for NBC, Centennial was a mammoth, twelve-parter, chronicling over 220 years of the history of a small Colorado town.

This mini series, directed by Virgil W Pogel, Paul Krasny, Harry Falk and Bernard McEveety, ran 21 hours, and was a truly monumental epic which made no attempt to conceal the savagery of America's past. Episode five, *The Massacre* focussed on bloodthirsty militia colonel, Frank Skimmerhorn (Richard Crenna) and his purging of a Native American village. This was based on the real life massacre at Sand Creek in 1864. *Centennial* condemned the butchery and emphasized the multicultural composition of the frontier.

In effect this all-star epic was a response to Henry Hathaway and John Ford's, *How the West Was Won* (1962).

Directors on the series included Harry Falk, Paul Krasny, Bernard McEveety, Virgil W Vogel. Writing credits include Charles Larson, James Michener, John Wilder and Jerry Ziegman. The series was produced by Howard P Alston, Alex Beaton and Richard Caffey.

Original Music was by John Addison. Cinematography was by Ronald W. Browne, Duke Callaghan, Jacques R. MarQuette and Charles W Short.

Stunts were by William H. Burton, David S. Cass Sr., Tony Epper, Leslie Hoffman, Terry Leonard, Neil Summers and Glenn R. Wilder.

The cast, too large to credit everyone, included stars such as William Atherton, Raymond Burr, Barbara Carrera, Richard Chamberlain, Robert Conrad, Richard Crenna, Timothy Dalton, Cliff De Young, Chad Everett, Sharon Gless, Andy Griffith, Merle Haggard, Gregory Harrison, David Janssen, Brian Keith, Donald Pleasence, Lynn Redgrave, Robert Vaughn, Dennis Weaver, and Anthony Zerbe.

# CHEYENNE

## 20 SEPTEMBER 1955

**CHEYENNE** became the first successful television series to be produced by the motion picture studio, Warner Brothers when they launched this one-hour classic western entertainment every week from 20 September 1955 to 13 September 1963. Cheyenne's eight-year run produced only 107 episodes, an average of 13 per season.

Originally it was one of the three rotating series in the studio's showcase, *Warner Brothers Presents*, but it emerged as a huge hit, helping fuel ABC's ratings ascent during the mid-1950's. ABC had fewer national affiliates than CBS and NBC, but in markets with affiliates of all three networks, *Cheyenne* immediately entered the top ten; by 1957, it had become the number one program in those markets, and was the show the audience wanted to watch. Although clearly successful, *Cheyenne* never stood alone as a weekly series, but alternated bi-weekly with other Warner Brothers productions, *Casablanca* and *King's Row* (1955–6), *Conflict* (1956–7), and two spin-off series, *Sugarfoot* (1957–61) and *Bronco* (1958–62).

Through the years the show's producers included William T. Orr, Roy Huggins, Arthur Silver and Harry Foster.

The 6'6" tall Clint Walker starred as Cheyenne Bodie along with Jack Elam who played Toothy Thompson. Cheyenne, a former army frontier scout, roamed the west just after the Civil War, doing an assortment of jobs including ranch foreman, Indian fighter and part-time lawman. He traveled without any particular motivation from one adventure to another, taking on any job and Walker certainly looked the way a rugged frontiersman should; tall, handsome, broad-shouldered, narrow-hipped and big-hearted. The series was held together not so much by its premise as by its charismatic star, who rose from obscurity to become one of the icons of the TV Western.

Essentially, the producers of *Cheyenne* changed the character's circumstances at will in order to place him in any imaginable conflict, although he was always a lone redeemer wandering from community to community through unrelated individual episodes. Several *Cheyenne* chapters were simply remakes of earlier Warner Brothers movies like *To Have and Have Not* (1944) and *Treasure of the Sierra Madre* (1948) with the character of Cheyenne simply inserted into the plot.

Each time Cheyenne entered a new community, he either witnessed or provoked a new story in which he can participate to varying degree. This structure particularly suited the Western's violent resolutions.

Walker battled the studio at every turn and no television series ever had such a tempestuous production history and survived.

For the 1957–8 season ABC offered to purchase a full season of 39 episodes, but Warner Brothers declined the offer. Since each hour-long episode took six working days for principle photography alone, the studio couldn't supply a new episode each week. Because Walker appeared in virtually every scene, it was also impossible to shoot more than one episode at a time. Consequently, Warner Brothers developed a second series, *Sugarfoot*, to alternate with *Cheyenne*. The show was only a slight variation on the *Cheyenne* formula. In *Sugarfoot*, Will Hutchins played Tom Brewster, a kind-hearted young drifter who travels the West while studying to become a lawyer.

In May 1958 Clint Walker demanded to renegotiate his contract before returning for another season. Among other things, he did not want to have to kick back 50 percent of all personal-appearance fees to the studio. He also wanted higher payment for reruns and wanted permission to make records for labels other than Warners' own record company.

He had signed his first contract at Warner Brothers in 1955 as a virtual unknown and had received an initial salary of $175 per week, which had risen gradually to $1250 per week. After the second season of *Cheyenne*, Warner Brothers capitalized on Walker's rising popularity by casting him in a feature film, *Fort Dobbs* (1958), and by releasing a musical album on which he sang.

Walker timed his ultimatum carefully, assuming that he had acquired some

## TRIVIA
Clint Walker is of one quarter Cherokee descent.

leverage and he requested more freedom to decide which projects to pursue outside the series.

When Warner Brothers refused to negotiate, Walker left the studio and did not return for the entire 1958–9 season. After meeting with ABC and advertisers, Warner Brothers decided to continue the *Cheyenne* series without its star. In his place the studio substituted a new charismatic drifter, a former Confederate captain named Bronco Layne (Ty Hardin), and managed to sustain an entire season without Walker – and still finished among the Top 20 programs – by interspersing Bronco Layne episodes with reruns of Walker episodes from previous seasons. If there was a difference between episodes of *Bronco* and *Cheyenne*, it was solely in the stars.

Eventually Warner Brothers did renegotiate Walker's contract, and *Cheyenne*

resumed with its star for the 1959–60 season. *Bronco* survived as a stand-alone series and alternated with *Sugarfoot* for the season. During the following season, the three shows alternated in *The Cheyenne Show*; and occasionally the characters would crossover into episodes of the other series.

By the end, the actors were numbed by the repetition of the scripts and by the dreary, taxing routine of production on a series in which one episode was virtually indistinguishable from another. Even after returning from his holdout, Walker disliked working on *Cheyenne* and complained to the press that he felt 'like a caged animal' pacing back and forth in a zoo. 'A TV series is a dead-end street,' he lamented. 'You work the same set, with the same actors, and with the same limited budgets. Pretty soon you don't know which picture you're in and you don't care.'

Will Hutchins also admitted to hoping *Sugarfoot* would be canceled. Its episodes, he complained, 'are pretty much the same after you've seen a handful. They're moneymakers for the studio, the stations, and the actors, but there's a kind of empty feeling when you're through.'

Walker is still active in the industry and lives in Grass Valley, California with his wife Susan.

Dell issued something like 25 *Cheyenne* comic books and they were all enormous sellers. Today, they are highly collectible and fetch upwards of $15 per comic.

# THE CHISHOLMS
## 1979

**THE CHISHOLMS** started life as a four-part mini series that ran through the spring of 1979, telling the story of a Virginia family who trekked across the 1840's wilderness in search of a new home following the legal battle that had taken their old home from them. The 60 minute show was shot in color on location at Bent's Fort, Colorado.

The ratings were initially so good that the CBS network ordered a follow-up series. This debuted on 26 January 1980. The shows were directed by Edward M. Abroms and Sigmund Neufeld Jr.

The family was headed by Robert Preston who played patriarch, Hadley Chisholm. His wife, Minerva was played by Rosemary Harris. Their long trip began in Virginia and continued to Fort Laramie and later onto California. Mitch Ryan starred as Wagon Master Cooper Hawkins. Ben Murphy, Brian Kerwin and James Van Patten played the Chisholm sons, Will, Gideon and Bo. The show also starred Delta Burke as Bonnie Sue Chisholm, Susan Swift as Mercy Hopewell, Devon Ericson as Betsy O'Neal, Reid Smith as Lester Hackett and Victoria Racimo as Kewedinak. Charles Frank starred as con man Lester Hackett.

Robert Preston died of cancer on 22 March 1987 at the age of 68. All the rest of the cast remain active in the industry.

Although the show was well written, beautifully shot and directed, it happened to be on air when Westerns were fast fading. It only managed a three month run, before going off on 15 March 1980.

# CIMARRON CITY

## 11 OCTOBER 1958

**PRODUCED** by Revue Productions for NBC, Cimarron City was an hour long show which debuted on 11 October 1958. The show ran for 26 episodes before leaving the air on 16 September 1960.

Cimmaron City in the 1890s was booming due to the oil and gold fields and there were hopes that it would become the capital of the future state of Oklahoma. Matthew Rockford, played by George Montgomery is the son of the city's founder. He was mayor and a major cattle rancher, and he wasn't deskbound by any means.

Audrey Totter played Beth Purcell, owner of the town's boarding house. Stuart Randall starred as Sherriff Temple. John Smith was the town blacksmith and deputy sheriff, Lane Temple and pre-Bonanza Dan Blocker played Tiny Budinger, a helpful townsman. Blocker left this show to head straight to the Ponderosa.

The show was directed by Virgil W. Vogel and was shot extensively at the Iverson Ranch, Chatsworth and also at Revue Studios.

Audrey Totter lives in Los Angeles. Dan Blocker died in 1972 following surgery. John Smith died in 1995 of cirrhosis of the liver.

Montgomery died on 12 December 2000 aged 84 at Rancho Mirage, California from heart failure.

Unfortunately, when this show first went out, it found itself up against a pair of Western heavyweights, *Have Gun Will Travel* and *Gunsmoke,* and it simply couldn't compete.

# CIMARRON STRIP

## 7 SEPTEMBER 1967

**THIS** show, boasting top locations, great stories, celebrity stars and first class writing ran for 90 minutes on CBS primetime between 7 September 1967 and 17 September 1968.

Very few other Westerns matched this one for quality although only twenty three episodes were made. Many of these featured top stars of the day but unfortunately critics saw the series as merely an attempt to recreate the success of *The Virginian*. CBS did re-run the show between 20 July and 7 September 1971.

Veteran Hollywood star, Stuart Whitman starred as Marshal Jim Crown who patrolled a 1,000-mile area of the Oklahoma panhandle known as the Cimarron Strip. *Cimarron Strip* ambitiously dealt with the effects of range wars and other problems faced by the pioneering cattlemen. Crown was often left to resolve bitter confrontations between settlers and the Indians in the Territory during the violent 1880's.

Although he worked single-handed most of the time, Randy Boone played Francis Wilde, a photographer who sometimes helped out, and Percy Herbert was iron-willed MacGregor, his good friend. Boone ended his stint on *The Virginian* to come to this series.

Crown lodged at the Wayfarer's Inn run by Dulcey Coopersmith, played by Jill

Townsend. The inn also served as the town jail, only tavern, restaurant and boarding house.

Whitman recently received a star on the Hollywood Walk of Fame. He lives in Santa Barbara. Townsend lives in the UK and Boone often stars in Western shows around America.

Percy Herbert died in England on 6 December 1992 of a heart attack.

Stuart Whitman Enterprises released most of the episodes on video.

The *Cimarron Strip* theme music was one of the few US TV themes written by French film composer Maurice Jarré, who was at the height of his popularity in the 1960s after scoring *Doctor Zhivago, Ryan's Daughter, Grand Prix, The Life and Times of Judge Roy Bean, Plaza Suite* and the TV mini-series *Shogun*. The theme, together with the magnificent camera work, lent a feel of the well made motion picture to the show.

*Percy Herbert*
*Stuart Whitman*
*Jill Townsend*
and
*Randy Boone*

# CIRCUS BOY

## 23 SEPTEMBER 1956

**THIS** black and white show ran on NBC early on Sunday nights from 23 September 1956. It ran for two years and after 78 episodes went off air in the autumn of 1958.

In 1955 producers Herbert B. Leonard and Norman Blackburn bought a South Carolina bankrupt circus for $55,000, including the wagons, tents, cages, and caliope. They then set up production of *Circus Boy* on 3 acres of the Corriganville Ranch.

The producers had hoped to attract a young audience, and it certainly proved to be a big hit with them. The half-hour mixture of comedy and drama, set at the turn of the 20th century, gave 12-year-old orphan Corky a chance to live out every kid's dream.

*Circus Boy* starred Mickey Braddock as Corky, whose parents were killed in a high-wire accident. The 12-year-old was adopted by the owner, Big Tim Champion and he travelled across America with the Circus. Corky rode his baby elephant Bimbo, dealt with his adolescent problems, and helped the adults keep the circus in the black as the show moved from town to town each week.

Corky shared screen time on the live-action *Circus Boy* with clown Uncle Joey and Pete. Corky's pet chimpanzee was called Bobo. Other featured animals were Sultan the tiger and Nuba the Lion.

Robert Lowery starred as Big Tim.

Noah Beery Jr., played Joey the Clown and Guinn Williams played Big Boy. Leo Gordon starred as Pete, Hank Miller played Billy Barty.

## TRIVIA

Mickey Braddock became Mickey Dolenz later in life and was drummer in the 60s pop band, The Monkees.

Directors included Fred Jackman, George Archainbaud, Robert G. Walker, Douglas Heyes. Writers included Max Lamb, Victor Mccleod, Jerome S. Gottler, Charles N. Stewart, Douglas Heyes.

Lowery died on 26 December 1971 aged 68. Noah Beery Jr., died 1 November 1994 and Williams on 6 June 1962.

Dell Comics published three issues of *Circus Boy* comic books.

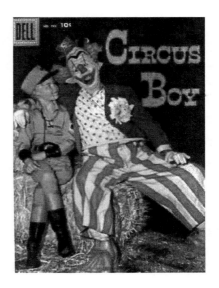

# THE CISCO KID
## 1950–1956

**ONE** hundred and fifty six color episodes of The Cisco Kid were shot for syndication between 1950 and 1956. Although this was long before many Americans even owned a color television set, it meant the series was easy to sell into syndication later. Most location work was shot at Pioneertown near Palm Springs. Directors included Eddie Davis and Leslie Goodwins.

The Cisco Kid was the Robin Hood of the old West and was played by Duncan Renaldo. The series also starred Leo Carrillo as lovable sidekick, Pancho. The two roving caballeros righted wrong and saved damsels in distress. The Cisco Kid's horse was called Diablo and Pancho rode Loco.

The Cisco Kid idea was originally penned by Oliver O'Henry as a short story, although his Cisco Kid was a much darker and more complicated character than the one who later featured in comic books, radio series, in films and on television.

Renaldo started making films for MGM in 1928 and had also worked for the Republic and Monogram studios, usually appearing as a sidekick or villain. Still, he was the perfect choice for a heroic action-adventure star and the spotlight on his film career was dimmed by the attention he won when he became the 'Cisco Kid' in the 1945 film series that later wound up on television.

Along side his faithful companion Pancho and in the grand tradition of the Lone Ranger, righting wrongs and fighting injustice wherever they find it, the duo stormed the west, taking care of bad guys, but in their own unique style. While most avengers

## TRIVIA

In the 1953 season Renaldo was hospitalized after injuring himself in a fall. He was unable to work through the following nine episodes. To cover for his absence on the show, the Cisco Kid was shown wearing masks, disguised as a ghost and in other situations where a double could be used. Some old unused footage was also cut in. Renaldo recorded his lines from his hospital bed.

of evil in the Wild West were rough, tough, no-nonsense hombres, Cisco Kid and Pancho were just the opposite. Unlike in today's violent films where dead bodies and needless bloodshed fill the screen, *The Cisco Kid* was prime family fare. The production design may have been simplistic, but there was still murder, intrigue and lots of action. The show always started upbeat with Cisco riding on Diablo and Pancho beside him on Loco, and it always ended on the comedic note, 'Oh, Pancho', 'Oh, Cisco.' Then as they rode away into the distance, Cisco yells 'Good-bye, Amigos!' as Pancho shouts, 'See you soon!'

Cisco rode into every town in his sleek caballero suit to charm everyone. Renaldo's mild manner and likeable charm infused his character with traits that made him wildly popular. Leo Carillo, on the other hand, had a round cherub face made for laughing. His comedy background was worked into the stories. From the moment he and Cisco rode up on their horses, during key moments of intrigue in the episodes and until that last goodbye when they rode off into the sunset, Renaldo and Carillo made audiences laugh.

Carillo died from cancer on 10 September 1961 in Santa Monica, California.

Renaldo died from lung cancer on 3 September 1980.

# COLT 45

## 18 OCTOBER 1957

**THE half hour show was shot in black and white and debuted on ABC on 18 October 1957 and left the lineup on 27 September 1960 after 67 episodes.**

This was the story of Government Undercover Agent, Christopher Colt who travelled to his assignments in the guise of a gun salesman peddling the frontier model, Colt .45, invented by his father.

Warner Bros hired rugged, 6'4" Wayde Preston to play Colt after seeing him in action in an episode of *Cheyenne.* For the next three years Preston struggled with contract problems with Warner Bros, demanding more money and less working hours. Warners recruited Donald May to star in some episodes as Sam Colt Jr. Although Preston returned to work, May eventually took over as full time lead after Preston finally walked off set after being denied the use of a stuntman.

Preston went to work in Europe and embarked on a lucrative career filming spaghetti Westerns through the 60's and 70's, before eventually returning to America to have surgery to remove a cancerous growth by his right temple.

In the mid 80s, after recuperation and reconstructive surgery, he appeared at numerous western film festivals and began accepting small movie rolls including the part of Jack in *Captain America* released in 1992.

Preston passed away on 6 February 1992, losing his battle against colon cancer. May went on to work in *All My Children.*

# COWBOY G-MEN

## 1952

**SYNDICATED** by Telemount-Mutual in 1952, each of the 39 half-hour slots was full of action and gunfire, shot in color, and, amazingly, the last 13 were in 3-D, anticipating new TV technology that to date hasn't materialized. Filming was mainly carried out at the Iverson Ranch, Chatsworth, California.

Jackie Coogan as horse-wrangler Stoney Crockett and Russell Hayden as cowboy Pat Gallagher, debuted in this short-lived series. Set in the West of the 1870's, the show was concerned with the exploits of two government undercover agents.

Russell Hayden died 9 June 1981 in Palm Springs. Jackie Coogan, at one time the top Hollywood child star, died 1 March 1984 following a heart attack.

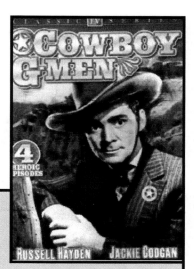

## TRIVIA

The theme music used for *Cowboy G-Men* was often referred to simply as 'Western Theme' or 'Western Theme Reel 3 (MUTEL Music Service Title)'. Its dramatic introduction deliberately resembled 'The Old Trail' theme by Rex Koury which had been used on the radio and TV series *Gunsmoke*. The orchestral introduction had also often been used by Gene Autry's Flying 'A' productions, and had been spliced onto the beginning of several Western series produced by the company, including *The Range Rider* and *Buffalo Bill Jr*. It had been used as a closing theme for *Annie Oakley*. Whilst its origins are not clear, The MUTEL (Music for Television) library of David Chudnow often hired B-picture composers to revise cues originally written for low budget films. Such cues were re-arranged for 40-piece orchestras and re-recorded in France under George Tzipine. It is not known if Joseph Mullendore was the sole composer of this piece or whether it was co-written with Herb Taylor, who was one of the MUTEL composers or even by someone else MUTEL hired.

# COWBOY IN AFRICA

## 16 SEPTEMBER 1968

**THE hour show was shot in color for ABC and premiered on 16 September 1968. It left the air after one season on 1 April 1968. Twenty six episodes were produced.**

Chuck Conner's third Western series was his least successful effort, perhaps because it was set in African rather than the Wild West. In it he starred as Jim Sinclair, a world champion rodeo cowboy, who finds himself working in Kenya for Englishman, Commander Howard Hayes, played by Ronald Howard (Leslie Howard's son). This was based on Ivan Tors' movie *Africa-Texas Style!* (1967).

Sinclair was hired to bring modern ranching methods to Hayes' game ranch.

Tom Nardini was a Navajo helper named John Henry, and Gerald Edwards played orphaned Samson.

Tom Nardini and Gerald Edwards are still alive.

Howard died in London on 19 December 1996 and Connors died of lung cancer on 10 November 1992 aged 71.

Whilst some of the background shots were filmed in Africa, much of the series was filmed at Africa USA Park in California.

# COWBOY THEATRE
## 1956–7

**HOSTED** by Monty Hall, this anthology program featured re-edited Western motion pictures produced by Columbia Pictures in the 1930–40's. (60 Minutes)

# THE COWBOYS
## 6 February 1974

**THE** short-lived Warner Brothers series of half-hour shows was produced by David Dortort and John Hawkins and shot in color. It debuted on the ABC Network on 6 February 1974. It left the air after 12 episodes on 14 August 1974.

Based on the John Wayne film of the same name this series failed to catch on, possibly because interest in the television Western was already declining, but may also have had something to do with the fact that audiences had not liked seeing the brutal murder of hero Wayne in the motion picture.

The show is a sequel to the movie and the young cowboys, hired by Wil Anderson, killed in the film by Long Hair, now work for Wil's widow, Annie, on the ranch. Annie is played by Diana Douglas.

The boys ages ranged from 9 to 17 and they worked under the supervision of Jebediah Nightlinger, (Moses Gunn) the former trail cook and now ranch foreman.

Marshal Bill Winter, played by Jim Davis, stops by from time to time, to check up on Annie and the boys. The cowboys are, as in the film, Slim played by Robert Carradine, Cimarron by A Martinez, Steve by Clint Howard, Hardy by Mitch Brown, Weedy by Clay O'Brien, Jimmy by Sean Kelly and Homer Wheems by Kerry MacLane.

# CUSTER

## 6 SEPTEMBER 1967

**THIS** 60 minute, color show from 20th Century Fox which was packed with stunts, action and incredible stories, debuted on ABC on 6 September 1967.

TV watchdogs immediately noted the level of violence in the show, and although the producer refused to alter anything, the show was forced off air on 27 December 1967 after only 17 episodes. Failing audience ratings were cited in the show's demise.

*Custer* stretched historical fact to breaking point. It dealt with the career of Lieutenant Colonel George Armstrong Custer through the years 1868 and 1875, the period of his life after the Civil War but before his error in judgement at the Little Bighorn. He has lost rank as the result of a court martial and been posted to Fort Hays, Kansas to take charge of a 7th Army Cavalry Regiment.

Wayne Maunder played Custer with Slim Pickens as Scout California Joe Milner, his trusted friend. Peter Palmer was Sergeant Bustard. Robert F Simon was General Terry, who although he disliked Custer and his methods and disapproved of his manner and even his hair, (when Maunder landed the lead role he had had to grow a moustache and his blonde hair long) he realized that Custer was doing an excellent job of pulling together the rag-tag 7th Cavalry. Grant Woods played Miles Keogh and Michael Dante was Crazy Horse.

Custer was devoted to curtailing the activities of Crazy Horse and his Sioux brothers.

---

## TRIVIA

Of historical note – 272 members of the 7th Cavalry died with Custer on 25 June 1876 at the Battle of Little Bighorn

---

The production was later titled *The Legend of Custer* for a USA theatrical release. Slim Pickens died in 1983 of a brain tumour and Robert F. Simon died in 1992 of a heart attack. Wayne Maunder lives in Southern California. Michael Dante lives in Palm Springs.

# THE DAKOTAS
## 7 JANUARY 1963

**A hard edged series, and one of the last of the hour-long television Westerns produced by Warner Brothers, The Dakotas debuted on ABC in January 1963. The series of one hour shows was shot in black and white. Despite being well written and produced, it ran for just 19 episodes before going off air on 13 May the same year.**

The show told the story of Marshal Frank Ragan and his three deputies who tried to keep law and order in the vast Dakota Territory just after the Civil war. It actually had its beginning in an episode of *Cheyenne*, which was telecast on 23 April 1962. In this episode, 'A Man Called Ragan,' Dakota Territorial Marshal Frank Ragan rides into Stark City to see his buddy Johnny Wilson, but cattle baron Ben Stark tells Ragan that Wilson has disappeared and that Ragan had better do the same. This is probably one of the only episodes where Clint Walker, as Cheyenne Bodie, did not appear.

This episode was so popular with the viewing audience that Warner Brothers launched it as a separate series.

Larry Ward starred as the marshal along with Jack Elam (chosen for his menacing looks) as Deputy J. D. Smith, Chad Everett (chosen for his striking good looks) as Deputy Del Stark and Michael Greene as Deputy Vance Porter.

Although the scripts were tough and unrelenting, usually featuring one of the four cast members prominently from week to week, the marshal and his deputies was basically a study in contrasts. Marshal Frank Ragan was the leader, a man totally dedicated to the law. Deputy J. D. Smith was a cynical, worldly ex-gunfighter, a supreme realist. Deputy Vance Porter was a man of extreme qualities ranging from violent and explosive anger one minute to gentleness the next. Vance was often too quick with decisions, too ready to take the world on by himself. Deputy Stark was 23-years-old, a young man with a great vision of the future, yet he was always willing to lay down his life to make his dreams come true.

The series was ruthlessly honest in character, as well as in depiction of the times. It presented the West as a hard and demanding place, where the rapidly growing population of the Dakota Territory struggled to build a world in a terrorized land. The deputies were portrayed to be earning $40 dollars a month, a large-enough paycheck for the times, but they only had a life-expectancy of three years.

The end of the series came when, in Episode 18, *Sanctuary at Crystal Springs*, Deputies Stark and Smith gun down two of the murderous Barton brothers, and the third Barton brother then takes the pastor of a church hostage. Deputy Smith manages to gun down the third brother in the church. A lot of people took a dim view of a shootout in a church, and with the adverse mail pouring into ABC's headquarters, the network dropped the show immediately. Only one more episode aired, on 13 May 1963.

Larry Ward died in 1985. Jack Elam died after winning a Golden Boot Award for his work in countless Westerns, usually as the baddie. *The Dakotas* was one of the only times he got to play a law abiding citizen. Chad Everett was most recently seen in an episode of *Without A Trace*.

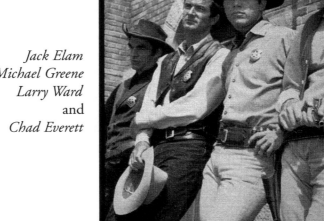

*Jack Elam*
*Michael Greene*
*Larry Ward*
and
*Chad Everett*

# DANIEL BOONE
# WALT DISNEY PRESENTS
## 1960–1

**SHOT** at an hour in length and color, the four part show went out through the 1960–1 season.

Hoping to strike gold as they did with *Davy Crockett*, Disney decided to produce a number of episodes of *Daniel Boone* for the ABC show *Walt Disney Presents*.

Dewey Martin starred as Boone. Mala Powers played Rebecca Boone. Richard Banke was Daniel's traveling companion and friend, Squire. Popular Disney child actors, Kevin and James Corcoran played Boones' two sons. Daniel Boone was typically well produced and has been released on video. Some episodes are also still occasionally found on The Disney Channel.

# DANIEL BOONE

## 24 SEPTEMBER 1964 – 27 AUGUST 1970

**THE** series which debuted on NBC on 24 September 1964, was broadcast first in black and white, but later it was shot in color. It ran for six years, finally departing the lineup on 27 August 1970. Much of the location work was shot around Kanab, Utah, and other filming was done at the Fox Ranch in Malibu Canyon, California.

Fess Parker, who also starred as Davy Crockett in Walt Disney's *Davy Crockett, King of the Wild Frontier*, once again hit ratings gold in this show about one of America's real life folk heroes.

Frontier hero Daniel Boone conducts surveys and expeditions around Boonesborough, running into both friendly and hostile Indians around the time of the Revolutionary War. Aiding him are his wife, Rebecca, played by Patricia Blair, precocious son, Israel, played by Darby Hinton and his daughter, Jemima, played by Veronica Cartwright.

His friends included Oxford educated half-breed Mingo played by Ed Ames, former slave Gabe Cooper, easy going oafs Yadkin played by Albert Salmi and Josh Clements played by Jimmy Dean, and Boonesborough tavern owner Cincinnatus played by Dallas McKennon.

Parker's portrayal of the two frontiersmen Davy Crockett and Daniel Boone impacted millions of young

## TRIVIA

In 1987 Parker purchased a 714 acre ranch 35 miles north of Santa Barbara, in the Santa Ynez Valley, where he promptly set about planning and establishing Fess Parker's Winery & Vineyard.

viewers in the late 1950's and 60's. The well written and exciting show was of course highly fictionalized.

During the six years *Daniel Boone* ran as one of the highest rated shows of its time, Parker not only starred in it but co-produced it and also directed five of its most popular episodes.

He continued to star in numerous box office hits for Disney, Paramount and Warner Brothers' Studios, while laying the foundation for his second career as real estate developer.

Salmi died from a self-inlicted gun wound on 22 April 1990.

Dallas McKennon died.

# DAVY CROCKETT
# KING OF THE WILD FRONTIER
## 15 DECEMBER 1954

**PRODUCED** by Walt Disney Studios for its NBC Disneyland Program, the show became a national phenomenon. The hour long show was shot in color and it could rightly be called the first miniseries of all time. The first installment, *Davy Crockett-Indian Fighter*, aired on 15 December 1954, *Davy Crockett Goes to Congress* on 26 January 1955 and *Davy Crockett at the Alamo* on 23 February 1955.

The 6'6" Fess Parker was personally chosen by Walt Disney to play Crockett. Veteran Buddy Ebson was hired as sidekick, Georgie Russel.

Of course, Crockett was killed at the Alamo, but by the time that show went out, all America was clamoring for more and Disney was forced to bring Crockett and Georgie back for further adventures, going back in time and make episodes about his earlier exploits. They made Davy Crockett and the River Pirates.

The show was also a merchandising pioneer as approaching $100 million coonskin caps were sold. The idea of selling tie-ins from a show is accepted practice now but it wasn't back then.

Parker went on to further fame and fortune as *Daniel Boone* in the long running series and Ebson moved onto two successful shows himself, *The Beverly Hillbillies* and *Barnaby Jones.* He died from complications of pneumonia on 6 July 2003.

By Parker portraying both Davy Crockett and later Daniel Boone so successfully on TV, many historians feel he caused a permanent blurring of the two real life men into one entity forever making each less distinct.

# DEADWOOD

## 21 MARCH 2004

*'Deadwood'* brings back the TV cowboy

THIS acclaimed 60 minute show was created by David Milch who is also the executive producer. The series was nominated for 22 Emmys; it won seven and also earned a Golden Globe Award in its first two seasons for Ian McShane. It was first screened on HBO on 21 March 2004. Thirty six episodes and two feature length films have been made to date.

Directors include Ed Bianchi, Gregg Fienberg, Dan Minahan, Mark Tinker, Dan Attias, Tim Hunter and Adam Davidson. Writers include David Milch, Regina Corrado, Ted Mann, Victoria Morrow, Alix Lambert, Kem Nunn, Nick Towne, Zach Whedon, W. Earl Brown and Bernadette McNamara

 Timothy Olyphant stars as Seth Bullock, a defiantly honest merchant. Ian McShane plays saloonkeeper Al Swearengen who curses and schemes all day, every day in an effort to keep his second-floor office-boudoir; in a town full of clapboard bungalows, second-floor inhabitants are royalty. Molly Parker plays widow Alma Garret, Jim Beaver is Ellsworth, W. Earl Brown stars as Dan Dority, Kim Dickens as Joanie Stubbs, Brad Dourif as Doc Cochran, Anna Gunn as Martha Bullock, John Hawkes as Sol Star, Jeffrey Jones as A. W. Merrick, Robin Weigert as Calamity Jane, Paula Malcomson as Trixie, Leon Rippy as Tom Nuttall, William Sanderson as E. B. Farnum and Dayton Callie as Charlie Utter.

Directors for the second season of *Deadwood* include Michael Almereyda, Ed Bianchi, Gregg Fienberg, Dan Minahan, Steve Shill, Alan Taylor and Tim Van Patten. Writers include: David Milch, Regina Corrado, Sara Hess, Ted Mann, Bryan McDonald, Victoria Morrow, Elizabeth Sarnoff, Steve Shill and Jody Worth.

At first glance, HBO's new drama from *NYPD Blue* scribe David Milch, screened on Movie Central and TMN in Canada, looks like an audacious throwback as it honors one the most saddle-worn of Western traditions by using the framework of history as a structure on which to hammer some lavish imagining. In this case, Milch takes the documented historical circumstance of Deadwood, South Dakota (which actually existed) in the weeks following the Custer massacre at Little Big Horn, and focuses on a dusty collection of characters, many of whom could have hoofed it directly to the set from any other screen Western. The town is a lawless sinkhole of corruption, with its outlaw gold-strike community that sprung up in the Black Hills in defiance of a treaty signed by the US Government with the Sioux at its centre.

Like many gold-rush towns, it grew fast, from nobody to 10,000 people in three months after gold was discovered. Deadwood even had the telephone before San Francisco. The Gem Bar was one of the most successful bars in American in 1876, bringing in $5,000 a day in revenue.

The cowboys, prospectors, prostitutes, Calamity Jane – just about everybody in Deadwood is rough and gritty and grimy. They all regularly use extremely vulgar language.

The show looks like it could have been shipped in from a much earlier time (except for the almost fetishistic reliance on particularly colorful profanities that you would never hear in any John Wayne movie).

Robin Weigert who plays Calamity Jane says, 'Deadwood is pushing the boundaries in many ways. If you're paying attention, you'll see, you'll feel, that it's like out of the muck, out of the mire, out of what appears to be the dregs, comes this incredible nobility of spirit. It's because everything is so harsh and seamy, each individual is able to find their goodness for a handful of minutes. The West was not won in a pretty way, in the way maybe other Westerns want you to believe, with handsome men who had clean showdowns.' In Deadwood, language is just another indication of human contradiction.

The profanity is used to show class lines, and Deadwood's classiest character, Widow Alma Garrett, never swears. David Milch attempts to separate the upper classes from the lower classes, and uses the profanity as somewhat of a literary device.

After all, this is a 21st century television Western, 'It's a really interesting blend of looking back at the old Westerns on TV, but taking the modern approach of filmmakers Sergio Leone or Sam Peckinpah in making it more edgy and realistic,' says Holly George-Warren, author of Cowboy: How Hollywood Invented the Wild West (Reader's Digest). 'That's what audiences want.'

Given that there hasn't exactly been an avalanche of successful TV Westerns in the last 10 years, it was quite a gamble. Milch's challenge may ultimately be less about whether an audience will accept something old and more about whether he can say anything new.

Take Olyphant's Bullock, who, despite a certain flair for the dramatically violent, is in many ways the classic Western brooder. Merciless with lawbreakers but not without sympathy for little children, his mind clearly sorts just violence from unjust violence without a lot of hesitation. He believes in order, if not law. He is *Deadwood's* link to traditional Westerns. Striding through town, Olyphant carries himself like Henry Fonda's Wyatt Earp in *My Darling Clementine*, arms slack, shoulders square, staring as if in a trance at the mean, difficult task before him.

While Olyphant and James Gandolfini could hardly be more different in type, there is a shade of Tony Soprano in Bullock's blend of brutality and fair process. The theme of *Deadwood*, after all, is lawlessness.

Westerns, ultimately, are somewhat formulaic by definition. The cues that are there are meant to be there; the well-timed tip of the hat, the card game with the bar-room piano playing in the background, and the toothless halfwit trying to put one over on the calm and unamused outlaw.

Milch understands the epic possibilities of Western storytelling in episodic TV, and he allows for a number of storylines to develop at once, for a number of characters to emerge and take shape, for a number of themes to find expression, and for the gradual articulation of one of the Western's most basic, touching and optimistic lessons; that the human drive to create community is stronger than the human drive to destroy, and that the best fertilizer for growing things is the waste of what went before.

The first thing that comes to mind for fans of *Deadwood* is probably not the score and indeed the music takes some looking-for.

While the usual TV Western surrounds its characters with dramatic, heroic anthems, the music for *Deadwood*, in fitting with the production's character, features subtly placed ditties of period instruments. The show started out with a few different composers, including Michael Brook and David Schwartz, the latter who is the writer of the show's evocative opening title theme. But since the middle of the first season, scoring duties have been in the hands of the musicians, Reinhold Heil and Johnny Klimek, who are more known for their work in the German techno world. 'They couldn't be less connected with the Western form,' comments Milch, 'But it's the mark of any artist that you submit yourself to the disciplines of the world, and these fellows work that way.'

There hasn't been time for the composers to meet with series executives and directors for a session to identify candidate scenes for music cues, 'They would send us a cut of the show and we'd watch it and take notes and make suggestions, or they'd send it with a few notes or a temp track,' says Klimek. 'Sometimes they might just ask us, 'Can you find some places?' or, 'What would you do?' So we'd make our own suggestions. Often, we gave them more than what was needed, and they would just use what they felt was appropriate.'

The sets created for Deadwood are extraordinarily detailed and realistic, series creator David Milch has been known to get ideas for the show by walking through the town's streets. 'David said he wanted the town itself to be a character,' says production designer Maria Caso.

It took a lot of research, a lot of attention to detail and a lot of dirt – 80 truckloads – to recreate the mining camp in all its muddy splendor.

Costume designer Katherine Jane Bryant remembers the first time she fit Keith Carradine in his full costume. 'He turned around to the mirrors,' she says. 'And he said, 'Oh my god! I'm Wild Bill Hickok'!'

Such transformations are common on the set of *Deadwood*, where Victorian ladies, New York dandies, road agents, Chinese laborers, saloon owners and lawmen all come to life in painstakingly researched period clothes.

The series was nominated for 11 Emmys and two Golden Globe Awards in its debut season.

McShane carried home the coveted 2005 Golden Globe Award for 'Best Actor in a Television Drama' for his versatile performance as Swearengen. The show also won the Television Critics Association's annual award for 'Individual Achievement in Drama.'

McShane has been named as one of GQ's 'Men of the Year'. The New York Times dubbed him, 'One of the Most Interesting Villains on Television' and Rolling Stone Magazine bestowed the title of 'Hot Barkeep' and described the character as 'played to perfection.'

McShane says, 'I play Al Swearengen who owns the Gem Saloon, but he also runs the dope, he runs the girls, he runs the liquor in Deadwood. Swearengen was in town six months before the show takes place in 1876, building up the camp. And since Deadwood was on Indian territory, Custer and his cavalry kicked him out. So then Custer gets killed by the Indians at the Battle of Little Big Horn and many of the soldiers deserted to gold mines looking to build another life for themselves. Swearengen is allowed back in and unofficially runs the town. He tries to look after the town and build it up; he's got a lot invested here, and he wants to keep on to what he has.'

# DEATH VALLEY DAYS

## 1952–1975

**THIS** long running syndicated anthology of half hour shows, produced by Darrell McGowan for Gene Autry's Flying A Productions, originally in black and white, supposedly told 'true' stories of the West. Early episodes were directed by Stuart McGowan. It was filmed on location between 1952 and 1975 and boasted almost 600 episodes. Some 20 new adventures were filmed each year. It had been a popular radio series from 1930.

'As the early morning bugle call of the covered wagon trains fades away among the echoes, another true Death Valley Days is presented by the famous Borax family of products – 20 Mule Team Borax and Boraxo.'

*Death Valley Days* hosts included many famous faces, amongst them, Stanley Andrews from 1952–65 (as The Old Ranger), Ronald Reagan succeeded him until leaving show business for politics in 1966. He was replaced by Robert Taylor from 1966 to 1968, and then Dale Robertson from 1968 to 1972 and John Payne 1972–1975. Merle Haggard hosted a short-lived revival in 1975.

Almost every top Hollywood star made appearances in the show including Guy Madison, Jane Russell, Rory Calhoun and Jeffrey Hunter. Some of the location work was done in Death Valley with other episodes shot in Lone Pine, California, Kanab, Utah and Tucson, Arizona.

*Stanley Andrews*

Stanley Andrews died in 1969 as did Robert Taylor of lung cancer.

John Payne died in 1989 of congestive heart failure.

Ronald Reagan died in 2004.

## TRIVIA

This show is best known for two things, its host Ronald Reagan, who was soon to become President of the United States, and its introduction (see above).

# THE DEPUTY

## 12 September 1959

**THE DEPUTY, a half-hour black and white show, premiered on NBC TV on 12 September 1959 and ran for 76 episodes before it went off the air on 16 September 1961.**

*Henry Fonda*

The show featured major Hollywood star Henry Fonda as Marshal Simon Fry, who kept law in Silver City in the Arizona Territory. He was also responsible for peace keeping in several other towns as well. This was Fonda's first venture into TV. *The Smith Family* in 1971 was his only other effort.

Obviously Fry wasn't the deputy of the title of the series. Clay McCord was the town storekeeper with a fast draw, but a man who bore arms with reluctance and who preferred to settle problems by peaceful means. He was sometimes recruited by Fry for special assignments.

Allen Case played McCord, the deputy. Although Fonda had top billing he actually only starred in a dozen episodes, appeared only briefly in others, and sometimes he only introduced the show.

*Allen Case*

Other regular cast members included Betty Lou Keim as Fran McCord and Read Morgan as Sergeant Hapgood Tasker, the one-eyed cavalry officer stationed in town to help keep order.

Wallace Ford played Marshal Herb Lamson through the first season.

Fonda died in 1982 of heart failure. Allen Case died in 1986 of a heart attack.

Robert Redford made his TV debut on the Deputy in an episode that went out on 30 April 1960, called *The Last Gunfight*.

# DESTRY

## FEBRUARY 1964

**THIS** series only ran from February through September 1964 on ABC. There were 13 hour long shows filmed in color.

John Gavin starred as Harrison Destry, son of famed lawman, Tom Destry.

He was yet another lawman famed for his dislike of guns. Naturally he could use them to devastating effect when the need arose.

Gavin left the industry after a handful of minor roles, but he then moved into politics and became the US Ambassador to Mexico. He married Constance Towers who amongst other things starred alongside John Wayne in *The Horse Soldiers*.

# DIRTY SALLY

## 11 JANUARY 1974

**ONLY** 13 episodes were shown on CBS from 11 January 1974 until 19 July 1974.

Jeannette Nolan starred as Sally Fergus in this half-hour spin off series from *Gunsmoke*. She played a hard-nosed, boozing, busy body who looked and smelled bad as she headed west toward the California gold fields. Travelling along with her was an ex-gunfighter called Cyrus Pike, played by Dack Rambo.

Besides Pike, Sally also talked to her mule, Worthless.

Rambo died of aids and Miss Nolan died on 5 June 1998.

# DR QUINN, MEDICINE WOMAN
## 1992

**THE high spirited hour long show debuted in color on CBS in autumn 1992, and ran for six years. Much of the filming was done around Agoura, California. The series was produced by Beth Sullivan for The Sullivan Company and CBS Entertainment Productions.**

Dr. Michaela Quinn, is a refined woman doctor who moved from the highly civilized world of mid-19th century Boston to a rough-hewn frontier town in 1860s Colorado Springs to start her own medical practice.

Played by film and television star, Jane Seymour, Dr. Quinn was betrothed to a man killed in the Civil War. She eventually wins the trust and respect of the townsfolk and the love of mountain man Byron Sully, played by Joe Lando.

She also adopts and raises three children, Matthew, played by Chad Allen, Colleen by Erika Flores and later Jessica Bowman and Brian Cooper by Shawn Toovey, after their mother dies of a rattlesnake bite.

In the later years, the show focused on Michaela and Sully who got married and had a daughter towards the end of the show's successful run.

While the headstrong Michaela was tough, Boston had never prepared her for the rugged world where folk were as coarse as the climate and their ideas came from another time. By having Dr. Quinn's sophisticated values clash with the antiquated mindset of her Western neighbors, the series explored situations and issues that remain part of life today. Whether championing the cause of gun control, exposing environmental polluters, battling disease or sexist cowboys, or liberating oppressed frontier women, she, at great personal risk, bucks the conventional wisdom of the Old West to emerge as more than just a pioneering feminist.

The popular show attracted a host of big guest stars including Willie Nelson and Johnny Cash.

CBS made two 'Dr. Quinn' movies after the show had left the air, and both won respectable ratings. Today fans are gathering together in an effort that a third movie is produced.

# DUNDEE AND THE CULHANE
## 6 September 1967

**ALTHOUGH** the hour long, color show was well written and acted, with lots of big name guest stars, it ran for just 13 episodes, between September and December 1967. It was shot on locations around Flagstaff, Apache Junction, and Old Tucson Arizona. The show was made by Mort Fine and William Friedkin, who were also responsible for *I Spy*, for Filmways Productions.

*Dundee and the Culhane* was created for famed British actor John Mills, who was more or less stuck in Hollywood while his daughter Haley fulfilled her multi-movie contract with Disney. The CBS series featured Mills as British lawyer, Dundee who travelled the frontier with Sean Garrison as The Culhane, his young partner, who was also a fast gun. Dundee's offices were in Sausalito, across the Bay from San Francisco, but the two wandered the West seeking out clients and trying to impose the rule of law in a lawless land.

For some reason, possibly the fact that it starred an English semi-classical actor and went out at 10 pm on Wednesdays the series failed to win over Western fans and it lasted only half a season. John Mills returned to making films and London. Sean Garrison left the industry.

# DUSTY'S TRAIL

## 1973

**THE half-hour color show was made by Metromedia Productions and debuted in syndication in autumn 1973.**

Sherwood Schwartz had already created sitcom *Gilligan's Island*, which was a cult hit and he attempted to repeat the formula with *Dusty's Trail*, set in the West of the 1880s. Bob Denver, was back and his character, the dunce-headed Dusty, was a clone of his earlier Gilligan persona. Virtually all the other roles were also mirror-images of *Gilligan* characters. Dusty was an assistant to wagon master, Mr Callahan, played by Forrest Tucker.

The wagon train was made up of rich socialites, the Carter Brookhavens, played by Ivor Francis and Lynn Wood, Lulu McQueen, the gold-digging dance hall girl, (Jeannine Riley) and a young school teacher, Betsy, played by Lori Saunders. Forrest Tucker died of throat cancer on 25 October 1986.

# EMPIRE

## 25 SEPTEMBER 1962

THE hour show, filmed in color around Santa Fe was made by NBC TV and premiered on 25 September 1962. It didn't do well and registered few viewers so NBC ceased production at the end of the first season. ABC TV picked it up and changed the title to Redigo, but this didn't help and it left the line-up on 16 September 1964 after 32 episodes.

Long before *Dynasty* or *Dallas*, there was *Empire*, a contemporary Western, set on the sprawling Garret ranch in New Mexico. Operations included oil, cattle, timber, mining, sheep and crop raising.

Jim Redigo, played by Richard Egan, was the foreman and responsible to owners, Constance Garret and her mother Lucia, played by Terry Moore and Anne Seymour respectively. Ryan O'Neil starred as impulsive son Tal.

Warren Vanders and Charles Bronson played the two loyal ranch hands, Chuck Davis and Paul Moreno. Richard Egan died of cancer on 20 July 1987.

## TRIVIA

O'Neil was diagnosed with Leukemia on his 60th birthday, but has recently had a recurring role in *Bones*.

# F TROOP

## 14 SEPTEMBER 1965

THE half hour F Troop ran for three years on ABC after its debut on 14 September 1965, both in black and white and color. Much of the filming was done on the Warner Bros. backlot. It left the air on 31 August 1967.

Set in the post Civil War West, the F Troop gallant bunch of misfits had been banished to forgotten Fort Courage in the Arizona territory, for this comedy series. Forrest Tucker starred as Sergeant Morgan O'Rourke, an enterprising man who ran many side deals with his partner Corporal Randolph Agarn, played by Larry Storch.

The hapless commanding officer was the wide-eyed, bumbling Captain Wilton Parmenter, who had been promoted from private and wrongly decorated for bravery during the closing days of the war when he accidentally led a charge in the wrong direction, toward the enemy. Hard-riding, fast-shooting cowgirl Wrangler Jane was played by Melody Patterson. She had her eye on Parmenter who was played by Ken Berry.

Unbeknowst to the captain, Sgt. O'Rourke had already negotiated a secret, and

## TRIVIA

Wild Eagle's brother-in-law was Sitting Bull and Geronimo was his cousin.

'Old Charlie' the town drunk, was thrown through the saloon doors or windows, bounced off a support post, pushed over the hitching rail, spun around to land on his face or back at least once an episode. Viewers assumed Charlie was a young stuntman in 'old man' makeup. In fact he was played by ace stuntman Harvey Parry, who at that time was 65 years old and had been a stuntman for almost 45 years.

highly profitable treaty with the nearby tribe of cowardly Hekawi Indians, from whom he also had an exclusive franchise to sell their souvenirs to tourists. The tribe was led by Chief Wild Eagle and his Medicine Man, Crazy Cat (Don Diamond). There was no peace treaty with the Shugs, however, and they sometimes caused trouble.

Other members of the troop included a survivor from the Alamo, Trooper Duffy, played by Bob Steele, an almost blind lookout, Trooper Vanderbilt, played by Joe Brooks, Private Hannibal Dobbs was played by James Hampton, and Private Hoffenmeuller by John Mitchum.

Frank DeKova, who played Wild Eagle has died.

Bob Steele died aged 82, from emphysema on 21 December 1988.

# FATHER MURPHY

## 30 November 1981

**THE** hour long show, shot in color, debuted on NBC on 30 November 1981 and left the lineup on 17 June 1984. Many episodes were filmed on the Little House on the Prairie set in California's Simi Valley. Series directors included William F. Claxton and Maury Dexter.

This series was created by Michael Landon and was all about caring and love on the American frontier.

Former pro footballer and frequent *Little House on the Prairie* guest, Merlin Olsen starred as Father John Michael Murphy, a drifter and freight driver in the 1870's. He settled in Jackson, a small town in South Dakota after he and his friend, miner Moses Gage (Moses Gunn) happen upon a school that had suddenly become an orphanage when an attack in town left many children parentless.

Katherine Cannon starred as Mae Woodward, a teacher at the orphanage who finally married Father Murphy. She had been struggling to keep the children from being split up and sent on to workhouses, which would have happened if the orphanage didn't have church support. John Murphy, posing as 'Father' Murphy in order to keep authorities at bay while helping Mae and Moses, cared for the children at the Goldhill school/orphanage.

A good collection of children made up the students of Goldhill, and the show regularly featured a select few, including oldest boy Will (Timothy Gibbs).

In addition to being the unofficial leader of the kids, Will also spent much of season two with a breaking voice, as in real life he had obviously done some growing up. Among the other young characters were brothers David and Matt (Kirk Brennan and Byron Thames), and brother and sister Ephram and Lizette (Scott Mellini and Lisa Trusel).

Gunn died on 16 December 1993 following an asthma attack.

# FRONTIER

## 25 SEPTEMBER 1955

THE half hour episodes were shot in black and white. It had its first showing on 25 September 1955. It ran on NBC for 39 episodes and went off the air on 9 September 1956. It was well made by producer Worthington Minor.

This anthology series starred character actor Walter Coy as the narrator and occasional star of episodes that featured different actors every week. The show illustrated the real hardship that pioneers had faced.

# FRONTIER CIRCUS

## 15 OCTOBER 1961

THIS hour long Western series, shot in black and white, debuted on 5 October 1961 on CBS and ended 26 episodes later on 20 September 1962.

It dealt with the encounters of a travelling circus in the Southwest of the 1880's. John Derek starred as Ben Travis, co-owner of the circus with Colonel Casey Thompson played by Chill Wills.

Richard Jaeckel filled out the cast as Scout Tony Gentry.

Whilst this show was primarily a circus show, there were also similarities to the earlier *Wagon Train*. The T&T Circus (for Thompson and Travis) traveled from town to town in a wagon train. And they had an advance man, scout Gentry who found good places for the circus to stop. The stories involved both the circus performers and the Westerners they ran across.

Chill Wills died on 15 December 1978, Richard Jaekel died aged 70 on 13 June 1997 and John Derek died in 1998 of a heart attack.

# FRONTIER DOCTOR
## 1957

**REPUBLIC** Studios produced 39 half hour black and white episodes of Frontier Doctor through 1957. They were sold individually to stations throughout Canada and the USA.

*Rex Allen*

Rex Allen starred as Dr Bill Baxter, a doctor in the Arizona Territory. Chubby Johnson starred as the Sheriff.

Rex Allen died on 17 December 1999.

Dell published one issue of a *Frontier Doctor* comic book.

Episodes of the series are still available on video.

# FRONTIER JUSTICE
## 1958

**THIS** series later became known as Western Theatre. The half hour episodes were hosted by special guest stars such as Lew Ayres through 1958, Melvyn Douglas through 1959 and Ralph Bellamy in 1961. The shows were shot in black and white.

# FURY

## 15 OCTOBER 1955

**T**HIS contemporary western about a boy and his love for a horse had a five year run on NBC, beginning on 15 October 1955. A total of 104 black and white, half hour episodes were made and after the show left the air it went into syndication from 1960 until 3 September 1966 under the name Brave Stallion.

*Peter Graves*
*Bobby Diamond*
and
*William Fawcett*

Peter Graves starred as Jim Newton, William Fawcett as Pete Wilkie, Ann Robinson and Bobby Diamond as Joey Newton. Other cast members included Jimmy Baird as Pee Wee (Rodney) Jenkins and Roger Mobley as Packy Lambert.

Joey was an orphan who had been involved in a street fight. This had been witnessed by Newton who had gone to court with the boy to confirm his innocence and to convince the judge to let him stay with him at the Broken Wheel Ranch.

Newton was a respected horse rancher who had recently lost his wife and children in an automobile accident.

He had finally captured Fury, a wild stallion, after three years of trying, and Pete his foreman named him during a conversation when he said the horse was full of 'Fire and Fury.' Joey soon made friends with the horse and became the only person who was able to ride him after saving his life. In fact, later Fury did let others occasionally ride him.

Each episode carries boy, horse and pals Pee Wee and Packy to new adventures.

The pilot and the first several episodes of *Fury* were filmed near Idlyllwild, California. There was a scripted fire in episode 5, *Scorched Earth*, in which the Broken Wheel Ranch burned down. Filming then moved to the Upper Iversons Movie Ranch north of Chatsworth and the Spahn Ranch. Interior scenes were filmed on the KTTV TV lot in Hollywood, which are now the Metromedia studios located at Sunset and the Hollywood freeway.

Graves commented, 'All the knowledge that had been gained in the history of motion pictures was used on *Fury*. We had to make our stories in a hurry for very little money, and we had the people to do it.'

Graves, the brother of James Arness, famously went on to star in the *Mission Impossible* series.

Fury, an American Register Saddle-Bred stallion, born on 4 March 1943 was 15 hands high and his weight was kept at around 1,000 pounds. He was owned and trained by Ralph McCutcheon. He was sired by Liberty Dale and his dam was Marian Highland. Interestingly enough Fury's ancestry consisted mostly of bays, browns, and chestnut colors. The only ancestors of his that were jet black were the studs, Rex McDonald, Gains McDonald, Black Squirrel, Black Eagle, and Washington Denmark all born back in the 1800's. McCutcheon bought the black stallion when he was eighteen months old. His registered name was Highland Dale. None of the cast or anyone involved with the show ever heard him called by any other name but Beaut. Even on his ranch, McCutcheon always called him Beaut.

Fury was never gelded, and was never bred either. Later in life he developed a breathing disorder, and he remained with McCutcheon until his death aged 29.

Fury had a great disposition and was trained on the reward system. He never tired of his favorite reward, carrots. He was permitted access to McCutcheon's swimming pool, among other things. Ralph and Fury often went on road trips in their trailer, and McCutcheon even bought a yacht he named 'Fury'.

When 20th Century Fox announced they were casting horses for *Black Beauty* there were black horses were in abundance in Hollywood and many were considered

---

# TRIVIA

An alternative title *Brave Stallion* was used in earlier syndication while the original title ran its duration on NBC.

The introduction to the show depicted the stallion running inside the corral and approaching the camera as the announer calls: 'FURY! The story of a horse and a boy who loves him.'

for the part. Fury was selected for the title role and although the picture did not turn out to be a very popular one, it established Fury as a reliable and capable performer.

Fury went on to play a number of bit parts, and whenever a black horse was needed for a picture he was inevitably the producer's first choice. As his fame grew larger in the role that made his name familiar Fury became the most publicized horse in films. His fan mail was as extensive as Trigger's and Champion's in their heyday. Before he died his gross earnings were far above $500,000 and he was second only to Lassie as a money earner in Hollywood' animal kingdom.

There were actually three horses that played the part of Fury in the television show. Each one of the horses had their own specific part. One would be used for long shots, one in scenes which had long dialogue where the horse needed to stand still for long periods of time, and another was used in riding scenes. There was also another special horse used for rearing scenes. Beaut was used for tricks. McCutcheon stood off camera and told Beaut 'Go pull the boy by his shirt, and pull him backwards'. Beaut never hesitated in carrying his orders out.

Bobby Diamond remains best known for his role as Joey, but he later went on to do guest appearances on other TV shows while still a young boy and had a couple of other roles in TV series. He attended US Grant High School, in Van Nuys. He appeared in several movies throughout the 50's and 60's and later went on to study law. He now practices Civil and Criminal Law. He has two sons from a marriage to Tara Parker.

William Fawcett got his big break at age 61 when he won the role of Pete Wilkey on the series, which he successfully played for five seasons.

*The Fury* Theme Song was by Ernest Gold.

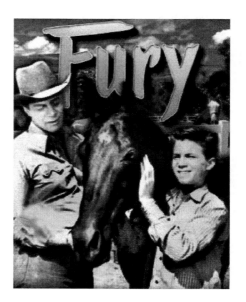

After Fury's run was over, Bill could still be seen in western movies and TV shows. One of his last being *Menace On The Mountain* a Walt Disney TV movie in 1970.

Fawcett passed away on 25 January 1974 in Sherman Oaks, CA. of circulation problems.

# THE GABBY HAYES SHOW

## JUNE 1950

**THE three quarter hour show ran on NBC from June 1950 to the summer of 1952.**

This series consisted of Gabby Hayes telling stories to children in a studio and running edited versions of Western films.

Gabby's first major role was portraying Windy Halliday, Hopalong Cassidy's sidekick at Paramount. *Three on the Trail* (Paramount, 1936) was his first attempt as Halliday, and he continued in that role through *The Renegade Trail* (1939). He went on to play Windy in 18 further Hoppy movies.

In 1939, Hayes switched allegiance to Republic Pictures and his first sidekick role with Roy Rogers followed in *Southward Ho* (Republic, 1939). He did 41 films with Roy Rogers, but these were separated into two groups – in between, he played the saddle pal to Wild Bill Elliott in his 1943–4 series as well as the first two *Red Ryder* oaters (which also starred Elliott). During his Republic days, Hayes generally went under the screen name of Gabby Whittaker. His last film with Roy was *Heldorado* (Republic, 1946).

Gabby's show was nominated for an Emmy award in 1952.

He was well known for his great sayings such as 'yer durn tootin', 'durn pernickety female', 'young whipper snapper' and 'Yessiree Bob'.

Hayes died of a heart attack on 9 February 1969.

# THE GENE AUTRY SHOW

## 23 JULY 1950

AUTRY'S own company, Flying A Productions, made this half-hour series for CBS. It aired between 7 July 1950 and 7 August 1956. a total of 91 episodes were filmed, 15 of which were shot in color.

Each episode of The Gene Autry Show was full of wholesome, rugged, exciting Western adventure with Gene's songs, usually one to a show, neatly blended into the plot. Music was an important part of any Autry project, and during 80 percent of each episode's action, background music helped set the mood. That was in sharp contrast to the average 30 percent use of background music on other television programs at that time. Carl Cotner, the musical director for The Cowboys CBS radio show, composed and conducted for Gene's television show as well.

When singing cowboy, Gene Autry rode the television range for CBS, he became one of the best known of all the cowboy stars. The show was mostly an opportunity for him to sing a bit but a lot of preparation went into each quality episode.

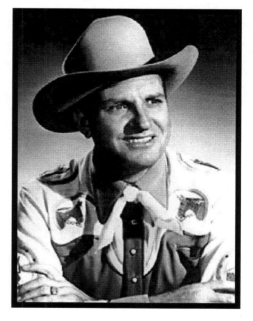

The series was sponsored by Wrigley's Doublemint Chewing Gum and followed the adventures of Gene, his Wonder Horse Champion, and his sidekick Pat Buttram, who travel the Southwest to maintain law and order. The series is a collection of stand-alone half-hour episodes; sometimes Gene and Pat know each other, sometimes they don't; some were set in the past and some are in the near present. Regardless, each one carried Autry's trademark mixture of action, comedy, and music. It also featured a wide range of guests, including the Cass County Boys, Alan Hale Jr., Sheila Ryan, and Gail Davis.

Before a single scene of the series was ever shot, Gene and his staff spent more than two years studying all angles of television production. They then made extensive preparations, including creating a new organization, Flying A Pictures, with Armand Schaefer as president and producer-in-charge. Armand's history with Gene began in 1934 with the serial *Mystery Mountain* and continued right through Autry's successful movie career.

Original scripts written especially for the television medium were purchased from well-known Western adventure writers, many of whom had also worked on Gene's features. A permanent filming location was established at Pioneertown, near Palm Springs, California. In 1952, filming was also done at the legendary Monogram Ranch in Newhall, California, which Gene would later purchase and rename Melody Ranch.

Special filming techniques, devised with the home viewer in mind, were adapted. They eliminated long shots and concentrated instead on close-up action to give the viewer maximum intimacy with the players. In riding sequences, horsemen were photographed at close range and shown traveling across the screen rather than toward the camera. White tones and lighter shades were emphasized and darker portions were kept deep gray rather than flat black. In order to assure the utmost quality, the producers captured everything on 35 mm film.

Autry's Flying A Productions also made *Annie Oakley, Range Rider, Buffalo Bill Jr.* and others. His Melody Ranch was used as the backlot for many Western scenes in both television and film and today the star's love of the West is still promoted at the Gene Autry Western heritage Museum in Griffith Park, California.

Autry himself had originally been concerned about starting a television career and said in 1950, 'Like everyone else in show business, I had become very much interested in the possibilities of television. And, in addition, I had a special reason for wanting to hit the video channels. During my three and a half years in the service, a whole new generation of children had been born. These youngsters are still too young to attend many movies (if at all), but they're not too young to watch television. And in these days, cowboy fans, like charity, begin at home.

'On the other hand, Hollywood has been mighty good to me for many years and, rightly or wrongly, Hollywood considers television a threat to its own business. This is particularly true of theatre exhibitors, the men and women who own and manage the movie houses where pictures are shown. So if I did go in for television, theatre men might consider this a definite affront, an evidence of disloyalty.

'Well, the problem plagued me for a good many months, but finally I reached a decision: to go ahead and produce a series of Western films for CBS television. I didn't want to make my TV debut in old serials of old movies in which I had appeared 10 or 15 years ago, so I made plans to star in a brand new series of half-hour movies especially designed for the needs and limits of television. And the reasons I decided to go ahead with this venture were: (1) Most of my movies play in small towns, whereas television sets are most numerous (per capita) in the large cities; thus, these areas of competition would not overlap to any considerable extent; (2) And more important, television can and will serve as a boon to the movie business. Children, and adults, too, who see a certain star on television become interested in him and, as a result, will also go to see his movies . . . or his rodeos, or his night club act. It has worked that way in every other phase of the entertainment business. Stardom on radio, records, or movies immediately stirs up interest in that personality in other mediums – and it is also going to be true of television. I firmly believe that.'

The year 1955 marked the end of Gene's onscreen career; he had concluded his movies in 1953 with *The Last of the Pony Rider*s. Although no longer starring in new programs for TV, Champion and Gene continued their popularity with television audiences through the 1960's and 1970's with syndicated episodes of *The Gene Autry Show* and edited versions of their much-loved feature films appearing regularly.

Autry is the only entertainer to have five stars on Hollywood's Walk of Fame, one each for radio, records, movies, television, and live performance including rodeo and theater appearances. Among the many hundreds of honors and awards he has received were Induction into the Country Music Hall of Fame; The American Academy of Achievement Award, the Los Angeles Area Governor's Emmy from The Academy of Television Arts & Sciences; and the Board of Directors Lifetime Achievement Award from the International Achievement in Arts Foundation. Gene Autry was also inducted into the Nashville Songwriters Hall of Fame, The National Cowboy Hall of Fame, the National Association of Broadcasters Hall of Fame, and he received The Songwriters Guild Life Achievement Award. He was also honored by his songwriting peers with a lifetime achievement award from ASCAP.

Gene Autry died at his home in Studio City, California on 2 October 1998 of lymphoma. He was 91 years old. Pat Buttram died in 1994 of kidney failure.

There were three 'official' Champions that performed in Autry films and several specialized Champions, including Little Champ, Lindy Champion, Touring Champion, and Champion Three. Other horses, for which there is no documentation at this time, served as doubles for movie stunts and personal appearances. The Original Champion was sorrel-colored, had a blaze down his face and white stockings on all his legs except the right front. His first onscreen credit was for 1935's *Melody Trail*. He died while Gene was in the service.

Gene's second screen horse was Champion Jr., a lighter sorrel with four stockings and a narrow blaze, who appeared in films until 1950. While onscreen with Republic, Champion Jr., was billed as 'Wonder Horse of the West,' and at Columbia, he was known as the 'World's Wonder Horse.' The third screen horse, Television Champion, costarred in Gene's last films and also appeared on television in *The Gene Autry Show* and *The Adventures of Champion* during the 50's. Also a light sorrel with four white stockings, he resembled Champion Jr. but had a thicker blaze. In the late 40's, Little Champ joined the stable. A well-trained trick pony, this blaze-faced sorrel with four white stockings appeared in three of Gene's films and made personal appearances with him.

Touring Champion and Champion Three were personal appearance horses. A darker sorrel with four white stockings and a medium-wide blaze, Touring Champion appeared at rodeos and stage shows in the late 40's and 50's and has his hoof prints next to Gene's handprints at Grauman's Chinese Theater in Hollywood. Champion Three appeared with Gene on the road from the late fifties until 1960, when he retired happily to

Melody Ranch in Newhall, California, where he died in 1990.

Throughout their careers, Gene Autry and Champion were featured in dime novels, children's stories, and comic books. Champion even received equal billing with Gene above the leading ladies on movie posters and lobby cards promoting Autry films.

Gene Autry's young Saturday audience wanted to be just like their hero and Autry responded by giving them his Cowboy Code, sometimes known as the Cowboy Commandments. Autry believed it was as relevant to children in the 1990's as when he was first turned into a hero:

1   The Cowboy must never shoot first, hit a smaller man, or take unfair advantage.

2   He must never go back on his word, or a trust confided in him.

3     He must always tell the truth.

4     He must be gentle with children, the elderly, and animals.

5     He must not advocate or possess racially or religiously intolerant ideas.

6     He must help people in distress.

7     He must be a good worker.

8     He must keep himself clean in thought, speech, action, and personal habits.

9     He must respect women, parents, and his nation's laws.

10    The Cowboy is a patriot.

# THE GRAY GHOST

## 1957

**THE** show was produced by Lindsay Parsons. 39 half hour black and white episodes were filmed and CBS stations syndicated it across America and Canada in Autumn 1957. Political correctness made sponsors nervous about portraying the Confederates favorably and the network cancelled the show after only one season. The Gray Ghost remained popular in syndication for over a decade despite the fact that so few episodes were made.

Confederate Officer John Singleton Mosby was The Gray Ghost, so called because of his lightening raids behind Union lines during The Civil War. *The Gray Ghost* was based on the true story of the major (later colonel), a young lawyer who joined the 43rd Battalion of the First Virginia Cavalry and eventually became the leader of a Confederate guerrilla unit.

Mosby was known for his cunning and stealth, the characteristics which earned him the name 'Gray Ghost.' The show was well made and remained remarkably true to historical fact. Virgil Carrington Jones, a noted authority on Mosby, was a consultant for some of the episodes.

Tod Andrews played Major Mosby, Phil Chambers was trusted Sergeant Myles Magruder, Phil Cambridge was Lt. St Clair and Ron Hagerty filled out the cast as a loyal trooper.

## TRIVIA

The real John Singleton Mosby was born in 1833 in Powhatan County, Virginia and died on 30 May 1916 in Washington DC at the age of 82. It was Memorial Day.

'We took our men from Texas, Kentucky, and Virginia; from the mountains and the backwoods and the plains. We put them under orders – guerrilla fighting orders, and what we lacked in numbers, we made up in speed and brains. Both Rebs and Yankee strangers, they called us 'Mosby's Rangers.' Both North and South they knew our fame. Gray Ghost is what they called me; John Mosby is my name.'

Andrews died in 1972 of a heart attack and Chambers died in 1993.

Dell issued two comic books of *The Gray Ghost*.

The real John Singleton Mosby was born in 1833 in Powhatan County, Virginia and died on 30 May 1916 in Washington DC at the age of 82.

*The Gray Ghost* theme song was by William Paul Dunlap

# GUN SHY

## 15 MARCH 1983

**GUN SHY was a short running, 30 minute, Western comedy produced by CBS.**

Set in the 1869 town of Quake City, California it told the story of the life and struggles of Russell Donovan played by Barry Van Dyke, a frontier gambler who won two children in a card game. The show was based on the Disney films *The Apple Dumpling Gang* (1975) and *Apple Dumpling Gang Strikes Again* (1979).

Tim Thomerson starred as Theodore Ogilvie, Geoffrey Lewis as Amos Tucker, Keith Coogan as Clovis (first four episodes), Adam Rich as Clovis, Bridgette Andersen as Celia, Henry Jones as Homer McCoy and Janis Paige as Nettie McCoy.

# GUNS OF WILL SONNETT

## 8 SEPTEMBER 1967

**THIS half hour show was produced by Aaron Spelling for ABC in color. The program debuted on 8 September 1967 and ran for 50 episodes before leaving the air on 15 September 1969.**

Seventy three year old Walter Brennan, three-time Academy Award winner, starred as Will in one of Aaron Spelling's first television series and what turned out to be his own last.

Dack Rambo played Will's Grandson, Jeff. The pair roamed the West of the 1870's looking for Jeff's gun-slinging father, James, a man he'd never known. James had left the infant Jeff in Will's care 19 years earlier. He was played by Jason Evers.

Will and Jeff ran into many people who claimed to know the elusive James. Some spoke well of him and others ill. The pair never caught up with him in the series although, in the last original episode, they did come across a man who claimed to have killed James.

While James Sonnett was a well known gunslinger, the elder Sonnett was no slouch with his gun either. Will had been a rifleman in the army and once explained to someone who was spoiling for a fight that he was an even faster draw than his famous son. He proved that fact in several episodes of the series as he pulled his grandson out of numerous scrapes, most of them started because of the family name.

After two months of searching, the viewers were finally introduced to the gunslinger in episode six, although it took Will and Jeff another year and a half to finally catch up to the prodigal Sonnett.

Unfortunately, despite a lot of heavy promotion, the series never really caught on with the viewers.

Although Evers was listed as a series regular, he was never included in the

*Walter Brennan and Dack Rambo*

opening titles but always got the primary guest star credit in each episode he appeared in.

*Guns of Will Sonnett* stood out among the other Westerns of the time because of the way Will summed up each segment and it was possibly the only action adventure series to ever end each episode with a trail prayer.

'We search for a man named Jim Sonnett and the tales folks tell may be true;
Most call him gunman and killer;
He's the son I hardly knew.

I raised Jim's boy from the cradle;
'till the day he said to me,
'I have to go find my father.'
And I reckon that's the way it should be.
So we ride, Jim's boy and me.'

Brennan died of emphysema on 21 September 1974 aged 80.

Rambo died of aids in 1994. He was the twin brother of Dirk Rambo, who died in 1967 in a fire.

# GUNSLINGER

## 9 FEBRUARY 1961

**THE** show ran for an hour and was shot in black and white for CBS.

It debuted on 9 February 1961 and ran for just 12 episodes before leaving the line up on 14 September 1961. This was an exceptional series that simply failed to take off.

*Tony Young*

The Gunslinger, played by Tony Young, went by just one name, Cord.

He was a fast gun who hired out for undercover assignments for the US Army in New Mexico after the Civil war.

Cord was under the command of Captain Zachary Wingate played by Preston Foster, at Fort Scott. Although he was a loner he had a few friends at the Fort, including Pico McGuire (Charles Gray), Billy Urchin (Dee Pollock) who wanted to learn all about the frontier from Cord, and Amby Hollister (Midge Ware), who ran the General Store had her eye on him.

John Pickard played Sergeant Major Murdock.

Preston Foster died in 1970. Tony Young died in 2002 of lung cancer after starring in an episode of *Quantum Leap* as Sam, chauffeur to Marilyn Monroe, who had to try to prevent Marilyn's tragic death.

# GUNSMOKE

## 10 SEPTEMBER 1955

AT ten o'clock in the evening of Saturday 10 September 1955 the first adult western from CBS premiered. Audiences turned on their sets expecting to see one more run of the mill Western. Instead they saw a familiar figure and heard the distinctive drawl of the greatest cowboy of them all when he introduced the show;

*Milburn Stone*
*Glenn Strange*
*Amanda Blake*
*James Arness*
*Ken Curtis*
and
*Buck Taylor*

'Good evening. My name is John Wayne. Some of you have seen me before. I hope so – I've been kickin' round Hollywood for a long time. I've made a lot of pictures out here, all kinds. Some of them are Westerns, and that's what I'm here to tell you about tonight – a Western. A new television show called *Gunsmoke*. I knew there was only one man to play it ... James Arness. He's a young fella and may be new to some of you. But I've worked with

**him and I predict he'll be a big star. And now I'm proud to present *Gunsmoke.*'**

**There were 633 total television episodes made: 233 half-hour episodes (1955–1960) and 400 hour long episodes (1961–1975). The first 11 seasons were filmed in black and white, the last nine seasons, color. There have been five *Gunsmoke* films produced since the show went off air in 1975.**

When Wayne made that announcement *Gunsmoke* had already been running as a successful CBS radio show for six years with a cast full of popular characters created by John Meston and Norman Macdonnell. That show, starring William Conrad as Matt Dillon, continued to air concurrently with the television program until 1960.

Still the question remained, despite Wayne's personal endorsement, how well would an adult Western fare in the relatively new medium of television? Throughout 1955 CBS executives had been getting increasingly nervous as they finally lined *Gunsmoke* up for the Fall schedule. But as with any good Western, when things were tough, in rode the hero. John Wayne had turned up to give the show an incredible boost by applying his personal seal of approval.

As the crew and cast of the new show gathered around the television in the home of James Arness – the new Dillon – to watch the show go out for the first time, they were surprised to see Wayne introduce it. Arness enthused, 'Of course that was an extremely gracious thing for him to do, and, boy, that meant a great deal. That had a lot to do with us getting off to such a great start. I don't know of any other television show that had a big movie star come in and introduce them like that.'

The vast majority of viewers were shocked that night at the opening scenes of the show, when instead of the hero saving the day, Matt Dillon was brutally gunned down. He was left lying on the dusty street to be tended by a dance hall girl and a seedy doctor whilst his limping deputy stood by helplessly. This was a far cry from the expectations of the comfortable home viewer, but Dillon immediately appeared more human, vulnerable and three dimensional than any television character they had seen before.

*Gunsmoke* went on to become the longest running dramatic series in the history of television. Two of its stars, James Arness and Milburn Stone, remained with it throughout the entire 20 seasons, with Amanda Blake running them a close second, departing after 19 years.

When the decision had initially been made to transfer *Gunsmoke* to television, CBS selected Harry Ackerman to direct the venture. It may have seemed more appropriate if Macdonnell and Meston had been handed the responsibility of re-creating their own program but CBS

executives didn't feel they had a suitable background for television and the producer's job was instead passed to Charles Marquis Warren, who they felt had the most impressive credentials, especially in directing Western films. His work included *Only the Valiant, Beyond Glory, Streets of Laredo* and *Springfield Rifle*. He had written and directed *Little Big Horn,* and produced *Hellgate* in 1952, (a movie featuring James Arness), before going to work at Paramount on the script for *Pony Express* and *Arrowhead.*

Meston continued writing half hour segments for both the radio and television shows, and Arness later insisted that all the best episodes were written by him. He churned out 38 scripts a season in his apartment in Paris or in a trailer in Spain as he followed the bullfight circuit. He said he could write *Gunsmoke* anywhere as he was writing legend not history. He was not interested in historical detail but rather preferred to capture the vitality and energy of 'the wickedest little city in America.'

Dodge City had certainly been that and had always had the reputation of being the most sinful of all Western towns and Meston had plenty of fuel to work with from the 1870's, (when the town's population grew from 300 to 700). There were 50 known prostitutes plying their trade there during the period when a ten minute dance with one of the girls cost cowboys 75 cents. *The Hays Sentinel* described Dodge City at the time, 'She is a merry town, and the only visible means of support of a great number of her citizens is jocularity. Here rowdyism has taken its most aggravated forms.'

To Meston, Dodge was 'a kind of arena for frustrated gladiators.' Between 1872 and 1873 there were 17 killings and the first burial on Boot Hill was in 1872. When developing *Gunsmoke*, Warren chose that barren hillside as the backdrop scene for each of the opening shots with Matt solemnly reflecting on the fates of the men buried there.

Macdonnell retained an executive role as associate producer and at the same time continued to produce and direct the radio show. Warren however, came to the show with a fresh vision and felt little commitment toward the radio cast or the creators of the show. Warren admitted he didn't like Macdonnell, 'I felt his resentment. You couldn't blame him… he thought, and rightly so, that he knew the characters. After all he had invented them, and I changed them.'

Casting the show had been Warren's first difficult task; the voices of Matt, Kitty and Doc were already loved in homes across America; their following was huge. Warren hesitated in the face of a fierce campaign to sign up the radio cast, but he knew he needed faces, not voices and he never seriously considered any of them for a principal role. He also argued that if he had selected any of them the radio show would have folded, as it was it continued its own successful and lengthy run unhindered.

Warren auditioned many actors and recalled that one of his toughest jobs was finding a suitable actor to play Matt Dillon, 'I've still got a copy of the first script, and the name of the actor is written in beside every role – except for Dillon. That was left blank because up to the last minute we didn't know who was going to get the part. When Arness was selected he was off shooting in Bermuda. I sent him a telegram saying, 'Hooray and congratulations! You are Matt Dillon'.'

Before Arness was chosen, several top actors competed for the role including Raymond Burr, Richard Boone and William Conrad, the voice of Dillon in the radio program. Warren said, 'During the tests Conrad and Burr were sitting down. When they got up, the chairs came up with them … that eliminated them.' Even though the Hollywood trade papers reported that a ground breaking adult-themed Western was under development in 1954, Arness hadn't even been in the running for the part at that time.

Ackerman himself took up the story, 'John Wayne called me one day and said, 'I've got just the man here to play Matt Dillon.' The next day Arness came in for a test'.'

Arness though was reluctant to audition, saying he wanted to make his mark in films even though at the time he had only had minor supporting parts. In 1948 he had landed a minor role in his first Western, *Whiplash* (Warner Bros) and following that break he had his first meeting with his destiny and John Wayne, 'I had gotten an interview with him as he was preparing to do a picture. He was at Republic Studios then, so I went out to meet him. There I was sitting across the desk from the great one! ...we talked a bit and he wasn't overly interested in all of the work I might have done. I think he was trying to see whether maybe I was the kind of guy that he'd like to have along on his company. Evidently I passed the test and got the part and it was great!'

The meeting led to a long term friendship with the star and soon after their picture was completed, Wayne's company Batjac signed him on a yearly contract. 'That turned out to be great because I got a steady income. I was there for three years and appeared in several of his pictures.'

Robert Totten, who directed many *Gunsmoke* episodes said that CBS had originally offered the part of Dillon to Wayne, "It's true. They believed Wayne would take a stab at it himself. They knew they couldn't use Bill Conrad. They were looking for a larger than life figure who could match Conrad's voice. Well, they were talking about one guy ... the one and only.

'So they went to John Wayne, and Duke didn't scoff at it at all. In fact, he once told me they flattered him by coming to him that way. But he knew this young guy who really needed a break. Television was new and so was James Arness. So Duke pushed for him and you know the rest of the story.' (Warren however, stated that contrary to the many rumors, he had never offered the part to Wayne, saying that Duke would have wrung his neck if he had.)

And neither was Arness sure that he wanted it either, 'I really wasn't all that sure that that was what I wanted to do right at that moment.' Initially he declined the offer, concerned that if the show failed he would then have a tough time finding roles in movies, 'But that was before I talked to Duke. He called me in and kinda leaned on me. He said I'd be crazy not to do it and that he thought it would really be good for me. And he surely as hell turned out to be right. He was wholeheartedly in favor of it. He convinced me thank God, that it was the thing to do.'

At six foot six inches, the commanding figure of James Arness was every bit the kind of stuff on-screen heroes were supposed to be. He looked and acted the way a frontier marshal should, he was tall, lean and taciturn, he added unparalleled depth and authenticity to one of pop culture's most commonly recurring characters.

Meston ensured that Dillon never fired a shot unless he was shot at and that he often agonized over the brutality he found himself embroiled in. He was a man who made the best decisions he could and lived with the consequences. Amidst evil and lawlessness he clung faithfully to his simple principles. He upheld the law that he was willing to die for along the frontier where lynch mobs were the norm. He had a reputation as a fair man and a quick draw. He faced cattle rustlers, fugitives, stagecoach bandits and gunslingers every day. He prefered to take these criminals into custody for a fair trial, but those who resisted inevitably wound up at Percy Crump's, the undertaker and furniture maker, and then on up to Boot Hill. But still, Dillon and his friends struggled against fate and frequently against forces beyond their control.

Arness described his character; 'Matt Dillon was a guy who not only had to see that the laws were carried out, but had to live by himself. He had to do the right thing. As a consequence, he always had to hold his own personal feelings or desires in restraint. To me, Matt is a fictional character in name only. He is something of a composite of the real life lawman; the Bat Masterson, the Pat Garretts and the Wyatt Earps. I've been reading every historical account I've been able to get my hands on and I know I'm not only getting the feel of the role but now I'm familiar with the temper of the times and that atmosphere of that period in American history. Dillon... after all, is truly a product of dramatic retrospect.

'When I first started *Gunsmoke* I thought, this is television and I can do this easily. But I found the workload was so tremendous. I'd never done anything that was even remotely as much work as that. I was in every scene and I was having to do about 15 pages of dialogue a day, and I began feeling overwhelmed. As an actor I had never been faced with having to do that much work in such a short period of time.'

For help in defining his role he got hold of as many of the old radio shows as he could, 'Listening to the old radio shows was tremendously helpful in establishing the feel of the guy. Norman Macdonnell and John Meston were right there on hand and we spoke practically on a daily basis in the first year or two.'

Whilst Arness always loved working on the show, his work schedule was certainly grueling. Every four days a half-hour episode was filmed. Matt was the central character and the stories revolved around him so Arness' presence was required most of the time. He worked ten to 14 hour days for nine months each season. Eventually he was compelled to ask for more time away from set and managed to get the writers to come up with some stories highlighting the other actors, 'I felt that Matt should be de-emphasized and used a little less. My feeling was that that would help give it longevity. And besides I had other things in my life that I was doing.' Fortunately for the writers and directors the other actors in the show were all strong and able to carry a show without his dominant presence.

Long term cast members included Amanda Blake as shapely red head, Miss Kitty Russell, Ken Curtis as Festus, Milburn Stone as alcoholic Doc Adams, Buck Taylor as Newly and Dennis Weaver as Chester Good. Burt Reynolds also put in some appearances as Quint Asper.

Milburn Stone will always be best remembered for his performance as Dr. Galen 'Doc' Adams. Appearing throughout the show's entire run, he filmed approximately 500 episodes in all and he was rewarded in 1968 with an Emmy for his portrayal. Bullet wounds were his bread and butter. He was one of Matt's closest friends and was greatly admired by the people of Dodge for his skill as a physician. Doc, of course, was only as capable as 1870's medical science permitted and whenever he was asked for a prognosis, he invariably replied, 'We'll have to wait and see.'

He was a bachelor who lived in his office in downtown Dodge, and when not practicing medicine, he visited Matt at the jailhouse, drank beer and talked with Kitty at the Saloon.

Amanda Blake was already working at CBS when she heard that *Gunsmoke* was being made for TV, 'I was in on the ground floor. They had to give me the part of Kitty – I drove everyone nuts until they did.' She was just 26 when she won the part of the feisty owner and operator of the Long Branch Saloon. Kitty was a savvy businesswoman with a tough exterior which belied her soft heart. She employed one bartender, Sam, and a variety of young women to make pleasant conversation and look pretty for her male customers.

A single woman, she had a warm affection for Matt, though it never amounted to a romantic on-screen involvement. Blake was nominated for an Emmy in 1958, but lost out to Barbara Hale of *Perry Mason*.

When the time came to cast deputy Chester Goode, Warren already had Dennis Weaver in mind, having worked with him on *Seven Angry Men* (1954), and he was the first principal actor signed. When Warren was fine tuning the character of Chester he felt he must be given some kind of infirmity to account for an apparently healthy looking young man being so sedentary and always hanging around the jail, 'That's why I gave Chester the limp.' For nine seasons Weaver dragged a bum leg

WHERE HAVE ALL THE COWBOYS GONE?

through Dodge City while serving as Dillon's trusted deputy. The lanky Weaver (6'2") recalls however that it was given to him to qualify him as a traditional sidekick, 'They wanted him to be nonviolent and he had to have something to keep him out of the action.'

However some thought the infirmity was to disguise Arness' real limp that stemmed back to the Anzio campaign. He had been wounded in the right leg by machine gun bullets and lay where he had fallen, in a freezing stream, until he was discovered eighteen hours later. He was confined to hospital for a year. When he became an actor some years later he consciously developed the rolling gate of the cowboy to cover the limp up.

Eventually Chester became a cult figure in his own right. Fans often wrote to Milburn Stone enquiring after Chester's health. Warren says that in one episode Weaver forgot to limp and no one noticed during filming, 'However, a million viewers spotted it.' CBS received thousands of letters from well-wishers saying, 'Thank God Chester is cured.'

Weaver didn't alter Chester's persona much over the years except that he allowed the 'country bumpkin' element to diminish over time. He certainly remained loyal to Matt throughout and idolized the man he felt was the most heroic of people. Warren said, 'Chester was like a puppy dog.'

In 1959 Weaver won the Emmy Award for Best Supporting Actor in a dramatic Series, but despite his success he became restless, 'I felt that if I stayed with it much longer I would have major problems. I recognized that I was doing a very unique character, and that Hollywood had a tendency to typecast and pigeonhole people.'

In an attempt to satisfy Weaver, the producers allowed him to direct four episodes. However, he finally left the show in 1964, saying, 'I would assume that they were somewhat disappointed when I left. But it didn't hurt the ratings particularly.'

After Weaver left, new character Festus Haggen (Ken Curtis) was introduced as Dodge City's Deputy Marshal. Festus was the pride of the Haggen family and the antitheseis of Doc. Although illiterate and often incoherent, the dog-eared Deputy had earned the respect of the townspeople as a capable lawman, and he was easily the most colorful resident of the frontier town. Just like Chester, Festus was fiercely loyal to Dillon and counted him as one of his two best friends – the other is his mule, Ruth. His meager salary as a deputy forced him to do odd jobs to make ends meet, so when he wasn't covering the Marshal's back, he might be found painting a barn or digging a well.

Festus was a confirmed bachelor, which was no great surprise given his educational background and lack of personal hygiene. In his spare time, he too could be found at the Long Branch Saloon, waiting for someone to buy him a drink.

Ken Curtis, the son-in-law of John Ford, won the role of Festus in 1964. Although he was cast to fill the void left by the enormously popular Weaver, Curtis' character was soon accepted by the fans and possibly even preferred. The rest of the cast and crew certainly found him a genial colleague and he and Stone became great friends over the years. He remained with the show for more than 10 years until its eventual cancellation.

Macdonnell and director Andrew McLaglen, chose him after he had worked a similar part for McLaglen in *Have Gun – Will Travel*. In that he had played the part of Monk, 'a skinner who smelled so bad they wouldn't let him stay in the cow camp.'

The dialect he developed for the role, whilst exaggerated, was quite natural to him, 'It's making two syllables out of one syllable words that does it. The word horse for example is pronounced hor-us.' Curtis called it a dry-land dialect which came from his home state, Colorado. He had also successfully played a similar character, Charlie McCorry in *The Searchers*, filmed by his father-in-law and starring John Wayne.

As the show entered its eighth season, ratings slipped and it was overtaken by *Bonanza* as America's favorite show. The producers decided to expand the episodes to a full hour and John Mantley was brought in to take control as writer and producer. Arness said there was a 'lot of horsefeathers' about demographics and he confessed that he found extending the show, '…tough to do. We did a year or two of those and had a lot of trouble making them all work. The audience didn't accept this change very well at first. Then I think it was two seasons after that they decided to shoot in color, and that in itself helped out a lot. About that time we also had a whole new production team come in that was fresh to the show and added a lot of new ideas and the thing picked back up again.'

During the 1967–8 season, *Gunsmoke* leapfrogged back above *Bonanza*. By coincidence it had dropped out of the Top 25 for the three seasons that *Bonanza* rode at number one, and in 1966–7 it had fallen to number 34.

CBS had actually served the citizens of Dodge City their papers, but fans were so outraged (it was even mentioned in Congress) that CBS network chief, William S. Paley, in an unprecedented move, suggested that the show be given another chance on a different night.

By switching to Monday and concentrating on topical themes, *Gunsmoke* attracted a whole new audience. Ironically, some critics suggested that *Gunsmoke's* new popularity had something to do with its borrowing a bit of the domesticity of *Bonanza*.

Under Mantley the show certainly made the transition into an anthology-type series, often featuring big stars such as Bette Davis, Bruce Dern, Ron Howard, Richard Dreyfuss and Harrison Ford (who fell on his gun during filming and lost several teeth) and Arness said, 'John Mantley is the guy who keeps the feeling of *Gunsmoke* going. Never lets it deviate from honesty. Mantley's so damned conscientious about our scripts.' (*Los Angeles Times* 3 December 1971)

Mantley had seen *Gunsmoke* as the dramatization of the American epic legend of the West, created from the standard elements of the dime novel and the pulp Western, and he didn't want it to die. He fervently pointed out, 'Matt Dillon was a gunman who was a benevolent dictator; Miss Kitty was a whore who had risen to be a saloon owner and madam; Doc Adams was a drunk and Chester (or his later equivalents Festus and Newly) the dim-witted town loafer.' How could it fail to entertain?

When CBS re-instated the show they ordered Mantley to eliminate the shootout, the violence and all the trappings of the traditional Western. Mantley said, 'We couldn't do the original type of show now. A funny thing; as the country grows more permissive and freer dealing with adult themes, television grows more puritanical. We're going backward.'

All he could do was to turn *Gunsmoke* into an anthology of stories that were incidentally set in Dodge City. Dillon, Miss Kitty and the rest had occasional shows but more often the plays simply featured the starring big guests.

Mantley said, 'I tell writers to forget plots and bring us scripts with strong character conflicts. I tell them not to worry about settling the story in Dodge City or fitting the narrative to our particular characters. That *we* can do, if the vital first element is there.'

When trying to explain the success of *Gunsmoke* Arness confided, 'It's a mystery… it's an unexplainable chemistry. I think our secret is harmony and happy rapport. We lucked out with a happy group of people alright. No personality conflicts…'

In April 1975 cast and crew were shocked to learn that *Gunsmoke* had been cancelled. Arness said, 'I was happy to be off for a while. I was planning to stay away from the tube but then they came up with *How The West Was Won* almost immediately.'

The first episodes of *Gunsmoke* cost only $35,000 each to make but by the time it left the air the cost for one segment had risen to $240,000. When Arness first pinned on the marshal's badge he took home $500 a week, but saw his salary soar to $60,000 a show plus a percentage of profits and residuals. Warren said, 'When the first episode of *Gunsmoke* was made in 1955, I figured it wouldn't last a year.'

Over the years some of Hollywood's most talented writers and directors such as Mark Rydell, Vincent and Bernard McEveety, Andrew V. McLaglen, Irving J. Moore, Harry Harris Jr., and Kathleen Hite, John Dunkel and Sam Peckinpah had helped perfect *Gunsmoke;* each one adding their own distinctive contribution. Each actor involved had also jealously guarded their character throughout the years, devoting a major part of their lives to the show.

After the success of *Gunsmoke*, Arness stayed with the television Western. From 1976 through 1979 he starred in *How the West Was Won*. His last television series was the police drama *Big Jim McLain* made in the early 1980's.

After Blake left *Gunsmoke* in 1974, her career quickly faltered into obscurity. She made a *Love Boat* appearance in 1979, and was featured in *Gunsmoke: Return to Dodge in 1987,* the first of several *Gunsmoke* TV movies. A longtime smoker, Amanda was forced to undergo oral cancer surgery in 1977. Seven years later, the American Cancer Society awarded her its Courage Award. She died of cancer in 1989 when she was just 60 years old.

In 1983–4, Ken Curtis appeared in another Western, *The Yellow Rose*, with Cybill Shepherd and Sam Elliott, before retiring to Fresno, California, where he died on 29 April 1991 at age 74.

Milburn retired in 1975 at the end of *Gunsmoke's* TV run. By that time, his 'Doc' title was official, and he had been awarded an honorary doctorate from St. Mary of the Plains College in – where else? – Dodge City, Kansas. He died of natural causes on 12 June 1980.

Weaver went on to star in *Kentucky Jones* (1964–5), *Gentle Ben* (1967–69), *McCloud* (1970–77) and *Buck Jones* (1987–8). He died 24 February 2006 from cancer.

In 1987, after a 12 year silence, a made for TV movie, *Gunsmoke: Return to Dodge*, was aired on CBS. Again produced by John Mantley, it was written by Jim Byrnes and directed by Vincent McEveety. It once more starred Arness, Amanda Blake and Buck Taylor. It was wildly received by fans, old and new.

Matt's buckskin horse was called Marshal throughout the series although the horse was replaced every four to five years. Arness said that after that time they became skittish around the cameras, but he always rode a buckskin for continuity purposes.

The only spin-off from *Gunsmoke* was *Dirty Sally*, based on the character Sally Fergus and her mule, Worthless, in the two-part episode 'Pike.' The TV show *Dirty Sally* ran from 11 January 1974 to 19 July 1974. Jeanette Nolan played the role of Sally all three times.

Today people continue to ask Arness why they are not still making *Gunsmoke,* he says, 'People really miss it… They miss that era of television I think.' Dennis Weaver also believed *Gunsmoke* continued to have relevance, saying, 'I think it's a timeless show because it is a period show. I think it certainly has entertainment value today.'

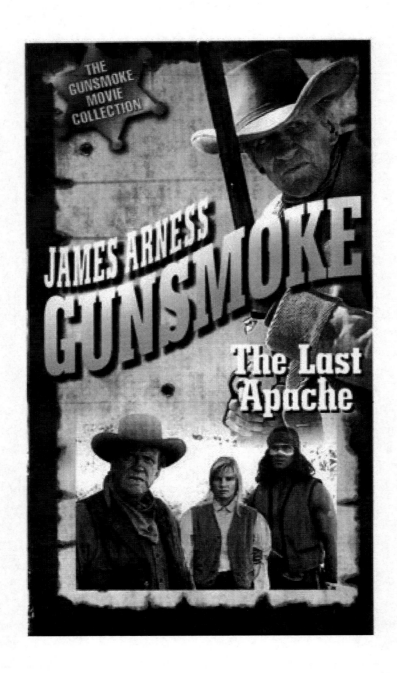

# HAVE GUN WILL TRAVEL
## 14 September 1957

**THE classic half hour Western series ran on CBS from 14 September 1957 until 23 September 1963. The show aired on Saturdays at 9.30pm, just before Gunsmoke. It opened as the number four rated show for the year, and followed that with three consecutive years at number three. A total of 225 episodes were filmed and are all are available on video from Columbia House.**

Richard Boone starred as Paladin, a wealthy man-of-the-world residing in the Hotel Carlton in San Francisco; he was also the black-clothed travelling gunfighter-for-hire. Paladin always carried a business card which somehow found its way into practically every episode. The card that he freely handed out stated simply, 'Have Gun-Will Travel'.

The unique title survives today, in countless incarnations through-out advertising and other media.

Paladin was highly moral and ethical, but a man to be crossed. He dressed all in black and worked from the hotel.

His standard modus operandi was the constant perusal of the scores of newspapers to which he subscribed, searching for potential clients in the turbulent stories of the times. He would pick one then send his card, along with a clipping of the story, to the person-in-need. Hey Boy, played by Kam Tong, brought Paladin his assignments in the morning mail.

His standard fee was $1,000, a hefty sum in those days, but he'd travel that many miles to get it.

Boone became 'The Knight Without Armor in a Savage Land', as sung by Johnny Western in the show's theme song. Each episode opened with him aiming his gun along with his words directly at the audience, and the series always featured a no-nonsense approach and intelligence rarely evident on the small screen since.

As the series progressed, it became clear that Paladin came from a well-to-do family, had served as a Union cavalry officer during the Civil War, then at some point left for Frisco to assume his double-life of civilized sophisticate/rough-and-tumble gunfighter. At the prestigious Hotel Carlton, he lived a life of leisure and luxury. He enjoyed the arts, fine food, brandy, cigars, gambling, acquiring knowledge, and he absolutely adored women. He dressed in the most expensive clothes of the day, and always had an appropriate quote at the ready, whether it be from Shelley or Montaigne, for a beguiling lady, or perhaps Socrates or Shakespeare for those of his own gender. He was able to speak several languages, play piano and compose his own symphonies, ascertain a bourbon's distillery with merely a small sip, and play chess (vs. himself, no less) according to the military tactics of various historical figures.

But things were different once Paladin changed into his work attire. Dressed completely in bad-man black, with a silver chess-knight on his holster and carrying a derringer under his belt, he hired out his services to those fortunate enough to be able to afford them. On many occasions, however, he did charity work, donating or waiving his fee for a good cause. He was a champion of justice, highly-principled and always concerned with 'what's right.' Frequently he switched his allegiance to his employer's opponent, after discovering his now ex-employer was up to no good. He was physically strong, and great with his fists (once duking it out bare-knuckled with a prize-fighter for dozens of rounds), but it was with his gun that Paladin truly excelled.

Not only did he always vanquish his foe in a gunfight, Paladin often decided beforehand whether he would merely wound the unlucky man or kill him – if his opponent was evil enough, he'd meet his maker. Paladin accepted the fact that he had the power of life and death, and did not take his responsibilities lightly. It was also clear he was, for all practical purposes, as talented at his craft as anyone. On occasion he would get wounded in a fair fight, but if he did, you could be sure his opponent would be shot dead by the end of the segment. Based on his demeanor and his deeds, Paladin feared no man; he reigned at the summit of the gun slinging pecking-order, and he understood that truth completely. (In one intriguing episode, events forced Paladin into a showdown with famed gunfighter Sam Tuttle; Paladin knew he couldn't beat him, but assured Tuttle that he would also die.)

He used a black, single-action Colt .45 with a long, rifled barrel; the gun was hand-crafted to his own specifications and had a feathery one-ounce trigger pull. He also carried a concealed derringer, which he often used to good effect some time after being told to 'drop your gun.'

Toward the end of the series the story of Paladin's origin was told in flashback. The Paladin-To-Be had incurred a huge gambling debt, and to pay it off he was forced by his IOU-holder; an evil land baron named Norge, to challenge an outlaw called 'Smoke' to a duel. Norge claimed Smoke was terrorizing the townsfolk of a settlement owned by the land baron, and has threatened to kill Norge if he ever set foot there. The man who grew into Paladin (the audience was never given name) sought out Smoke. But Smoke found him first and knocked him unconscious. When Paladin awoke he was in a secure pen, imprisoned by a steep cliff on one side, unscalable rock-faces, and a wall of long, pointed wooden poles.

Smoke (also played by Richard Boone, with gray hair and no mustache) was dressed completely in black; the future Paladin's outfit. He watched his prisoner from a ledge above and questioned him, remarking that he was merely the latest in a long line of assassins sent by the land baron. Impressed, however, with P-T-B's passion to fulfill his sworn obligation and kill him, Smoke mused that 'in the books, there's a name for someone like you... a paladin....'

From then on, he sarcastically called the hero by that name. Smoke told his 'noble paladin' that he would get his duel.

While Paladin practiced his quick-draw he noticed Smoke's persistent cough. Eventually Paladin shouted that Smoke faced imminent death, one way or the other. The night before the big event, Paladin sat before a smoky fire, thinking. The next morning, Smoke tossed him a few bullets, and Paladin loaded his gun. He placed some bushes into the smoldering fire and fanned the flames, producing a cloud of irritating smoke which drifted ominously upwards. The two men prepare to draw, then the smoke hit Smoke (so to speak), and he started coughing. Realizing Paladin's ploy, he draws quickly, but his aim is badly affected.

Meanwhile, the late-drawing Paladin scored a critical hit, and Smoke fell off the ledge to the ground below. Paladin rushed to the dying man, who asked, 'Now you think you've slain the dragon? You know what you've done? You've turned the dragon loose.... The one decent thing I ever did in my life was... chain him away from these people... Who's gonna stop Norge now? You? Oh, your armor does shine brightly, and your arm is... strong enough... but, where is righteousness, noble paladin? Where is your cause? You remember, there's always a dragon loose... somewhere.'

The townspeople held a memorial service for Smoke, while Paladin stands in the background.

From their words it became clear they valued him and had considered him their protector, while they regard his hired killer as a contemptible subhuman, Paladin was stricken with grief... and also with new resolve.

The next scenes showed Norge riding up and Paladin called out 'Norge! Stay there!' Paladin was now dressed in the clothes of Smoke, sneering in disgust. A new hero had emerged, and a new era dawned.

*Have Gun Will Travel* has seldom been seen in syndication over the last 25 years, apparently because it was filmed in black-and-white, and also because of its violent content.

After six years of portraying Paladin, he hosted and appeared in his personal 'dream project', *The Richard Boone Show,* a repertory theatre featuring the same actors in different plays every week. The show quickly proved too highbrow to gain a big following and it was canceled in mid-season.

In the early 70's, he played the title-character in *Hec Ramsey*, another Western TV series, and once quipped that 'Hec Ramsey is Paladin, only fatter.' The two characters were vastly different, of course, and of the two, Paladin was by far the more popular.

Boone appeared in motion-pictures throughout his television career, and was nominated for the best-actor Emmy five times. He also directed various film and television productions, including episodes of *HGWT*.

Boone died of throat cancer on 10 January 1981, aged 63.

Gene Rodenberry polished his writing skills on this show!

# HAWKEYE

## 1994

**THE** hour long, color show was full of action and shot amongst the fabulous scenery around Vancouver. It was produced by Stephen J. Cannell Productions, but only ran through the 1994 season.

The syndicated series was also loosely based on James Fennimore Cooper's *Tales of the Early American Frontier*. Lee Horsley starred as Hawkeye. Rodney A Grant played his Indian blood brother, Chigachgook. Lynda Carter starred as storeowner Elizabeth Shields.

In 1755 the quiet land of the Hudson Valley was enmeshed in the turmoil of the French and Indian War.

Hawkeye was the fair-minded woodsman and unbeatable marksman who lived off the land and in harmony with Chingachgook, the only survivor of the Mohicans.

Elizabeth Shields had entered the land with her husband, William, to run a trading post at Fort Bennington. She was afraid that the frontier life would prove too much for her ailing husband; and her fears were confirmed when he was captured by the French while out on a trading expedition. When William's double-crossing brother refused to help her, she set off on her own to rescue her husband and was joined along the way by Hawkeye. But treachery was everywhere and they had to forge a strong friendship to survive the many hardships that awaited them in a land at war.

## TRIVIA

Horsley had a musical theater background prior to arriving in Hollywood and TV in the late 70's. He toured in such shows as *West Side Story* and *Oklahoma!* He is an expert horseman and outdoorsman, and he even participated in rodeo events over the years.

# HAWKEYE AND THE LAST OF THE MOHICANS

## 1956

**THE** half hour black and white episodes of this show were filmed around Toronto and ran on CBS through the 1956–7 seasons. The Independent Television Corp and Canadian Broadcasting Co made 39 episodes.

Shot entirely on location in Canada the syndicated series told the story of the white man, Hawkeye and his Indian blood brother, Chingachgook and it was very loosely based on the James Fenimore Cooper novel. The series was set in New York's Hudson Valley during the French and Indian war in the 1750's.

White trapper and scout, Nat 'Hawkeye' Cutler was played by John Hart and Chigachgook, the last member of the Mohican tribe, by Lon Chaney Jr.

Lon Chaney Jr., died in 1973 of beriberi and liver failure.

*John Hart* and *Lon Chaney Jr.*

# HEC RAMSEY
## 8 OCTOBER 1972

**HEC RAMSEY, starring Richard Boone, alternated with McCloud, Columbo and McMillan and Wife on NBC's Sunday Mystery Movie franchise from 8 October 1972 to 25 August 1974. The show ran 90 minutes and was shot in color.**

Ramsey was a former gunslinger who had settled down to become the deputy sheriff of Prospect, Oklahoma. He used the new science of criminology to solve various crimes. He still used his gun if necessary, but preferred to use new technology.

Other cast members included Harry Morgan as Doc Coogan and Richard Lenz as Sherriff Oliver Stamp.

# HERE COME THE BRIDES
## 25 SEPTEMBER 1968

**THE hour long show, which debuted on 25 September 1968 on ABC TV, was shot in color. After a two year run, it left the air on 19 September 1970. Produced by Screen Gems, Here Come the Brides was fun and boisterous.**

The comedy/adventure story was set in the boomtown of Seattle in the 1870's. Jason Bolt and his younger brothers, Jeremy and Joshua risked losing their timberland at Bridal Veil Mountain because their 152 loggers are in revolt over the lack of women in nearby Seattle.

Jason was sent to find 100 women for the men and he sailed off on Capt. Clancey's ship back to New Bedford, Massachusetts. He returned with the women, all prospective brides for the loggers, who have agreed to try living in Seattle for one year.

6'4" Robert Brown played Jason Bolt. Teen idol Bobby Sherman was Jeremy, David Soul was Joshua and Joan Blondell was Lottie Hatfield, owner of the local saloon. Mark Lenard played the rival sawmill owner, Aaron Stemple.

Rounding out the main cast were Bridget Hanley, Mitzi Hoag, Susan Tolsky, Patti Cohoon, Bo Svenson and Henry Beckman.

The show was a springboard for Sherman's singing career which took off in 1969 with the releases of *Little Woman*, *La La La (If I Had You)*, *Easy Come, Easy Go*, and *Julie, Do Ya Love Me*.

David Soul went on to immortal stardom as Detective Ken 'Hutch' Hutchinson of *Starsky and Hutch*.

Mark Lenard remains best known as Sarek, Spock's father, on *Star Trek*. He died in 1996 of multiple myeloma. Joan Blondell died in 1979 of leukaemia.

# THE HIGH CHAPARRAL
## 10 SEPTEMBER 1967

**THE HIGH CHAPARRAL** premiered on NBC in color on 10 September 1967. It left the air on 12 March 1971

*Cameron Mitchell, Linda Cristal, Leif Erickson, Mark Slade* and *Henry Darrow*

David Dortort created *The High Chaparral* to follow up his huge hit, *Bonanza*. He knew *Chaparral* couldn't hope to match that record, but he still managed to notch up 98 episodes between 1967 and 1971. The show's main theme; empire building in the Arizona Territory during the 1870's, was set against a backdrop of cactus, intense heat and the precarious relationships between the white man, the Apache Indian and the Mexican. Dortort ensured all races were portrayed with dignity and honor.

The scripts for each segment were way above average, and each episode was action packed. Nearly all the action sequences were coordinated by famed stuntman Henry Wills, and almost every episode showcased a guest star of major repute.

Some 22 nations bought the rights to *The High Chaparral* even before the show went out in America and the pilot was released as a feature film to the overseas market. Throughout Europe, it was the top-rated show being imported at that time.

The series was shot almost entirely on location in and around Old Tuscon, Arizona, and rarely did any western reflect such an intentionally realistic air. Filmed in 100 plus degree heat, it was not unusual to see huge sweat stains streaking the shirts of the regulars. The wardrobe people were kept forever busy changing clothes ordered during a hot day's filming. Each actor had 12 identical shirts, six pairs of pants and three pairs of boots every season. The viewer could almost feel the heat and the dust after an hour spent down on *The High Chaparral*.

Dortort insisted on realism and even built the ranch house to specifications of 1870 Arizona using real adobe and materials native to the area. The natural desert and mesa land around Old Tucson was where the Apache leaders had battled Spaniards, Mexicans and American settlers over a hundred years before. That authenticity was exactly what persuaded Dortort to film *The High Chaparral* there.

He hired Mexicans to play Mexican roles and real Apaches to play Apaches. Perhaps his greatest coup was the hiring of Nino Cochise, grandson of the fabled Cochise, to play the part of his famous grandfather. At that time, blue-eyed Nino was 94-years-old, missing one leg, and needed to be helped into and out of the saddle.

Director and producer had screened dozens of prospects before they arrived at Nino. Director Bill Claxton was shocked when the old man gave his name as Cochise, 'No; you're up for the part of Cochise... what is *your* name?' Claxton pressed impatiently.

'Dammit. I am Nino Cochise. I am the grandson of Cochise.'

Dortort authenticated the old man's identity and was happy that he had stumbled upon Nino, (literally 'The Little' Cochise). The great Apache leader, Cochise had died two months after the birth of his grandson.

Whilst much of the location filming was carried out in the adobe pueblo of Old

Tucson, occasionally the cast and crew were ferried to Vasquez Rocks instead, a park just 43 miles out of Los Angeles and an area that closely resembled the Mexico-Arizona borderlands. Again the bush-covered ridges were dry and hot and full of dying yucca trees. When filming there, cast and crew often drank more than 70 gallons of water a day; twice the amount they got through when they were in Arizona. Realistic and very uncomfortable for all concerned.

The producer had methodically pored through the archives at the UCLA library, studying old diaries, letters and military reports and re-reading books and documents dealing with Western lore and the story of the Apache nation's struggle for survival. He developed great sympathy for their fight against the overwhelming odds of the 1870's.

His research had shown him that the Apache nation had been far from the depraved society so often shown in Western movies and he also wanted to give some recognition to the advanced Mexican culture, 'We're trying to make restitution to what I feel are damaged reputations. *The High Chaparral* is based on the truth. We have a commitment to authenticity'

Dortort continued, 'We don't have to concoct those ridiculous, phony, fictional stories that you see on the air all the time. *The Virginian*, for example, is a disgrace. It's sloppily done. It's dull… my shows have the look of authenticity.'

When Dortort had been assembling the cast, only Leif Erickson was ever considered for the part of grizzled John Cannon, a character he modeled on General George F. Cook. Erickson always had a great deal of confidence in the show and in Dortort and he worked hard to ensure the producer's requirement for authenticity was fulfilled; he received a broken wrist, several cracked ribs and assorted other bruises for his effort. When he was asked by the Press why he kept getting hurt when he had a stunt double to hand at all times, Erickson laughed, 'You should see my stunt man. He's really busted up!' The fact that filming was done in Old Tucson where the ground was baked hard meant that every fake fall was likely to get out of hand.

John Cannon believed that Apaches, American settlers and Mexicans could all get along in harmony as he strove to establish his cattle empire in the rugged land, but he ruled the ranch with an iron fist. He also demonstrated compassion and savvy for what it took to survive the harsh elements. And he didn't stand alone; he had an innate understanding that survival in such a hostile environment depended on the help of good and reliable people; he surrounded himself with such and refused to admit failure or defeat.

Along with his wife, Victoria, played by Linda Cristal were his younger brother, Buck, played by Cameron Mitchell, his son, Billy Blue, played by Mark Slade, and Manolito Montoya played by Henry Darrow.

After his first wife's death, John married Mexican heiress, Victoria Montoya, daughter of Don Sebastian Montoya (Frank Silvera). The mutual arrangement between the two landowners brought some stability to the fraught area. It also brought Victoria's brother Manolito north of the border to The High Chaparral. Initially he came to ensure that Victoria was properly respected but he soon became a permanent part of the household. Henry Darrow says, 'The kind of guy Manolito is, is that he likes nothing better than to get in a two-against-one fight. Especially if he's one of the two. He's what you might call a devout chicken.'

In the first episode, Buck and Blue rode into Tucson to hire the bunkhouse guys, led by Sam Butler (Don Collier), who became the ranch foreman and Cannon's 'left arm of The High Chaparral.' The rest of the bunkhouse consisted of Sam's brother Joe (Bob Hoy), Reno (Ted Markland), Ira Bean (Jerry Summers), and Pedro (Roberto Contreras). Vaquero (Rudolfo Acosta) is also acquired in the first episode as the household help. The bunkhouse crew was the glue of the series and several episodes were devoted entirely to their antics.

Although there were cast changes, most notably in the fourth season with the sudden unexplained disappearance of Blue and Don Sebastian, together with the addition of Wind (Rudy Ramos) and Don Domingo Montoya (Gilbert Roland), Ira Bean disappeared at the end of the first season, and both Reno and Vaquero disappeared at the end of the second season, all the rest of the cast remained throughout the entire run.

Most of those selected, including Leif Erickson, Cameron Mitchell, Frank Silvera, and Gilbert Roland were already well known movie actors, Rudolfo Acosta was a veteran Mexican actor, and Linda Cristal was well-known in both American and Mexican films. Don Collier was an established actor who had his own successful television Western *Outlaws* and he had made numerous television appearances as guest star in some of the highest ranking shows. Mark Slade came from the television series *The Wackiest Ship in the Army*. Bob Hoy and Jerry Summers were both stuntmen turned actors, and they continued working both sides of the fence through their entire careers. Henry Darrow was really the only unknown, but he certainly shot to fame on the back of this series. Ted Markland was a well-known stand-up comedian before turning actor, and Roberto Contreras was well-known in both films and television as a character actor. The cast and characters of *The High Chaparral* were all outstanding and so well developed here that they constantly displayed entirely human traits and audiences were able to empathize with them and their problems of survival; it was escapism of the highest order.

Leif Erickson, born William Wycliffe Anderson, had seen his career sputter many times before being chosen to play Big John. He had appeared on Broadway with Deborah Kerr in *Tea and Sympathy*, but had never really made it to the star's dressing room. By the time Dortort found him he had all but given up and was selling boats in Marina del Rey.

Dortort had first seen him in an episode of *Bonanza* in 1961 playing a man who believed he was God. Erickson said that stardom hadn't found him sooner because, 'I wasn't focused enough. No aura. No sense of direction… I just wasn't ready…'

'*The High Chaparral*? That's different. I've got a goldmine by the tail and it's something we all want to protect. We knock ourselves out… Linda Cristal… now there's a woman with zap! She'll sit in the sun all day and not complain… Cam Mitchell…tough customer…we understand each other…Good kid, Mark Slade…'

Erickson enjoyed everything about working on the series, 'I like to work hard; I'd rather be working than not working; I like the location shooting out in the open; I like the recognition, the fame… and I like the money.' Cameron Mitchell, born Cameron Mizell, is remembered today almost exclusively for his role as Buck Cannon although he actually made many films. He came from a long line of Presbyterian ministers, but had broken with family tradition to develop his career as an actor. He made his film debut in the John Wayne movie, *They Were Expendable*.

He was also a stage performer and successfully played Lucky in Miller's *Death of a Salesman* on Broadway in 1949 and then later in the film version. Before being chosen for the role of Buck he had spent some years working in Europe and even behind the Iron Curtain. He also made Spanish and Italian films. But Buck was certainly a very special role for Mitchell. He could out-drink, outshoot, outfight, and when motivated, outwork any man alive. The part had originally been established largely to give brother John, some kind of verbal back up against the hot headed Mexicans they lived with on the ranch. He was also often used for comic relief and his forays into Tucson with the other hired hands usually ended in drunken brawls. Still Mitchell managed to invest this unpromising supporting role with depth and dignity and a gentle mournfulness which was accentuated by dressing permanently in black. In 1973 Mitchell made a bad financial gamble when he formed his own production company along with Ray Spinks, Camray Productions, to film a Civil War epic in South Carolina. Mitchell was going to play General Robert E. Lee. He planned a cast of thousands and said it would be one of the biggest ever assembled. The loan he took out to cover the production was tied to his residuals in *The High Chaparral*. After 12 months, with no finished film, he was forced to declare himself bankrupt with debts of almost $2.5 million. At the time his assets totaled just $306. He spent the rest of his career playing roles beneath him to try and cover repayments.

Mitchell confessed to being hard headed and to fighting with all the show's regulars admitting that he, 'managed to alienate everybody... Everybody on the show hates me, except David Dortort.' In fact Dortort says the cast all got on well and that there was only ever one incident between Mitchell and Erickson, and he believed that was settled amicably off set.

Billy Blue was in his early 20's and his mother had been killed off in the first episode; he was troubled and rebellious. Dortort said he based the misunderstood character on his own son, Fred, 'When I started *Bonanza*, my son was ten years old. We had a real father-son thing... Now we don't see eye to eye on anything...' It had struck Dortort that for some time television had ignored a common affliction of society; the generation gap, 'What about families like mine, where father and sons are having trouble communicating? I thought this might be interesting in terms of *Chaparral*.'

Mark Slade, who played the sensitive son of John Cannon, left the series in 1970. NBC said the arrangement was amicable, 'He is involved in film production which is keeping him occupied.' But Slade himself let it be known that was not the full story. He had been writing and producing a film of his own, *Better Times Are Coming*. Originally he had planned to work with his partner, Hollywood scriptwriter William Lansford, during the four month break in the shooting of *The High Chaparral*. Slade had asked NBC if they could keep him out of the first two weeks of shooting the new series so that he could finish his film. NBC informed Slade that he had to return to work for the opening week. He chose instead to finish his own film because he had sunk his money into the venture. NBC didn't renew his contract.

He had been discovered by Elia Kazan in 1960 and been brought to Hollywood to work on his film, *Splendor in the Grass*. He also appeared in *My Three Sons*.

Just as Dortort attempted an accurate representation of Tucson and its environs in the 1870s so Henry Darrow tried to bring authenticity to the character of Manolito Montoya, the carefree adventurer, 'I am trying to create a character who is familiar with the Apache.' Darrow had himself studied Indian folklore and language for a number of years, 'I've always done dialect work… I learned some Apache… it is guttural, aspirate, it comes from the throat.'

Born Henry Thomas Delgado in New York in 1933, his first movie work was the difficult art of dubbing nine American feature films for release in Mexico.

He came to the series after a career spanning 12 movies and more than 75 television appearances. Dortort saw Darrow in the Ray Bradbury play, *The Wonderful Ice Cream Suit* and knew he had found his Manolito.

Manolito was soon established as the *Chaparral's* most dashing figure; always remaining part of the family, he was equally at home with the bunkhouse boys. He always does his share of work alongside them although his father despairs of him ever growing up and he is recognized as a ladies' man. He is also a man of fierce honor and dignity, loyalty and bravery. Originally the irresistibly charismatic Manolito was meant to be a skulking villain, but Darrow's own charm altered him into a good character, and many viewers felt that his was the role that was the high point of the show.

Ironically Darrow's success in the part of an overtly Latin character came after he spent several years doing his best to avoid that image; he had even changed his name from Delgado to Darrow. His Puerto Rican heritage had typed him as a Mexican too often.

Even as one of the main stars of *Chaparral*, Darrow never felt that he was treated equally, and put this down to his heritage. When the producers of the show cut eight shows from the schedule Darrow grew angry. All his co-stars were paid for the full twenty six segments whether they did them or not; he alone received no pay for those eight programs. He said angrily, 'In the Mexican Community *Chaparral* was known as a program that portrayed a Mexican with dignity, as a man of substance and worth… it was also a program that employed many Chicanos. But with the cutback in the number of the shows, they will shrug and say, 'It is to be expected; what is good for Chicanos will be destroyed'.'

Darrow went on to create an impressive list of television appearances after *The High Chaparral*, co-starring with David Janssen in *Harry-O*, *The New Dick Van Dyke Show*, *Petrocelli* and *Brock*. He guested on *The Waltons, Hawaii Five-0, Hart to Hart* and *Kojak*. He also served in numerous capacities to advance opportunities for ethnic minorities; he is a former Vice President of Nosotros where he worked alongside Ricardo Montalban, Anthony Quinn and Desi Arnaz Sr, trying to promote a more positive Latino image in the film and television industry, and worked with Dennis Weaver on the Ethnic Minorities Committee of the Screen Actors Guild.

Darrow donated all his costumes from *Chaparral* to the Gene Autry Western Museum. When he was asked to be Grand Marshal at the Wrightwood Rodeo he had to buy himself a new outfit.

Linda Cristal fought off hundreds of hopefuls for the part of Victoria. She was one of the last to turn up at the casting conferences and once there she refused to read the lines given to her saying she could prove she was right for the part by doing a one-girl show ad-lib. David Dortort went along and signed her as the first regular female he had ever worked with. It had been his rule that any female arriving at the Ponderosa in *Bonanza*, had to be gone by the end of the show. He now actively encouraged the inclusion of his female lead and made Linda's part pivotal.

Universal-International first brought Cristal from her native Argentina to Hollywood and she had co-starred with James Stewart in *Two Rode Together* and with John Wayne in *The Alamo*. She also guest starred on television shows such as *Iron Horse* and *Voyage to the Bottom of the Sea*.

Dortort had been a magazine writer and novelist before hitting Hollywood as a film-writer. He had worked on many other Western series including *Restless Gun* with John Payne.

The producer of *Chaparral* was James Schmerer. He also worked on the John Mills Western *Dundee and Culhane* as well as serving as the Story Editor on *Daniel Boone*.

Harry Sukman created many of the musical compositions for the show. David Rose, who also worked on *Bonanza*, was musical director. At one point his music was being used on up to 22 television programs.

All the horses came from the Myers and Wills stable in California and altogether 14 of them regularly traveled between the California and Arizona locations.

During the first year Darrow rode El Diablo, but the horse was too excitable and he was soon changed for a ten-year-old sorrel called Mackadoo. Cameron Mitchell's horse was Prince, an 11-year-old bay which occasionally stole the show. He would let Mitchell know he was getting bored by nibbling his arm. Erickson rode a horse called Billy and Mark Slade's horse was called Soapy.

Darrow says, 'When the series began I thought I knew how to ride. I had taken some lessons a few years earlier doing a *Wagon Train* segment… however, with all the riding *High Chaparral* requires, I found I had a lot more to learn. I took a couple of months taking lessons from Stevie Myers.' He even attempted to learn how to rope and handle a whip although apparently Macadoo didn't much like the idea.

Whilst *The High Chaparral* rode consistently high in the Top 20 of the American national ratings, it was also increasingly lambasted by the growing anti-violence lobby and as filming of the series went on an edict against violence on television was passed by television's controllers.

Although many observers believed this would lead directly to the demise of the Western, Erickson argued, 'One thing about this edict… it's giving us the best scripts we've ever had. I suppose it's because it's a real challenge to the writers. No longer can they resolve a situation with a gunfight or banging someone over the head.'

However he also added, 'I don't know how the public will go for them.' Erickson really felt that the new scripts were more interesting and kept actors on their toes, 'Scenes and characters are more fully developed, there is a more honest sense of reality.'

As it turned out the public didn't go for it at all and the show, which had consistently been one of the best of the television Westerns, left the air after just four years. Re-runs round the world however ensure that it can still be seen today by the

fans. Erisckson died of cancer 29 January 1986, aged 74. After *Chaparral* ended, he had gone on tour in 1976 with Rock Hudson and Claire Trevor in a production of Stephen Vincent Benet's *John Brown's Body*; a show directed by John Houseman, but he had been semi retired ever since *Chaparral* ended. He spent most of his time sailing.

Mitchell died of lung cancer, aged 75, on 6 July 1994.

Rudolfo Acosta, Frank Silvera, Gilbert Roland and Roberto Contreras have all died. Linda Cristal and Jerry Summers retired. Mark Slade left acting in the early 1980's, and his whereabouts is unknown. The others are all still acting.

# HONDO

## 8 SEPTEMBER 1967

**MGM made the hour long show in color for the debut of the series on ABC on 8 September 1967. It was well produced and action-packed by Andrew J. Fenady. No matter how good the show was, it ran for only 17 episodes and prematurely left the air on 29 December 1967.**

Rugged Ralph Taeger starred as Hondo Lane, a cavalry dispatch rider based at Fort Lowell, Arizona in the late 1860's. Hondo had been a Confederate officer who went to live with the Apaches under Chief Vittorio after the war. But his Indian bride, the Chief's daughter, had been slain in an army massacre. He then went to work for the army again as they attempted to avert further bloodshed.

Kathie Browne starred as Angie Dow, manager of the store at the fort, and Buddy Foster played her young son, Johnny.

Noah Beery Jr was Scout Buffalo Baker; Gary Clarke played Captain Richards, the fort commander; William Bryant was General Crook and Michael Pate was the Apache Chief, Vittorio.

The series was lifted from the Louis L'Amour story and the 1953 John Wayne movie of the same name.

Buddy Foster is Jodie Foster's brother.

Noah Berry Jr., died in 1991 – but not before audiences came to love him as Jim Rockford's father!

# HOPALONG CASSIDY

## 6 JUNE 1949

**THE** half hour, black and white series started life as an edited version of the B-feature *Hopalong Cassidy* films that had starred silver haired William Boyd. The series ran on NBC from 6 June 1949 until 23 December 1951, and in syndication for years after that, even though much of the show was narrated and lacking in action.

It was the first significant Western to appear on network television. Eventually 40 new episodes were shot, with Edgar Buchanan arriving later as Hoppy's sidekick, Red Connors.

Boyd had played the Hopalong character in 66 movies between 1935 and 1948.

In *The Hopalong Cassidy Show* on television, Hoppy was still owner of the Bar 20 Ranch. Red Connors was the perfect foil for Cassidy, who, unlike most cowboy heroes, dressed all in black and, with snow-white hair, cut a dashing figure riding his white horse Topper.

William Boyd died on 12 September 1972 of Parkinson's disease and heart failure and Edgar Buchanan on 4 April 1979 of a stroke.

All Cassidy related merchandise remains highly collectible and eagerly sought.

## TRIVIA

Sagebrush Books of Tarzana, California has recently announced it is publishing a brand new Western adventure featuring 'the most amazing man ever to ride the trails of the early west!' *HOPALONG CASSIDY RIDES AGAIN!*

# HOTEL DE PAREE
## 2 OCTOBER 1959

**THERE were 33 half hour black and white episodes made which debuted on CBS on 2 October 1959. It went off the air on 23 September 1960.**

Hotel de Paree was a fancy establishment in Georgetown, Colorado and was also the residence of Sundance.

Earl Holliman, who went on to play Lt. Bill Crowley in *Police Woman*, appeared in this show as Sundance, a man released from prison after serving 17 years for accidentally killing someone. Returning to the town after all that time, he became a partner in a hotel run by Annette Devereaux and her niece, Monique; two relatives of the dead man. They have been threatened by town bullies and a ruthless business man who wants them out on the street.

Sundance's lightening draw made him handy to have around. He was also one of the first television cowboys to have a gimmick; his hatband was circled with shiny oval discs that could be used to blind an adversary.

Jeanette Nolan starred as Annette Devereaux and Judi Meredith as Monique.

The only other regular was Strother Martin as Aaron Donager, one of the only friends that Sundance has left. Martin is perhaps best known as Percy Garris in *Butch Cassidy and the Sundance Kid*.

Strother Martin died in 1980 of a heart attack and Jeanette Nolan in 1988 of a stroke.

# HOW THE WEST WAS WON

## 12 FEBRUARY 1978

**THE series, filmed in color, debuted on 12 February 1978 and ran until 23 April 1979. It comprised two three-hour segments followed by one hour weekly shows. The two three hour segments were the longest single-story television programs made at the time. Its producers boasted that it was the longest motion picture ever made.**

In 1976, just after long running show *Gunsmoke* was axed, its producer John Mantley went to MGM to work on a TV pilot; he said the film was 'in the Western tradition'. Mantley became the executive producer of *How The West Was Won* and John G. Stephens was line producer. The 1,200 page script was largely written by Mantley himself and a team of writers including, Calvin Clements and Earl W. Wallace. Directorial assignments were divided between Bernard and Vincent McEveety, the

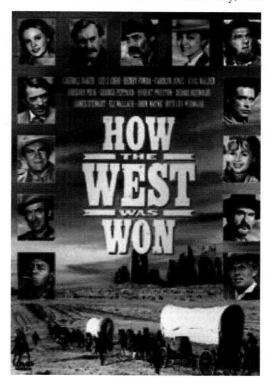

brothers who had directed so many episodes of *Gunsmoke*. Mantley also persuaded James Arness to go to work for him again on the series.

The first six hour movie was called *The Macahans* and was set in 1861 and was complete with Arness as mountain man, Zeb Macahan, the head of a pioneer family trying to settle in the West. Arness no longer died his hair dark as he had done for 20 years playing Matt Dillon; now he was resplendent with long curly blonde hair and a handlebar moustache.

The film concluded at the close of the Civil War.

*How the West Was Won,* a complex, 20 hour story broadcast over 15 weeks on ABC, followed the exploits of Zeb after his brother, Timothy (Richard Kiley) was killed and Zeb went home to Virginia to help move the whole family to Wyoming.

Filming was done on location all over Arizona, Utah, Colorado and California and many of the first several hours were filmed in the restored Bent's Fort in Colorado.

A preview of the show by James Brown for *The Los Angeles Times* on 2 October 1978 stated, 'This program, at least in its premier, is a storehouse of déjà vu. It contains the legacy of the Indian Nation and its ever diminishing land, kidnappings and search parties, 'Indian Hating' scouts and brick witted cavalry, innocents on the run from the law, kind hearted sheriffs trying to uphold the law, hot-tempered but warm hearted young women and cartoon-like villains'.'

Eva Marie Saint starred as Kate, Bruce Boxleitner was eldest son, Luke, who was on the run for killing three men in self defense. Kathryn Holcomb played Laura, Vicki Schreck played Jessie and William Kirby Cullen was Josh. In the second series Fionulla Flanagan showed up as Aunt Molly.

Arness himself wasn't enamored by what he called, 'long form' television, 'It's too damned hard. It takes too much stomach lining. The mental stresses are too much.' But he went on, 'After 20 years of portraying Matt Dillon, I wanted a chance to create an entirely new character,' and said, 'Zeb Macahan came from an era when men were the law unto themselves. He was a free spirit, made his own rules. He was used to taking everything over and not consulting anybody. Except that after the Civil war – the stage we've got him at now – it's more civilized times and he's running into a little trouble. He is a free thinker and a free spirit. He lives by the code of what's right is right.'

When *Gunsmoke* was first cancelled and then re-instated, Arness had demanded the entire crew was brought back intact and when Mantley approached him for *How the West Was Won*, he again made sure that many of the same faces went to work with him, 'All of us had been ready for one more season of *Gunsmoke* when they dropped the axe. Some horsefeathers about demographics. We knew it couldn't last forever. Still, we were left hanging by the ropes. The cancellation took us by surprise, but the day it happened… the fellows developing *How the West Was Won* called and said they were ready to go. I fell in love with the script and said, 'Forget Matt Dillon. This Macahan guy's more colorful.' What really appealed to me was that here was an interesting character completely different from Matt Dillon… he's pretty much of a free spirit as opposed to living within the law and its restrictions, which is what Matt Dillon had to do'.'

In March 1973 Arness was honored as *Man of the Year* by the Hollywood Radio and Television Society.

# INTO THE WEST

## 10 JUNE 2005

**THE** sprawling epic Into the West was a miniseries produced by Steven Spielberg, Larry Rapaport, David A. Rosemont and Spielberg's company, Dreamworks. It runs six episodes of two hours each. The series was first broadcast in the US on Turner Network Television (TNT) on six consecutive weeks starting on 10 June 2005. It is directed by Robert Dornhelm, Sergio Mimica-Gezzan, Timothy Van Patten, Michael W. Watkins and Simon Wincer. Segments were written by William Mastrosimone, Cyrus Nowrasteh and Craig Storper. The music is from Geoff Zanelli, cinematography is by William Wages and editing by Mark Conte and Sabrina Plisco.

The rich account of the opening of the American West begins in the turbulent 1820's and is told mainly through the third person narration of Jacob Wheeler (Matthew Settle) and Loved By the Buffalo (Joseph M. Marshall III).

'It takes place during one of the most dramatic periods in American history,' Spielberg explained and continued, 'We're painting on this huge canvas in order to tell a story that explores the Gold Rush, the transcontinental railroad, the Wild West and the Indian wars – leading to the tragedy at Wounded Knee. These are all facets of the American and Native American experience. It's the story about opportunity and the clash of cultures and the eventual overwhelming of one nation's way of life over another.'

The clash of cultures follows the story of two families, one white American, one Native American, as their lives become mingled through the momentous events of American expansion. The Wheeler clan hails from Virginia and their tale centers on Jacob, a spirited adventurer who heads west. He married a Native American called Thunder Heart Woman (Tonantzin Carmelo) along the way.

The other family is a plains Native American family of the Lakota tribe. Thunder Heart Woman is a member of this family. Her brothers are Loved by the Buffalo (Simon R. Baker), who has been given a spiritual vision about the future of his people; Dog Star (Michael Spears), who holds to the traditional ways; and Running Fox

(Zahn McClarndon), who believes the only way to survive is to adapt to the white man's ways.

Throughout the series, the two families experience the historical and cultural events that led to the inevitable clash of cultures.

The show had a large cast with about 250 speaking parts and featuring well known performers including Wes Studi, Irene Bedard, Russell Means, Graham Greene, Raoul Trujillo, Gordon Tootoosis, Gil Birmingham and Sheila Tousey.

Advisers on the production included Charlie White Buffalo, a Lakota Studies professor at Oglala Lakota College; George P. Horse Capture, senior counselor to the director and special assistant for cultural relations at the National Museum of the American Indian; Kay-Karol Horse Capture, a specialist in ethnographic and material culture objects; Kerry Scott, a teaching assistant in the department of Native  American Studies at the University of Letterbridge, Robin Whortman, a specialist in native economic development and corporate relations and Joseph Marshall, a published author and Native consultant for film and television.

*Into The West* received 16 Emmy nominations in 2006; more than any other program in its year, for:

Outstanding Miniseries

Two for Outstanding Cinematography for a Miniseries or Movie (episodes *Dreams and Schemes* and *Wheels to the Stars*)

Outstanding Art Direction

Outstanding Casting

Outstanding Sound Editing (episode *Manifest Destiny*)

Two for Outstanding Single Camera Sound (episodes *Dreams and Schemes* and *Hell on Wheels*)

Outstanding Music Composition (Dramatic Underscore): Music by Geoff Zanelli

Outstanding Costumes (episode *Hell on Wheels*)

Outstanding Special Visual Effects (episode *Hell on Wheels*)

Two for Outstanding Make-Up (non-prosthetic) (episodes *Wheel to the Stars* and *Ghost Dance*)

Outstanding Prosthetic Makeup (episode *Wheel to the Stars*)

Two for Outstanding Hairstyling (episodes *Manifest Destiny* and *Casualties of War*)

# IRON HORSE

## 12 SEPTEMBER 1966

**THE** series ran for two seasons on ABC, debuting on 12 September 1966 and running for 47 episodes until 6 January 1968. Location work was carried out at Sonora.

Dale Robertson starred in the one hour long, color series as gambler Ben Calhoun who had won an unfinished railroad in a card game. Ben had to complete the Buffalo Pass, Scalplock and Defiance line in the West of the 1880's.

Helping him was construction engineer, Dave Tarrant, played by Gary Collins, clerk Barnabas Collins, played by Bob Random and Swedish crewman Nils Torvold played by Roger Torrey. Ellen Burstyn starred as Julie Parsons who ran the Scalplock General Store.

Robertson lives in Yukon, Random in Sausalito and Collins in Beverly Hills. Torrey died of a brain haemorrhage.

Dell published two *Iron Horse* comic books to tie in with the show.

# JEFFERSON DRUM

## 29 APRIL 1958

**THE** series of half hour, black and white shows debuted on the NBC Network on 29 April 1958. Screen Gems produced 26 episodes and it left the air on 23 April 1959.

Jefferson Drum was a courageous frontier newspaperman living in the wild town of Jubilee in the 1850's. He hoped his pen would resolve conflict, but when it didn't, he was handy with a gun as well.

Drum, a widower with a young son, wanted to build a decent, law-abiding community. He was the owner and editor of *The Star*, a paper that fought corruption and helped the community.

Jeff Richards was cast as Jefferson Drum and Eugene Martin played his son Joey.

Veteran actor Cyril Delevanti was Lucius Coin, the printer and Robert Stevenson played Big Ed, the friendly bartender.

Delevanti and Stevenson both died in 1975.

Richards died on 28 July 1989.

# JOHNNY RINGO

## 1 OCTOBER 1958

**THE half hour Western was Aaron Spelling's first production for CBS. It debuted on 1 October 1958 and left the air on 29 September 1960 after 38 episodes. The show was screened on Thursday nights in the 8.30 timeslot vacated by Yancy Derringer.**

This black and white show was everything a good Western ought to be; boasting a superlative cast, it was well written, full of action and top guest stars that included child star Ron Howard, James Coburn, Buddy Ebsen and Burt Reynolds. Don Durant starred as fast gun and lawman Johnny Ringo. It also had a great theme song, written and performed by Durant himself; the song was recorded in a few days with Durant singing both the harmony and lead via multi tracking. RCA Victor released the record.

Johnny used a trick gun, the Le Mat special; a custom made seven-shooter. It had an extra barrel that fired a single shotgun shell out of the bottom barrel. He was given the gun in the first episode so he would have an edge as he faced the villains alone. Originally the gun had been designed by Confederate Colonel LeMat and it held nine .42 percussion rounds. The separate shotgun barrel was approximately 18 gauge. The gun Johnny used was a reworked version of the real gun.

Durant had learned to rope and ride on a cattle spread in Nevada when he was a child and when he later served in the Special Services in Korea, he developed his singing and performing as he entertained veterans. In 1953 he appeared at various big name venues such as the Sands in Las Vegas. In 1954 he signed with CBS Television and was given small roles. He often appeared in as many as five shows a night and became a familiar face on *The Jack Benny Show, The Red Skelton Show, Shower of Stars,* etc. He also sang jingles for adverts and with the Frankie Carle and Tommy Dorsey orchestras.

Mark Goddard played Cully, the eager deputy of Velardi, Arizona. Karen Sharpe was Laura, who was smitten with Johnny. She pursued him through the series. Cyril Delevanti played her father and a storekeeper in town, Case Thomas. He was a man who loved his whiskey.

---

# TRIVIA

Johnny Ringo was based very loosely on the real-life exploits of John Peters Ringo (3 May 1850 – 13 July 1882), better known as Johnny Ringo, a cowboy who became a legend of the American Old West through his affiliation with the Clanton Gang and the Gunfight at the OK Corral. The outlaws that hung around Tombstone were commonly referred to as 'the cow-boys' and Ringo himself as 'the King of the Cowboys'. Unfortunately for the reputation of this supreme gunfighter, there is no record that he ever actually had a single gunfight (although he is known to have shot several unarmed men) and even his violent death may have been at his own hand. On 14 July 1882 the body of Ringo was found beneath a tree in West Turkey Creek Valley with a bullet in his right temple. His body had been there around twenty-four hours, and his boots were found tied to the saddle of his horse, which was captured two miles away. His death was officially ruled as a suicide. However through the decades many people have been suspected of his murder including Wyatt Earp, Doc Holliday, a gambler named Johnny O'Rourke A.K.A Johnny-behind-the-Deuce, Buckskin Frank Leslie, or Lou Cooley. The 1993 film Tombstone, features a dramatic showdown where Doc Holliday shoots Ringo dead. Ringo's body is buried at the same spot where his body was found.

---

The town was rife with lawlessness and run by the evil saloon owner. Ringo was hired by the mayor to clean the place up, but he gets no help from the citizens and he is forced to hire Thomas, the town drunk as his deputy. Of course, even though he sobers up, he's no match for the villains.

Dick Powell, when hosting the series *Zane Grey Theater*, had offered Durant the lead role as Johnny Ringo in an episode of the Theatre entitled *The Loner*. The segment had been written by Spelling and he eventually penned a follow-up pilot called *The Arrival* which was based on *The Loner* and re-shot using different actors. A second episode, *Kid Adonis*, served as Part Two and the series was under way.

Although there was a real gunfighter turned lawman named Johnny Ringo, the show itself was highly fictionalized.

Durant had his motion picture debut under Raoul Walsh for Warner Brothers in *Battle Cry*. His fast developing career then saw him guesting on *Gunsmoke*, *Wagon Train* and *Perry Mason* before he won the role as Johnny.

*Johnny Ringo* drew ratings high enough that the Marx Toy Company produced the Johnny Ringo Playset including a special mold of Durant. Although more toys and collectibles are associated with Johnny Ringo than any other TV Western, and despite the ratings, the fact that cast got along well and the show made profits, in 1960 the sponsors, Johnson Wax decided it was time to get rid of Westerns. They wanted a new situation comedy to replace it. Aaron Spelling had left and, with no one to champion its cause, *Johnny Ringo* bit the dust. Everyone involved with the show was stunned.

In 1962 Durant signed a new contract with Universal's Revue Studios. They promised to find him a new series, but *The Plainsman*; a proposed show starring him as a young Buffalo Bill, failed to sell. He had also been promised the lead in *The Virginan* that role eventually went to James Drury. He was offered a few guest parts but he soon decided that Revue weren't committed to him. Durant walked out of Revue, confronting Hollywood's most powerful studio boss, Lew Wasserman, telling him he wanted to end his contract. He left the business and went into real estate and property development over 40 years ago, but continued to draw the crowds whenever he made guest appearances.

Mark Goddard got a better job as Don West on *Lost in Space* following the death of *Johnny Ringo*.

Terrence De Marney died in 1971.

Durant died 15 May 2005 of lymphocytic leukemia, leaving his wife Trudi and his daughter Heidi and son, Jeff.

Goddard and Sharpe are all still alive.

# JUDGE ROY BEAN
## 1955

**SELF appointed Judge Roy Bean, played by Edgar Buchanan, administered the only law west of the Pecos in this single season series of half hour black and white episodes filmed for syndication during the 1955–6 season.**

The irascible judge held court in Langtry, Texas, a town named for Lillie Langtry, but the show stretched history about as far as it could go.

Co-starring as Bean's deputy, Jeff Taggert, was Jack Buetel and Jackie Loughery played the judge's niece, Lettie Bean.

The show was produced by actor Russell Hayden, who also appeared in some of the 39 episodes which were shot around Pioneertown, California.

Edgar Buchanan died on 4 April 1979, Russell Hayden in 1981; and Jack Beutel in 1989.

The real life character was later the subject of a 1972 movie starring Paul Newman.

# KLONDIKE
## 1960

**THE series was based on Pierre Benton's book, Klondike, about the Gold Rush. The 60 minute show, shot in black and white by ZIV TV Productions, debuted on 10 October 1960 and went off the NBC schedule on 6 February 1961 after failing to find a big enough audience.**

This gold rush Western was set in Skagway at the turn of the century. Ralph Taeger starred as adventurer Mike Halliday who was looking for women, gold and excitement. Mike had many lady friends.

James Coburn played the roguish Jeff Durain who owned the local hotel. Many a miner lost his money in card games there. Kathy O'Hara, played by Mari Blanchard, owned the honest hotel. Joi Lansing completed the cast as Goldie, Durain's accomplice. Kathy and Mike had their hands full trying to keep track of Durain.

Taeger lives in Camino, California.

Mari Blanchard died in 1970 of cancer as did Joi Lansing in 1972.

Coburn died 18 November 2002 of a heart attack.

# KODIAK

## 13 September 1974

**THE** half hour color series was filmed in Alaska and shown on ABC. Sadly, the show only lasted for nine episodes, between 13 September 1974 and 11 October 1974.

Clint Walker played Cal 'Kodiak' McKay in this contemporary Western set in Alaska. He was an Alaskan State Patrol Officer and his beat stretched over 50,000 square miles.

Other cast members included Maggie Blye as Mandy and Abner Biberman as Eskimo, Abraham Lincoln Imhook.

Biberman has died. Maggie Blye lives in LA. Clint Walker is still active.

# KUNG FU
## 14 OCTOBER 1972

**KUNG FU was filmed in color by Warner Brothers Productions. The hour long show debuted on the ABC Network at the height of the martial arts craze on 14 October 1972. It had soon attained cult status and continues to be seen thanks to endless re-runs. The pilot movie, Kung Fu was scripted by Ed Spielman and Howard Friedlander and screened on 22 February 1974. It ran 74 minutes uncut.**

The unusual series was created by Ed Spielman, produced by Jerry Thorpe and developed by Herman Miller. The advisors for the show included David Chow and Kam Yuen. Thorpe was nominated for an Emmy for both outstanding new series and outstanding drama series and he later became Executive Producer. Miller later also filled in as one of the show's producers.

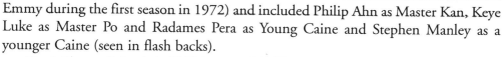

The regular cast was built around David Carradine as Kwai Chang Caine (he was nominated for an Emmy during the first season in 1972) and included Philip Ahn as Master Kan, Keye Luke as Master Po and Radames Pera as Young Caine and Stephen Manley as a younger Caine (seen in flash backs).

Kwai Chang Caine is half-Chinese and half American Shaolin priest and also an expert in the Chinese art of Kung Fu. He had been raised by Master Kan and Master Po at the Shaolin Temple in the Honon Province in China, but he fled the country for America after killing the Emperor's nephew (who had murdered Master Po).

When he arrives in America he learns that he has a half brother, Danny Caine. He travels the American South West in the 1870's searching for him but the story is also often carried back to China in a series of flashbacks.

Caine does his best to stay out of trouble and adhere to a non-violent code but he is being sought by Chinese assassins, members of the Chinese Imperial Guard, and also American bounty hunters who want the $10,000 reward that China has put on his head.

Caine said, 'The taking of a life does no one honor,' but needless to say, trouble and death aplenty usually found him.

Guest actors appeared throughout the series playing different roles.

Some of the flashbacks were reused, sometimes with different dialogue added.

Keye Luke died on 15 January 1991, aged 86. David Carradine made a revival called, *Kung Fu, The Legend Continues.*

# LANCER

## 24 SEPTEMBER 1968

**THE hour long color series debuted on CBS on 24 September 1968. 20th Century Fox TV made 51 episodes for its three year run. The last season was made up entirely of choice reruns from the first two seasons. That last original episode before the third season reruns began was Lifeline, which aired on 19 May 1970.**

Ageing ranch owner and widower Murdoch Lancer, played by Andrew Duggan, struggled to hang on to his sprawling spread in the San Joaquin Valley in California in the 1870's in another lively Western about a ranching family in the spirit of *The High Chaparral* and *Bonanza*. His only ally was his ward, Teresa O'Brien played by Elizabeth Baur.

Desperate for help to protect his 100,000 acre cattle and timber empire against land pirates, he sent word to his two estranged sons from different marriages, Scott, played by Wayne Maunder of *Custer* fame, a college graduate and Johnny Madrid Lancer, played by James Stacy, a gunslinger. Murdoch offered them each one-third of the land if they would help him fight off the bad guys.

The boys had never met before and coming from widely different cultural backgrounds and harboring animosity toward each other, the series made for some interesting conflicts. Gradually, they all learned to respect each other as they settled in together as family.

The only other employee on the ranch is the cook, Jelly Hoskins played by Paul Brinegar.

The show attracted top guests, including J. D. Cannon, Dennis Cole, Shelley Fabares, Billy Mumy, Keenan Wynn, Pernell Roberts, Joe Don Baker, and Warren Oates, but it was too similar to *Bonanza* to win over huge audiences.

Andrew Duggan died of cancer on 15 May 1988.

Maunder became a writer and producer in Los Angeles. During the 70's he appeared in *The Seven Minutes* and on television in *Kung Fu* (1972) and *Chase* (1973). In 1981, *Porky's* was his only other reported role. He now spends his time behind the camera, producing independent films.

Stacy lives in Ojai, California. In 1973 he was riding a motorcycle with his girlfriend when they were struck by a drunk driver. The girlfriend was killed and Stacy lost his left arm and left leg. Both his ex-wives, Connie Stevens and Kim Darby, plus friends pitched in to help him with his medical bills. He continues to act but only in roles he feels appropriately represent the handicapped.

Baur lives in Marina Del Rey.

# LARAMIE

## 15 September 1959

THIS solid series of hour long shows ran for four years on NBC. Produced by Revue Productions, it premiered with Stage Stop on 15 September 1959, and hung up its boots with The Road to Helena on 21 May 1963. In between, 124 episodes were made. The first 93 episodes were filmed in black and white, and the next 31 were in color.

*John Smith, Hoagy Carmichael, Robert Fuller* and *young Robert Crawford*

John Smith starred as Slim Sherman and Robert Fuller as Jess Harper. Together they operated a stagecoach way station outside Laramie, Wyoming in the 1870's.

Regular cast members included Hoagy Carmichael as Jonesy, a handyman at the station and Robert Crawford Jr., as Andy, Slim's 14-year-old brother. Through the 1961 season Spring Byington signed on as Daisy Cooper, a housekeeper and Dennis Holmes played orphan Mike Williams after Carmichael and Crawford left the show.

Slim and Andy had been left by themselves to run the Sherman ranch in Laramie, Wyoming during the 1870's after their father had been killed in a gunfight with a land-grabber.

In the first episode Slim is offered a contract from the government to use the ranch as a relay station for the Great Overland Mail Stage Lines. A young drifter with a lightning-draw named Jess Harper wanders in and helps Slim out in a gunfight with outlaws. Slim, grateful for the assistance, persuades Harper to stay on. His fast gun comes in handy throughout the series.

In 1961, Andy was written out of the cast and two new members were added: Daisy Cooper, a housekeeper and surrogate mother to the all-male household, and orphan Mike Williams whose parents were killed in the proverbial Indian attack.

Running a stagecoach relay station proved to be a great way of bringing in guest stars each week, and *Laramie* alwas pulled in top Hollywood names. Among them were Dan Duryea, Clu Gulager, James Coburn, Julie London, Ernest Borgnine, and Vera Miles.

*Laramie* was well-written and had the advantage of having two stars who were both excellent cowboys. John Smith came to *Laramie* directly from the successful *Cimarron City* but he retired right after *Laramie* finished.

*Laramie* also boasted some of the finest Western directors including Les Selander and Joe Kane. Fuller commented, 'They were tough, they were good, old time directors who knew how to make a Western just as easy as 1-2-3.' Kane had worked with Herbert Yates at Republic Studios. Fuller recalled he always had trouble working with blonde actresses, 'Whenever we had a blonde on the show he went ballistic. He wore an old green fedora and smoked a cigar. When a scene didn't go right he would take the fedora off and throw it on the ground and jump up and down on it.'

Fuller, a former stuntman, remains active and versatile in the industry. *Laramie* was his first starring TV series but he went on to play many cowboy roles. He began his career in musicals as a chorus dancer, under contract at MGM in 1952. He danced with Mailyn Monroe in *Gentlemen Prefer Blondes*. Recently he voiced the part of Harold in Disney's *All Dogs Go to Heaven*. Today's youth know him as sullen *Emergency's* top doctor, Kelly Brackett.

Fuller confessed, 'It was a big jump. I had had my heart set on another Western and no desire to work on a medical series.' He initially turned the part of Dr Brackett down but producer Jack Webb eventually persuaded him. Fuller says, 'When Webb

died they broke the mold. He gave me a medical dictionary which I still own. We ran for seven years. I don't know who else would have cast me as a doctor right out of Westerns. He must have seen something and it worked.'

His depiction of Jess was tough, rugged, mean and noble, a knight in tarnished armor. Jess was half outlaw, half good-guy. He was a gunfighter and his wardrobe indicated that.

Immediately after his four year run on *Laramie*, Fuller moved on to *Wagon Train* where he portrayed Cooper Smith for two years, leading settlers west with John McIntire. Fuller had been a guest on *Wagon Train* when Ward Bond was wagon master, 'I used to share a dressing room with Ward Bond, Terry Wilson, Frank McGarth and Lee Marvin at Universal Studios. Everyone called it Whiskey Row. But we worked long days and drank to get loosened up.'

Westerns ruled the airwaves in '60 and '61 with 32 programs running in prime time. Fuller kept busy during the period working as a cowboy on several shows at once including *Johnny Ringo, Lawman, Rin Tin Tin* and *Wyatt Earp*.

Between guest appearances plus his own Western series, Fuller worked for 8 years without a break, 'I had 30 days a year off. For those 30 days they packed me off to do publicity in New York, Chicago and Philadelphia. If I was lucky I'd get four days with nothing to do. That ain't bad for a young actor… I was working.'

Reflecting on his golden period and pondering whether Westerns will ever come back Fuller said, 'It's not that the era died out… it just ended… and it was politics. Westerns were supposedly too violent. If you had a gun, right here on your hip, it was 'No, you can't do that'. That was it, they stopped us. They made me sick.'

Fuller has appeared in *Dan August, The Fall Guy, Matt Houston, Murder She Wrote, Renegade* and *Diagnosis Murder*. With the reemergence of Westerns on TV he has also worked more recently on *Paradise, The Adventures of Briscoe County, Jr*, and the contemporary *Walker, Texas Ranger*. He did cameo work on the 1994 *Maverick*. 'On that picture I spent three weeks playing poker with my dear friend Doug McClure and Jodie Foster. We had a good time.'

Fuller has won five Ottos (Germany's Emmy) for best actor and he was the first American to receive the Japanese Golden Order of Merit!

Smith's horse was named Alamo and Fuller rode Hoot.

John Smith (real name Robert Van Orden) died in 1995 of cirrhosis and heart problems on 25 January 1995, aged 63.

Spring Byington died of cancer on 7 September 1991 and Hoagy Carmichael died after a heart attack on 15 December 1981.

The *Laramie* theme song was written by Cyril J. Mockridge and the lyrics were by Bill Olafson.

Bobby Crawford (Andy) is Johnny Crawford's (*Rifleman*) older brother.

# LAREDO

## 16 September 1965

**FIFTY** episodes were filmed in color and debuted on NBC TV on 16 September 1965 and concluded on 1 September 1967. Laredo came from Universal, the studio that produced the longer-running series Bonanza and The Virginian.

*William Smith, Philip Carey, Peter Brown, Neville Brand*

This show was a lot of fun, full of excitement and splattered with bawdy humor. The stories centered round three Texas Rangers in Company B and their exasperated Senior Officer, Captain Parmalee, who monitored their assignments and tried to keep a check on them.

The Rangers were Reese Bennett, played by Neville Brand, Chad Cooper played by Peter Brown and Joe Riley played by William Smith. Robert Wolders was added to the cast later as Ranger Erik Hunter. Parmalee was played by Philip Carey.

*Laredo* maintained a consistently light tone comparable to the humorous episodes of *Bonanza*. Despite that it just barely cracked the Top 40 at 8.30–9.30 Thursday nights in competition with *Bewitched, My Three Sons* and 'The Thursday Night Movie'. It didn't do as well following its move to 10 pm on Friday in the slot vacated by *Man From Uncle*, opposite *Twelve O'Clock High* and 'The CBS Friday Night Movie'.

When *Laredo* debuted it was as an episode of *The Virginian* and it was set up as a Western version of Dumas' Three Musketeers with Trampas as d'Artagnan. Trampas (Doug McClure) was sent to Mexico by way of Laredo to pick up a prize bull for Judge Garth. In Laredo he had run-ins with Texas Rangers Reese, Chad and Joe. Violence was only averted when the Rangers were sent to locate an overdue train transporting gold. Trampas helped them rescue a baby, fight off Yaqui bandits, expose gunrunning Mexican soldiers and recover the stolen gold.

With the addition of some footage from the 2nd season *Virginian* episode *Ride a Dark Trail* about Trampas' life leading up to Shiloh and another snippet from a 1st season *Laredo* episode, the pilot was cobbled together and released as the feature film, *Backtrack*, mostly for the European market.

*Laredo* had a lot of potential as a Western action series but somehow it struggled to live up to its promise.

The show was written by top author Borden Chase, directed by Earl Bellamy and often had top guest stars including Ida Lupino, Fernando Lamas, Rhoda Fleming, and James Drury.

Chad Cooper was the clever, well educated Ranger, although he rarely outsmarted Captain Parmalee. He was a ladies' man, a manipulator, a fast talker, a schemer, a lover of the usually unattainable good life and, as with his buddies, he threw a mean fist in a brawl. Chad rode a flashy black 'Sunday horse' with fancy tack while the others were satisfied with more mundane accoutrements. (His horse Amigo was actually Brown's own horse.)

Unlike Erik Hunter, Chad wore 'sensible clothes' on the job but had what Reese called, 'fuddadiddle clothes' for special occasions.

Cooper was recognized as the fastest draw in the Rangers. In the first season, Chad sported a cross-draw, wearing his revolver backwards on his left hip like Billy the Kid. Brown thought it would be an interesting difference from the standard draw he had used in *Lawman*. However, although known as one of the best gun handlers in TV Westerns, he never mastered the cross draw. So audiences never saw him draw his gun during *Laredo's* first year, although he did a very fancy spin when returning it to the holster. The second year he returned to the standard draw.

Chad was a New Orleans man with a background that gave him some expertise in fencing, boxing, literature and fine manners. He didn't bother with a Southern accent in every show, usually just bringing it out to impress the ladies. He was almost always partnered up with Joe. Even when the three Rangers went out together, it was usually Chad and Joe who manipulated or mocked Reese.

Robert Wolders as Erik Hunter was added to the Laredo cast in the second season, an addition in keeping with the outlandish direction some of the plots took them. Erik came to Company B from Europe by way of Company A, where, it was said, there were two ways of doing things, the Ranger's way and Erik Hunter's way. That meant he would fit right in with Chad, Joe and Reese. As in most Western series, the Rangers wore the same clothes in every episode. Erik, however, had a bottomless saddlebag of outlandish outfits.

He gave Chad competition in every way; with women, scheming, fast talking, manipulation, he also gave Chad someone he could talk to without dumbing down his vocabulary. They were occasionally paired off on Ranger assignments. More often, if not working alone, Erik was paired with Chad and Reese said of Chad and Erik, 'Putting you two in the same place with one girl is like throwing a pork chop between a lion and a tiger.' The Captain referred to them as 'God's gift to the working girl.'

Erik was sometimes teamed with Reese because the contrast between them provided opportunity for comedy. He was rarely partnered with Joe perhaps because the writers had not written Joe as educated enough to play off Erik verbally or as enough of a buffoon to provide a humorous contrast.

Reese Bennett was the oldest of the Rangers. He had joined up to get immunity from a prior life of crime in other states. An old cohort described him as 'Tough, plenty tough, maybe not too smart, but tough.' He was constantly being duped into the schemes of the others, especially Chad who always had a plan to avoid work, strike it rich or make time with a lady. Reese constantly reminded the others how proud they should be to be Rangers. No matter how tough things got, Reese felt the $40 a month and the prestige he got as a Ranger made life worthwhile and made up for all of his other disappointments in life.

Brand himself could be very difficult to work with and he lacked the discipline for a costarring role in a weekly series, something he admitted in a 1966 TV Guide interview. His drinking was a problem although he was reportedly likeable when sober. He was certainly never the favorite of the directors nor of the other actors, all of whom were consummate professionals. Carey and Smith always knew their parts; Brown frequently memorized the whole script and could irritate Brand by feeding him his missed lines. There was some talk of replacing him on *Laredo* with Claude Akins who had a recurring role as Ranger Cotton Buckmeister, but Brand's character

# TRIVIA

Between 1993 and 1999 Philip Carey was nominated for four Soap Opera Digest Awards all for his efforts in *One Life to Live*.

was very popular, especially with the older viewers. Brown, who because of his own perfectionism would be expected to have been the most irritated when Brand held up shooting, said that when Brand was sober, doing a scene with him was as natural as having conversation because he was just so good.

In fact Brand was the fourth most decorated soldier in America. He had won the Silver Star, America's third highest combat decoration, when the armored division he was with found itself held up by a German 50-calibre machine gun nest. With no thought to his own safety, he had maneuvered through enemy fire, entered the rear of the lodge housing the machine guns, and sprayed the place with his own gun. He arrived in *Laredo* after a successful stint as Al Capone on the hit series *The Untouchables* starring Robert Stack.

Brand died of emphysema on 16 April 1992, aged 72.

Captain Parmalee was a demanding father figure who kept the difficult Rangers in line. He was clever enough to figure out most of their schemes but he was usually willing to look the other way when things turned out for the best. A stereotypical tough but fair leader, he was not quite strait-laced. He had a fondness for good 'sippin whiskey' and he kept a private stock (although only for off-duty indulgence). In several episodes, he ended up with the lady while his Rangers were assigned stable duty or some other onerous task.

At 6'6" Philip Carey towered over his costars, even the formidable 6'2" William Smith who had slimmed down for *Laredo* from his competitive body-building days. In 1979 Carey left Hollywood for New York and moved into steady daytime drama employment when he became patriarch Asa Buchanan in *One Life to Live* where he resides to this day.

*Laredo's* Ranger Joe Riley was an orphan raised by Indians. It was this childhood which helped him become the best tracker in the Rangers and made him deadly with the knife he always wore in a sheath on his pant leg. He also had an eagle eye for long-distance rifle fire.

Although *Laredo* was the story of three Rangers (2nd season four) it was Chad and Joe who were the driving force of the team. In fact, it was fortunate that William Smith and Peter Brown got along so well because their characters were essentially joined at the hip throughout. In most episodes they played almost every scene together, especially in the first year.

Brown and Smith remain active in the industry. Brown made a number of appearances in TV series, TV Movies and feature films before embarking on a successful career in daytime drama. He starred in five soaps, starting with *Days of Our Lives* in 1971 and ending with *The Bold & The Beautiful* in 1992.

After leaving the show Wolders married Merle Oberon in 1975. After her death he moved to Switzerland where he became Audrey Hepburn's companion. He had a few unimportant roles in unimportant movies and a few TV series guest appearances.

# LASH OF THE WEST
## 14 January 1953

**THE** King of the Bullwhip came to TV on 14 January 1953 in a 15 minute series called Lash of the West. It ran on ABC until 26 April 1953.

At the start of each episode, Lash appeared and related how his grandfather and sidekick, Fuzzy, cleaned up the West.

Excerpts from his earlier feature films would then be run before Lash reappeared to invite the audience back the following week.

Lash LaRue died on 21 May 1996 of heart failure and emphysema.

# LAW OF THE PLAINSMAN
## 1 October 1959

**THE** show, which portrayed the Apache as honorable and dignified, debuted on 1 October 1959 and ran for 34 half-hour black and white episodes until 24 September 1960. Four Star Productions, who produced The Rifleman, made this series.

Apache born lawman, Deputy Marshal Sam Buckhart, worked in the New Mexico Territory in 1885. Michael Ansara had played the same unique role in an episode of *The Rifleman* where he apprehended a couple of murderers in North Fork and NBC ordered the series on the back of his performance.

He had nursed a cavalry captain back to health after he had been wounded in an Indian ambush. The soldier had been so grateful that, upon his death, he financed young Buck Heart's (as he was known to the Apache) education which culminated at Harvard.

When he returned to his native New Mexico, he went to work for Marshal Morrison in Sante Fe. Buckhart successfully brought together a respect for both Indian and white cultures to the work.

Martha ran the boardinghouse where he lived and Tess was an orphan he rescued from a stagecoach accident.

Other cast members included Dayton Lummis as Marshal Andy Morgan, Sam's boss; Nora Marlowe as Martha Commager, the owner of the inn where Sam stayed when in Santa Fe and Gina Gillespie as Tess Morgan, her young daughter. Robert Harland played Deputy Billy Lordan.

Nora Malowe died in 1977. Dayton Lummis died in 1998.

Ansara lives in California and is still active in the business.

# LAWMAN
## 5 OCTOBER 1958

**THE half-hour black and white no-frills series from Warner Bros. debuted on ABC on 5 October 1958 and was immediately earning top ratings. Lawman ran for four years before closing on 2 October 1962.**

In the opinion of many, *Lawman*, along with *Maverick,* represented the best of Warner's Westerns which dominated ABC in the late 50's and through the mid-60's. Each episode was a straightforward adventure, which used no gimmicks or tricks to draw in its audience. The stories were intentionally kept taunt and simple, and were always about desperadoes brought to justice by the long arm of the law. *Lawman* may initially have been ABC's attempt to emulate the success of CBS' *Gunsmoke*, but it succeeded all by itself in becoming one of the top-rated shows ever put on television. And where *Maverick* was a delightful, light-hearted romp with occasional serious moments, *Lawman* was a serious Western with occasional light moments. The half-hour format, almost unheard of today in television drama, required a compact storyline and there was little time for romance or the development of secondary characters.

The show was set in Laramie in the 1870s and the lawman in charge was Marshal Dan Troop. His eager deputy was Johnny McKay. When they were in town, people towed the line or suffered the consequences.

For most of its run it followed *Maverick* at 8.30 pm on Sunday nights and was paired with *Colt .45.* or *The Rebel* and opposite that Sunday night classic, *The Ed Sullivan Show*. In *Lawman's* final season, *Maverick*, which was then struggling without its star, James Garner, was moved to 6.30 pm on Sundays (Sunday prime time started earlier then) and *Lawman* was isolated between two short-lived, one-hour, non-Western dramas: *Follow the Sun* and *Bus Stop* for most of the season. In April 1962 it moved to 10.30 pm until its demise. Despite constantly running against high-powered competition and the sheer number of Westerns airing at the time, *Lawman* still generally achieved decent ratings, hitting No. 15 in its second season. It might well have continued its run had ABC not decided to play a two-hour movie on Sunday nights. When the producers were offered a less desirable time-slot by the network, they declined and one of the best Westerns to appear on the small screen was cancelled.

Veteran actor, John Russell was Troop and Peter Brown was Johnny. Russell, a 6'4" ex-Marine with the most compelling steely gaze on television, embodied the courageous, no-nonsense marshal. He reportedly modeled the character after one of his superiors in the Marine Corps. Russell was 37 when the series started, only 14 years older than his young co-star. However, he portrayed Troop as an experienced lawman in his mid to late forties. To that end, he added gray to his hair and played the character a decade older than he was himself.

Peter Brown, a lean, handsome six footer, had no problem playing a character four or five years younger than his already youthful 23. The producer said that Johnny McKay was intended to be only 18 when the series started. The series debuted on Brown's 23rd birthday which means he was 22 when the first episodes were filmed. In the third season episode *Cornered*, Johnny tells someone he's 21.

Together the two men portrayed a classic mentor/protégé team that fell just shy of a father-son relationship. The series generally avoided sentimentality, but for those who looked for it, the bond between the two characters was stronger than the words exchanged suggested. The promos for the series described Dan Troop as a lawman of strength and purpose and Johnny McKay as the boy he trained to fight by his side. Despite its limitations, the series did a good job developing the two main characters and their relationship.

The stand-out quality of the show can be attributed in great part to the efforts of the two stars both of whom came to the series as excellent horsemen and gun handlers as well as actors dedicated to their craft. They were perfectly cast and together conspired to maintain the consistency and integrity of their characters in the face of constantly changing writers and directors, tight budgets and frantic shooting schedules.

In the second season Peggie Castle joined the regular lineup as saloon owner, Lily Merrill.

Russell died of pneumonia on 19 January 1991, aged 70. His lingering death was a cruel heritage from the years he smoked the cigarettes that sponsored his most successful role. (*Lawman* was sponsored by Camel cigarettes.)

Brown went on to star in *Laredo*.

*Lawman* theme music was by Jerry Livingston with lyrics by Mack David.

Merrill died 11 August 1973 of cirrhosis of the liver.

# THE LAZARUS MAN
## 1996

**THERE were 22 hour long, color episodes shot around Santa Fe, New Mexico for the 1996 syndication season.**

Robert Urich starred as fast gun, The Lazarus Man, an amnesiac soldier of fortune, in this modern Western series.

He wandered the West just after the Civil War. He had been pistol-whipped and could not recall his identity, but he unfailingly came to the aid of all the unfortunates who crossed his path.

Although a second series was ordered, Urich had a cancer scare and the show was brought to an early close.

# THE LEGEND OF JESSE JAMES
## 13 September 1965

**THIS half-hour, black and white series produced by 20th Century Fox TV, debuted on ABC on 13 September 1965. It ran for 26 episodes until 15 September 1966**

The show about the notorious Frank and Jesse James was hardly based on fact, and the brothers were portrayed here as latter day Robin Hoods.

Christopher Jones played Jesse and Allen Case was Frank.

Don Siegel, who was closely involved in the show had some difficulty making the notorious robbers and killers into believably sympathetic characters, and confessed, 'The trouble is that the producers, having decided to give us an outlaw for a hero, then produced script after script to make him, if not an in-law, at least not all bad.'

Robert J. Wilke rounded out the cast as Marshal Sam Corbett, who believed the boys were innocent and he tried to get them to turn themselves over to the law.

Wilke died of cancer on 28 March 1989.

Chris Jones hasn't been active in the industry for some time.

# LIFE AND LEGEND OF WYATT EARP
## 6 SEPTEMBER 1955

**SOME** 226 half hour episodes were made for ABC and they ran from 6 September 1955 to 26 September 1961. The series aired for its entire six-year run on ABC on Tuesday nights from 8.30–9 pm, and was scripted throughout by Frederick Hazlitt Brennan.

*The Life and Legend of Wyatt Earp* was *the* first adult Western on television, beating *Gunsmoke* for that distinction by four days. Hugh O'Brian starred in this series as real-life Marshal Wyatt Earp. Unlike *Gunsmoke*, *The Life and Legend of Wyatt Earp* was upbeat and fast-paced.

The first episode was titled, *Mr. Earp Becomes a Marshal* and depicted Earp assuming the job of his lawman-friend who had been gunned down, as he sets out to avenge his death.

O'Brian was the only actor to appear in all six seasons but he was supported at various times by a large cast including Morgan Woodward, Myron Healey, Mason Alan Dinehart and Douglas Fowley.

Many a bad man's skull felt the crack of Earp's Buntline Special, a long-barreled pistol that O'Brian weilded round Tombstone.

O'Brian and Woodward remain active and Healey now lives out in the Simi Valley.

The film *Return to Tombstone* saw O'Brian reprise his role as Earp.

# LIFE AND TIMES OF GRIZZLY ADAMS
## 9 FEBRUARY 1977

**GRIZZLY ADAMS** was filmed in color by Sunn Classic Pictures and ran for an hour. It was aimed primarily at a young audience. Location work was done in Payson, Arizona and Park City, Utah. It aired on NBC between 9 February 1977 and 26 July 1978.

The show starred Dan Haggerty as Adams, a man accused of a crime he hadn't committed. He fled to the wilderness where he rescued a bear cub from a ledge. He christened the cub, Ben, and it grew into a massive grizzly.

Although Adams enjoyed solitude, he allowed two people to get close to him, Mad Jack, a trapper, and Nakuma, an Indian blood brother.

Denver Pyle was Mad Jack and Don Shanks played Nakuma.

Pyle died on 25 December 1997. Haggerty still works in TV movies as Adams.

# LITTLE HOUSE ON THE PRAIRIE
## 11 SEPTEMBER 1974

**SHOT** in color and running an hour, Little House On the Prairie, debuted on NBC on 11 September 1974. Michael Landon served as writer, producer and director for the series. The program was a long running ratings winner until leaving the air on 23 March 1983. The show still goes out in syndication all around the world.

Landon's first post *Bonanza* project was directing a segment of NBC's *Love Story* and he followed that up by directing *It's Good to be Alive*, and it was more than a year after *Bonanza* left the air before he made it back before the camera as pioneering family man, Charles Ingalls. He developed, directed and starred in the adaptation of Laura Ingalls Wilder's children's classic, *The Little House on the Prairie* first a TV Movie of the Week, where he was the head of the Minnesota farming family in the 1870's.

Ed Friendly had bought the rights to the series of books written by Wilder. Friendly and Landon were long-standing acquaintances and had been neighbors in Encino. Friendly was also a close friend of actor Lorne Greene. In fact they had all often dined at Greene's house in the years before *Bonanza* was cancelled. Friendly had seen the 1969 *Bonanza* episode *The Wish* when it aired and was highly impressed with Landon's direction of the story.

Friendly and Landon had a meeting and they then contacted NBC with their ideas and finally pre-production of the pilot for *Little House on the Prairie* got underway in December 1973. Landon, who had been turning down various offers to play cops in new shows, had approached Friendly to ask if he might portray Charles Ingalls himself. The answer, needless to say, was a resounding 'Yes.'

Before Friendly formally offered him the part however Landon sought the permission of *Bonanza* creator-producer David Dortort to take Kent McCray, Hal Burton and the entire *Bonanza* film crew to work on the new project. Filming of the interiors got underway on stages 31 and 32 at Paramount Pictures, and the outdoor location scenes were shot in Farmington, Mother Lode foothills and the Stanislaus National Forest in California.

Paramount Studios had been home to *Bonanza* for many years, and it still had a two-story Western set that had been used in various TV series including *Gunsmoke, Have Gun; Will Travel* and many famous Western films. When Landon was looking for a set for *Little House*, he chose the one he was familiar with. By the late 70's it was rather shabby and run down and it was finally demolished in 1979.

Unlike on the *Bonanza* series, Landon now found himself in total control of the show. In addition to being actor, writer and director, he was also now the executive producer.

He got the pilot assembled after a two-week filming shoot although it wasn't due to air until later in the season. On 30 March 1974 the show finally went out and it won higher ratings than any other NBC pilot ever. The network immediately ordered 13 episodes and if those proved as successful, they would take a further 13.

The series of course was an instant hit and audiences were thrilled to see Landon playing a mature man who was responsible, compassionate, sensitive, caring and a hard-working father and husband every week. *Little House* was packed with his heartwarming adventures and life-affirming lessons.

Series filming was done in California and Arizona, and local exteriors were filmed at Big Sky Ranch in Simi Valley, which had been used in *Bonanza's* later years, with other locales such as Bronson Canyon and Golden Oak Ranch in California. Fat Jones Stables were used for the rentals of horses, livestock and other equipment until they closed in 1975.

The family oriented, non-violent, value driven enterprise had been given little chance of success during the violent seventies. But Landon's hard work, care and dedication transformed the gamble into eight seasons of TV drama and he was firmly established as one of TV's premier stars.

Charles' wife, Caroline, was played by Karen Grassle; Laura, their daughter, by Melissa Gilbert; Mary, another daughter, by Melissa Sue Anderson, and their youngest daughter, Carrie was played by identical twins, Lindsay and Sidney Green Bush.

In the conception of the series, Landon hired his friend and character actor, Victor French for the role of Mr. Edwards. They had met in the late 60's, when French was a guest star on *Bonanza*. NBC wanted a star name for the role, but Landon insisted on French and he got his man for the pilot. French thought Landon wouldn't want him for the series since he stole the pilot episode from him, but the new producer insisted he stay on as a regular. It was a great break for French as over the past 15 years he had been typecast as murderers, rapists and mob bosses.

By the end of 1981–2 season the *Little House* cast were much older and all ready to move on, so Landon wrote them all out. He brought in a completely new cast for

*Michael Landon as Charles Phillip Ingalls, Karen Grassle as Caroline Lake Quiner Ingalls, Lindsay Green Bush as Caroline Celestia 'Carrie' Ingalls, Melissa Sue Anderson as Mary Amelia Ingalls and Melissa Gilbert as Laura Elizabeth Ingalls.*

the 1982–3 season which saw the show re-titled *A New Beginning*. He had also written out Merlin Olsen and given him a series of his own entitled *Father Murphy* which made its fall premiere on 3 November 1981.

French died aged 54 on 12 June 1989, of cancer. Gilbert was elected President of the Screen Actors Guild.

In 1984 Landon approached NBC head Brandon Tartikoff with a new idea. Tartikoff felt Landon would be laughed off the air as an angel who came to Earth to help people and he warned him no audience would accept it. Landon had enough clout by then to push it through anyway and he stated that he wanted to bring a show that was positive, uplifting and inspirational to TV. *Highway to Heaven* successfully ran five seasons, and was only cut short by the untimely death of Landon's co-star Victor French.

When *Highway* went off air in summer 1989 Landon immediately began work developing a new project, *Us*, a series about an absent father struggling to reconnect with his family. It was whilst working on this series that Landon began to suffer stomach pain. He feared an ulcer but in 1991 he was diagnosed with pancreatic cancer. He immediately established two cancer research foundations which still run today. Landon died three months after diagnosis on 1 July 1991.

# THE LONE RANGER
## 25 SEPTEMBER 1949

**PRODUCTION** on the series started on 21 June 1949 and the first episode aired on 15 September 1949. For the first two seasons The Lone Ranger was budgeted at $12,500 per episode, rising to $15,000 in 1951, $17,000 in 1952 and $18,000 by 1954, 'we were really masters at stretching a buck back then.'

'A fiery horse with the speed of light, a cloud of dust and a hearty, 'Hi Yo Silver!... It's THE LONE RANGER. With his faithful Indian companion Tonto, the daring and resourceful masked rider of the plains led the fight for law and order in the early west. Return with us now to those thrilling days of yesteryear. The Lone Ranger rides again!'

In 1929, George Washington Trendle, a motion picture distributor, expanded his empire, buying radio station WXYZ in Detroit. The station played melodramas and many of its best programs were written by Fran Striker. Trendle and Striker got together to work on the idea for a Western series, *The Lone Ranger*. The show was to be aimed at children because Trendle wanted to win over some extra revenue from promoting toys and souvenirs. He decided the hero of the show must therefore be wholesome, pure and upstanding. He was also to be mysterious.

Trendle set up creative sessions and many of the WXYZ staff were involved. They pooled ideas like the hero having a white horse called Silver. Little by little their ideas came together until Striker decided to adapt and use one of his earlier series, *Covered Wagon Days*. This became the working title for the new show for a while. Striker also wrote a booklet describing the various traits of his masked man; this became the building block of every Lone Ranger show ever broadcast. It defined how the Lone Ranger felt about patriotism, tolerance, sympathy, religion and speech. For example, he wrote, 'Tolerance: The Lone Ranger's friend is Tonto, a Comanche Indian. If the Lone Ranger accepts the Indian as his closest companion, it is obvious to the child listener that great men have no racial or religious prejudice. Concerning religion: The Lone Ranger is shown not to be a member of any specific church, but he is definitely a respecter of all creeds, and the only man besides Tonto who knows him is a Catholic Padre of a mission.' The Lone Ranger would always use proper English, be respectful of women and children, and never kill anyone. However, there would always be plenty of action in his show.

*The Lone Ranger* was taking shape.

Throughout the entire radio show, which ran from 2 February 1933 to 1954, Tonto, the Lone Ranger's sidekick, was played by Shakespearean actor, John Todd.

When the first episode aired it crashed out to the majestic strains of Rossini's William Tell Overture and announcer, Fred Foy, calling out, 'A fiery horse, with a speed of light, a cloud of dust, a hearty laugh-the Lone Ranger.' (The hearty laugh was later refined into, 'Hi Yo Silver! Away!') The show caught an immediate audience.

Clayton Moore was already 18 when it went out, but it was soon his favorite show, 'I tried not to miss an episode.'

The first masked man was George Stenius, (he later changed his name to Seaton) but he only stayed with the show briefly, and he went on to become a screen writer. In 1947 he won an Oscar for *Miracle on 34th Street.*

In 1941 Earle Graser, who had been playing the Ranger since April 1933, was killed in an automobile accident. To ensure the show went on, Striker wrote some scripts where the ranger had been wounded and was bed ridden whilst Tonto got on with the action. When the ranger recovered it was with the voice of Brace Beemer. Beemer remained in the role until 1954, and was so loved that when Moore took on the TV role he tried to imitate him, 'I tried my best to duplicate Beemer's powerful voice and distinctive way of speaking.'

Clayton Moore and Jay Silverheels assumed the roles for Trendle's television show which began in 1949. While Moore shaped the masked man in his own image, Beemer upheld the tradition on the radio. So for five years there were two Lone Rangers and fans even accepted it when Jay Silverheels went out on personal appearances with Beemer!

Into a stark landscape of craggy rock gallops a brilliant white stallion. On his back is a figure in a blue suit, white hat and black mask, immediately mysterious and mythic. Pausing at the summit of an incline, the stallion rears magnificently, pawing at the air with his front hooves.

And so the Lone Ranger rode onto TV screens around the world with his loyal and faithful friend. He was a real hero, equal to any task. He became the American archetype; brave, honest, compassionate, patriotic and inventive.

*The Lone Ranger* is probably the greatest fictional Western legend of them all, and Clayton Moore became synonymous with the role.

Generations of American children grew up believing that Clayton Moore *was* the Lone Ranger, they regarded him with reverence and he seemed to embody the spirit and essence of the character he played. No one could have been as consistently noble as the Lone Ranger and Moore himself always played a hero to his fans.

Whilst Moore's status as the one and only Kimo Sabe is celebrated, several actors have played the part in radio, television, motion pictures and on the stage.

Between 25 September 1949 and 12 September 1957, Moore and Jay Silverheels brought justice to the West in 221 half hour, black and white and color episodes and two feature films.

When Trendle first created *The Lone Ranger* he laid down a strict code of conduct for the masked man; The Lone Ranger must never smoke, never use profanity and never use intoxicating beverages. He was a man who could fight great odds, yet always took time to treat a bird with a broken wing. The Lone Ranger believed the sacred American heritage which allowed every individual the right to worship God as he desired. Gambling and drinking scenes were to be played down as much as possible, and The Lone Ranger was kept out of saloons. The Lone Ranger at all times used precise speech, without slang or dialect. His grammar must be pure. He must make proper use of 'who' and 'whom', 'shall' and 'will' 'I' and 'me' etc. The Lone Ranger never shot to kill. When forced to use guns, he aimed to maim as painlessly as possible. In addition he had to be as respectful to people as possible.

Clayton Moore added his own further rule, refusing to appear in public without the mask.

Later, when young new producers decided the rules were outmoded, Moore argued it was their loss, 'People remember the character and what he stood for. He is a reminder of a time when they were still optimistic.'

Moore had been working at various studios through his early career; mostly making cheap serials, but he said, 'I was seriously considered for the part of the Lone Ranger before I knew anything about it.'

When his agent rang him in 1949 to tell him he was being considered for the leading role in a proposed TV version of the story he was thrilled. Trendle himself was going to produce it and had already auditioned a few actors before being shown the tapes from *The Ghost of Zorro*. Moore was immediately asked to go to see Trendle who asked about previous roles. Trendle was also interested in his trapeze background. His athletic ability was a definite plus. Eventually Trendle asked, 'Would you like the part of the Lone Ranger?'

Moore says he responded, 'Mr Trendle, I am the Lone Ranger!'

Trendle confirmed, 'The job is yours.'

Moore went on, 'By appearing in this show, I would be a part of history: *The Lone Ranger* was the first Western ever produced for television. The networks were already showing *Hopalong Cassidy* and other Western heroes, but those programs were edited versions of movies originally shown in theatres.'

*The Lone Ranger* was only one of two major roles in the series, and his equally important sidekick, Tonto was played by the tall, regal Jay Silverheels. Moore says of first meeting Silverheels, 'We instantly understood each other perfectly. We would remain close friends for the next 30 years.'

Silverheels was a full-blooded Mohawk from Ontario, Canada, who started out life with the very un-Indian-sounding name, Harold J Smith. His name wasn't legally changed until 1971. No one else was ever considered for the part of Tonto.

Moore then chose his white horse and said, 'They had two white horses for me to consider, but we never used the second one. The first horse was the stallion that I used. He was a gentle and good-looking stud. Although his name was Silver on the screen, on the set we nicknamed him Liver Lip. You can see in some of the publicity pictures he had a big bottom lip. We made fun of him because the bit he used had a copper roller and he would tongue that copper roller so his lip would hang down. When we went into production we had to tape the roller down because the sound department was picking up the clatter as he rolled it against his teeth.'

Liver Lip had a dark spot on his hindquarters that had to be dyed before filming. The second horse had a black spot on his left ear, the only dark spot he had on his entire body. Moore sometimes took horse two on tour, with rubber shoes fitted so as not to damage school halls and stages, 'Silver Two was very camera wise. Sometimes we used a motor to start the camera and his ears would twitch when he heard it; he knew when the camera was on.'

Tonto's horse was a brown paint called Scout.

The Lone Ranger's first mask was made of plaster and molded to Moore's face, 'In previous movies, masked men had trouble moving around because the mask hindered their vision. But with this mask I had no trouble at all. I could see a punch coming from the side, or I could look down and see my toes.'

The first mask was purple, not black. For the early black and white shows, the purple color gave a better textured effect. According to TV lore the mask was made from the vest of the Lone Ranger's slain brother.

'With so much of my face covered by the mask, it was especially important for my eyes to register effectively. They used a little magenta light, called a hinky-dink, that was set up next to the camera and directed at my eyes. In close ups, the hinky-dink helped to bring my eyes out.'

The opening episode of the television version in September 1949, explained how the Lone Ranger got his name and his mission in life to correct the wrong-doings of others.

He had been one of a posse of six Texas Rangers tracking a gang of desperadoes led by outlaw Butch Cavendish and his Hole in the Wall Gang. The Rangers were ambushed in a canyon and five of them were killed. The sixth, young John Reid, was left for dead, but he managed to crawl to safety near a water hole, where he was found and nursed back to health by the friendly Tonto. Reid had once helped Tonto, so the Indian vowed to stay with the 'lone' Ranger. Tonto recognized Reid by a medallion he wore around his neck which had been made from Tonto's ring, which he had given to him in return for his earlier kindness. Kemo Sabe means 'Trusty Scout'. Reid buried his past in the graves of his friends, one of whom was his brother Dan, donned a mask, and set out with Tonto to avenge wrongs throughout the Old West. He had no visible means of support except for the proceeds from a silver mine that he and his brother had discovered. Periodically, he returned to the mine, which was run for him by an honest old man, to collect enough silver to stock up on his silver bullets.

The locations for several episodes were shot at one time. Back in 1949 camera trucks and sound trucks could be taken up into really rough country around Chatsworth and nearly all the exteriors were filmed at Iverson's Ranch. The rugged location had provided the backdrop on hundreds of great Westerns. At the summit of one of Iverson's hills is a unique grouping of large rocks known as Garden of the Gods. Those rocks concealed many a bad guy. The opening scene of Silver rearing up was shot at what has become known as Lone Ranger Rock.

As a money saving device Trendle used some of the same action scenes in several episodes. Viewers could count on seeing footage of runaway stagecoaches in several episodes.

The interiors for the show were all filmed in Culver City at the old Hal Roach Studios and there was a Western street there along with a sheriff's office and farmhouse.

Trendle had told Moore right at the start that he didn't want a superman, but a real, authentic, true-to-life hero and Moore says, 'I think audiences sensed that the Lone Ranger, although brave and resourceful, was only human and could be placed in real danger. An audience roots harder for a vulnerable man than for some superhero.'

## The Lone Ranger Creed

I believe that to have a friend, a man must be one. That all men are created equal and that everyone has within himself the power to make this a better world. That God put the firewood there but that every man must gather and light it himself. In being prepared physically, mentally and morally to fight when necessary for that which is right. That a man should make the most of what equipment he has. That 'This government, of the people, by the people and for the people' shall live always. That men should live by the rule of what is best for the greatest number. That sooner or later... somewhere...

somehow… we must settle with the world and make payment for what we have taken. That all things change but truth, and that truth alone, lives on forever. In my Creator, my country, my fellow man.

*The Lone Ranger*

It must have come as a big shock in 1952 when Trendle suddenly fired Moore from the role that meant so much to him, 'No one connected with *The Lone Ranger* ever told me why I had been fired – and I never asked.'

John Hart replaced Moore and Jay Silverheels stayed with the job.

Moore went on to film more serials and features like *Gunfighters of the Northwest* before Trendle eventually came back in 1953 saying he wanted him back. Just as he had never been told why he had been fired, he also never heard why Trendle wanted to get rid of Hart. Perhaps it had something to do with the way Moore had inhabited the role, but by June 1954 he was back in the saddle anyway, 'It was like old times… if anything, things were better than ever. The new scripts offered me more opportunities to play different characters besides the masked man… in one episode, *The Return of Don Pedro O'Sullivan*, which aired in October 1956, I played three separate roles, including a Mexican bandit and a red-haired Irishman'.'

In August 1954 Trendle sold all the rights to the show and to the Lone Ranger character to Jack Wrather for $3 million cash.

Wrather approached Moore to ask if he wanted to make any suggestions, 'Just before I was released from the show in 1952, the mask had suddenly become much larger. I now believe this was done deliberately because they knew they were going to replace me and wanted a mask that would hide John Hart's face as much as possible… 'Jack,' I said, 'I would really like for the mask to be made smaller. This larger mask has always seemed to me like something an outlaw would wear. I don't think it's appropriate for the Lone Ranger.'

'You know, you're absolutely right,' he said. 'I want you to get with the wardrobe people and get a mask that you think is just right.'

'I never had problems with Jack Wrather. I could always talk matters over with him.'

In 1956 they started shooting the series in color. There were few people then who owned color TV sets, but Wrather wanted to ensure the program could show in reruns for years to come. *The Cisco Kid* and *Superman* were also changing to color at the same time. Naturally there was more location work to make full use of the color. More filming was done at Lone Pine and Sonora and the more distant scenic areas lent a spark of something new to each episode.

Wrather was anxious to take the adventures to the big screen and *The Lone Ranger* went into production in summer 1955 at Warner Bros Studios in Burbank. *The Lone Ranger and the lost City of Gold* later opened in 1958.

The last new episode aired on 6 June 1957, and Moore and Silverheels never again starred as Tonto or the Lone Ranger. In 1964 Moore said, 'Since I no longer had any interest in performing on television or in films as any character but the Lone Ranger, there didn't seem to be much point in staying near Hollywood. I was touring the country making personal appearances, but this allowed me to live anywhere.

'I enjoyed meeting the fans'.'

Silverheels had a stroke in 1974 and never really recovered. In 1980 he took a turn for the worse and eventually passed away on 5 March 1980 from complications of pneumonia. He was 62 years old. His ashes were scattered over the Six Nations Reservation in Canada.

Clayton Moore died 28 December 1999, of an apparent heart attack at West Hills Hospital in West Hills, California. He lived in Calabasas, California and right up to his death Moore was busy on book signing tours. In 1987 he had received his star on the Hollywood Walk of Fame. In cement next to his own name, 'The Lone Ranger' is written. It is the only star on the Walk that mentions a specific character. Moore had been inducted into the Cowboy Hall of Fame in 1990.

In 2000 a collection of Clayton Moore's Lone Ranger memorabilia was sold by Sothebys in an online auction. The mask was expected to raise up to $60,000.

John Hart is alive and well and in retirement.

To understand the whole Lone Ranger experience, it has to be understood that by the time *The Lone Ranger* was 20 years old in 1953, he was still being broadcast three times each week on 249 radio stations, he achieved the highest rating of any Western program ever, and had a weekly listening audience of twelve million people. At that same 20th anniversary, he was being broadcast on 90 television stations and was the highest rated Western on TV, being seen by five million viewers. He also appeared in 177 daily papers, 119 Sunday papers and was being read by 71 million people in comic strip fashion. This is in addition to the many novels and series books that had also been written by this time. He was perhaps the first character that was truly a multi-media entity, having a very broad spectrum of appreciation, not to mention the toys and clothing that were sold.

*'Who was that masked man?'*

# THE LONER
## 18 SEPTEMBER 1965

**THE LONER ran on CBS between 18 September 1965 and 30 April 1966. The 26, 30 minute episodes were shot in black and white.**

*'In the aftermath of the bloodletting called the Civil War, thousands of rootless, restless, searching men traveled west. Such a man was William Colton. Like the others, he carried a blanket roll, a proficient gun, and a dedication to a new chapter in American history... the opening of the West.'*

*The Loner* centered on the exploits of a battle weary and introspective ex-Union cavalry captain named William Colton, played by Lloyd Bridges, who worked his way Westward in search of himself and some meaning to life after the Civil War. In each show he confronted significant, ethical issues that were as relevant in 1965 as they had been a century earlier. *The Loner* took his position and stood by it.

With its focus on characterization and philosophy the series was unconventional, but it still had plenty going for it with its proven film and television star in Bridges, a wealth of capable guest stars, established and respected directors, even a catchy theme song by renowned composer Jerry Goldsmith and Alexander Courage before they boldly went on to work together on *Star Trek*.

The project was conceived and written by Rod Serling, fresh from the successful network run of his legendary *Twilight Zone* series. *The Loner* is not all that surprising a creation for Serling who revisited many of the themes prevalent in his earlier writing including the horrors of war, moral ambiguity, bigotry, and the pressures of command and responsibility.

However the show was given a 9.30 Saturday evening time slot, which did not bode well. It was scheduled to run against ABC's popular Hollywood Palace; a variety show filmed in color, in an era when the novelty of such a broadcast was a great weapon in the publicity wars. The journey of *The Loner* proved to be an uphill ride and despite being well written and acted, it was panned by critics who never grasped the idea. *TV Guide* critic Cleveland Amory began his review of *The Loner* 'Rod Serling, who has done some fine things on TV, evidently felt there was a crying need for another TV Western.' The show failed to catch an audience and it went off air after just six months.

Bridges died in 1998.

# LONESOME DOVE
## 1989

IN total the show's runtime was 384 minutes / Brazil: 145 minute (video version). It was shot in color. Originally the eight hour show aired on CBS between 9pm and 11pm four consecutive evenings.

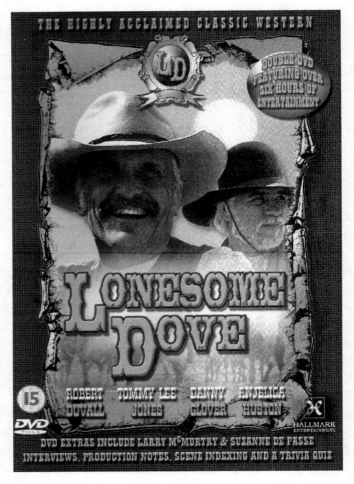

*Lonesome Dove* told the epic story of two retired Texas rangers who decided to move cattle from the south to Montana with the intention of becoming cattle barons. Gus McRae and Woodrow Call had been content to live out their remaining years in the tiny Texas town of Lonesome Dove until their old friend Jake rode back into town, and tells them about the incredible opportunities for cattle ranching in Montana. Encouraged by this, Call convinces Gus and many other townspeople to join him on a perilous cattle drive through the state.

Gus had his own agenda though: his former sweetheart now lives in Nebraska, and he hopes for a second chance with her. As the drive struggled on it took on an epic scale and ultimately became the central event in the lives of all involved

McCrae and Call run into many problems on their way, and the journey doesn't end without numerous casualties; the show burst at the seams with separated lovers, lost children and numerous death scenes. As Call attempted to escape the memory of his careless disregard of the woman who bore his unacknowledged son, Newt Dobbs (Ricky Schroder), the boy yearns for a father. July Johnson (Chris Cooper), a young sheriff from Arkansas, has taken his son searching first for a murderer and then for his own wife, Elmira (Glenne Headly), who has run off to find her lost love.

Pretty Lorena (Diane Lane) was also looking for love but ignored devoted Dish (D. B. Sweeney) in favor of the undependable Jake Spoon (Robert Urich), who is always searching out trouble, 'I'd a damned sight rather be hung by my friends than by a bunch of darned strangers.' Blue Duck (Frederic Forrest), a bloodthirsty renegade Indian, wants men to skewer and women and children to abuse. Coincidence and pathos are spilled as they all criss-cross one another's tracks through a sparsely populated continent.

The renowned mini-series was packed with memorable performances and two sequels, a prequel, and one or two syndicated series followed in its tracks.

Robert Duvall starred as McCrae, Tommy Lee Jones as Call, Danny Glover as Joshua Deets, Diane Lane as Lorena Wood, Robert Urich as Jake Spoon and Anjelica Huston as Clara Allen.

*Lonesome Dove* was originally written by Larry McMurtry in 1971 as a movie script. He intended John Wayne to play Woodrow Call, James Stewart to play Gus McCrae and Henry Fonda to play Jake Spoon, with Peter Bogdanovich directing. Wayne turned it down, and the project was shelved. Ten years later McMurtry bought the script back and wrote the book (on which the series was based).

William D. Wittliff wrote the teleplay and the show was directed by Simon Wincer. The show won two Golden Globes.

# LONESOME DOVE: THE SERIES
## 9 SEPTEMBER 1994

**THIS** sequel to Lonesome Dove which ran 42 minutes was directed by George Mendeluk and Mark Sobel. It was shot in color and went out originally on CTV on 9 September 1994.

Writing was by Larry McMurtry and Susanna Styron. Scott Bairstow starred as Newt Call, Christianne Hirt as Hannah Peale Call, Eric McCormack as Col. Francis Clay Mosby and Ron Webber as Dog Faced Gambler.

Set in the small western town of Curtis Wells, *Lonesome Dove: The Series* follows first the romance and later the marriage of Newt Call and Hannah Peale, and the obsession that Clay Mosby, who owns most of the town, has with young Hannah, who looks remarkably like his late wife, Mary.

In addition to the talented regular Canadian cast of actors, the show also featured the recurring players, Dennis Weaver as legend Buffalo Bill Cody, Diahann Carroll as innkeeper and widow Ida Grayson, Paul Johansson as newspaperman and family member Austin Peale, and Paul Le Mat as Hannah's father and the editor of the local paper.

The last episode, *Buffalo Bill's Wild West Show,* in which Newt and Hannah head to the big city to catch Buffalo Bill's Wild West show saw Hannah stepping into the show, aired on Saturday 18 March 1995.

# LONESOME DOVE:
# THE OUTLAW YEARS
## 1995–1996

**THE** series originally went out on CTV (60 minutes) on 1 September 1995. The last episode, Love and War, aired on Thursday 16 May 1996.

The show was directed by Penelope Buitenhuis and Ken More and was written by Elizabeth Keyishian and Larry McMurtry. Again set in the small town of Curtis Wells, *Lonesome Dove: The Outlaw Years* begins two years after the death of Hannah

Call and follows what happened to the townspeople. Hannah's death had forever changed the lives of her husband Newt, father Josiah, brother Austin, and Clay Mosby, the man who loved her because she reminded him of his dead wife. Much darker than the original series, *The Outlaw Years* intended to show what happened when people lost everything, and there was nothing left that mattered to them.

After two years spent bounty hunting, womanizing, and drinking away the painful memories of his late wife, Newt returns to town to find many things have changed. His brother-in-law, Austin, is an alcoholic sheriff, his father-in-law, Josiah, is the town mayor.

The town is under the iron fist of Clayton Mosby, who cannot forget Hannah and The Lonesome Dove hotel, opened in the mini-series by Ida Grayson, now belongs to Amanda Carpenter.

Scott Bairstow again stars as Newt Call and Eric McCormack as Clay Mosby, Kelly Rowan is Mattie Shaw, Paul Johansson is Austin Peale and Tracy Scoggins is Amanda Carpenter (1995–6). In addition to the talented regular Canadian cast this season added American import Tracy Scoggins, and Paul Le Mat as Hannah's everchanged father Josiah Peale, Frank C. Turner as the sweetly innocent Unbob Finch, Bret Hart as bounty hunter Luther Root, Guylaine St-Onge as the soiled dove Florie and Sam Khouth as the local town doctor Ephraim Cleese.

# LUCKY LUKE
## 1991

**TERENCE** Hill starred in and directed this tongue in cheek Spaghetti Western series through the 1991–2 season. The hour long show was syndicated worldwide and was shot in color around Santa Fe, New Mexico.

Hill starred as Luke who became sheriff of the tough town, Daisy Hill. Co-starring as saloon owner, Lotta Legs was Nancy Morgan, and Ron Carey played the head of the Dalton Gang.

# MACKENZIE'S RAIDERS
## 1957–1959

**THE** 39 half-hour, black and white episodes were filmed by ZIV Productions for syndication in autumn 1958.

This series was set on the Mexican border of the 1870's and concerned the efforts of Colonel Ranald Mackenzie to protect American soil from Apaches and Bandidos.

Colonel Mackenzie, the commander of the 4th Cavalry Regiment at Fort Clark, Texas in 1873, has been given secret orders by President Grant and General Phil Sheridan to cross the Rio Grande to chase marauders back into Mexico. This was illegal and the colonel knew he and his men must never get caught on the Mexican side of the river.

Richard Carlson played Mackenzie. Jack Ging was his junior officer and Riley Hill played the capable sergeant. Other raiders were played by Morris Ankrum, Kenneth Alton, Charles Boaz, Jim Bridges, Louis Jean Heydt and Brett King.

Carlson, who was better known for his portrayal of Herbert Philbrick in *I Led Three Lives*, died in 1977.

Heydt died in 1960, Ankum died in 1964 of trichinosis, and King in 1999 of leukaemia.

# THE MAGNIFICENT SEVEN
## 1997

**THE hour long, color series ran occasionally on CBS through the 1997–8 season. The show was cancelled by CBS after the first season, but it was later renewed thanks to a large internet campaign to save it and CBS agreed to air the remaining six episodes that had been made. Unfortunately ratings faltered and CBS only aired two of the six before cancelling the program again.**

This show was loosely based on the five-movie series (but mostly the first two) from the 60's and 70's, which were in turn based on the 1954 Japanese film *Seven Samurai* by Akira Kurosawa. The Magnificent Seven are now hanging around, semi-retired, with Chris still their leader. They live together on a small spread.

When trouble flares and guns are required the seven are once again called to action. The series starred Michael Biehn as Chris and Andrew Kavovit, Ron Pearlman, Eric Close, Dale Midkiff, Rick Worthy and Anthony Starke. Robert Vaughn, who had starred in the film, made some guest appearances.

Following the cancellation Michael Biehn went on to star as explorer Judson Cross in the syndicated series *Adventure Inc*. Eric Close now plays FBI agent Martin Fitzgerald in the ensemble cast of the CBS series *Without a Trace*. Close also appeared in the ten-part series *Taken*.

Ron Perlman appears in the film *Nemesis* – the latest instalment of the enduring *Star Trek* saga – and has the title role in the feature film *Hellboy*.

Rick Worthy had a role in the ABC series *Push, Nevada,* which unfortunately became one of the first casualties of the 2002/2003 season.

Dale Midkiff appeared in the new *Nancy Drew* series. Andrew Kavovit has the lead role in the film *Meeksville Ghost* in which he co-stars with Judge Reinhold.

Anthony Starke worked on the hit series *Charmed, Angel,* and *CSI*.

# A MAN CALLED SHENANDOAH
## 13 SEPTEMBER 1965

**THE series ran for 34 half-hour, black and white episodes from 13 September 1965 to 5 September 1966.**

Robert Horton starred as an amnesiac wandering the untamed West, searching for his identity after being shot in an ambush. Two buffalo hunters find him and thinking he may have a price on his head, they carry him to town. Although he is not wanted, when he comes around, he cannot remember who he his. He calls himself Shenandoah.

Although Horton turned in some memorable performances and even sang the theme song over the end credits, he was not rewarded with a renewal from ABC and the show was cancelled before audiences ever learned his true story.

# THE MAN FROM BLACKHAWK
## 9 OCTOBER 1959

**THE half hour show, made by Screen Gem Productions for ABC, debuted in black and white on 9 October 1959 and closed on 23 September 1960. Although some episodes can be obtained in America on video, the show hasn't been seen on TV in re-runs. Only 37 episodes were made.**

Robert Rockwell starred as rugged insurance investigator, Sam Logan who worked for the Blackhawk Insurance Company of Chicago. He travelled through the West investigating claims and searching out fraudulent scams.

Although he dressed in city clothes and didn't shoot a gun, he did get in a few fist fights. He was a man well able to look after himself on the wild 1880's frontier.

Robert Rockwell died in 2003 of cancer.

---

## TRIVIA

Robert Rockwell starred in over 200 commercials and voiceovers, most notably as the grandfather treating his grandson to a piece of candy in the Werthers Original Candy spot. He was also a founding member of the California Artists Radio Theatre.

---

236

# MAN WITHOUT A GUN
## 1957

**THIS syndicated black and white half hour Western was produced by 20th Century Fox Television. The show went into production in October 1957 and through 1959, 52 episodes were shot.**

The series starred Rex Reason as Adam McLean, a hard-hitting newspaper editor in the rugged Yellowstone, Dakota Territory of the 1880's. He wanted to prove that the pen was mightier than the gun!

He never carried a gun but was aided in his struggle to bring law to town by Marshal Frank Tallman, played by Mort Mills. Other cast members included Harry Harvey as Mayor George and Dixon Forrest Taylor as Doc Brannon.

Forrest Taylor died in 1965, Harry Harvey died in 1985 and Mort Mills died in 1993.

Reason continues to travel the American countryside attending Western festivals.

# THE MARSHAL OF GUNSIGHT PASS
## 12 MARCH 1950

**THE half-hour, black and white ABC series ran from 12 March 1950 to 30 September 1950.**

The early short-lived show lies all but forgotten except by real television Western fans. Riley Hill, a veteran bad-man, finally had the chance to play the hero when he was cast as the marshal.

Comedian Roscoe Ates played the marshal's sidekick. He died from lung cancer on 1 March 1962 in Hollywood, California.

Hill reportedly lives in New Mexico.

# MAVERICK

## 22 SEPTEMBER 1957

**WARNER** Bros produced their amiable hour long western for ABC. They made 124 episodes, running from its debut on 22 September 1957 to 8 July 1962, when it went off the air.

James Garner played Bret Maverick, the devious card sharp hero, a self-centered, smooth talking ladies man more interested in fancy duds and serious violence avoidance than truth, justice and the American way in the series. Garner won the role after being spotted by Bill Or, an executive at Warners, in the film *Sayonara* with Marlon Brando.

Garner had to be proficient with a gun and a deck of cards and he said, 'I've handled guns ever since I was a kid. Shot rabbits all over Oklahoma. And my closest pal during the Korean War was a Reno black-jack dealer. He showed me quite a few things. I don't need a stand-in to do card tricks on *Maverick*. I can do my own.'

Creator Roy Huggins laughingly sent up the rugged myth of the West, 'I wanted to see how many rules we could break and get away with.' Garner agreed, '*Maverick* isn't a hoss opera in the classical tradition; if it could be categorized it could be described as an Eastern-Western.'

Warners avoided paying royalties to Huggins for the first screened episode, *War of the Silver Kings*, by using a 'studio-owned' book as the basis for the plot and the actual pilot was the second episode screened, *Point Blank*. Huggins was never given any on-screen credit as the creator until the 1994 movie, starring Mel Gibson and Jodie Foster, was released.

*Maverick* was sponsored by Kaiser Aluminum and Chemical Company. The company had been looking for scheduling to compete with the *Ed Sullivan Show* (CBS-TV) and the *Steve Allen Show* (NBC-TV) during Sunday evening prime time. When the show premiered public response to it was unprecedented and Garner, at least, expressed surprise when the ratings for the show surpassed both the Allen and Sullivan shows, 'When we started *Maverick* we thought we'd do well up to a point. We didn't foresee topping Sullivan.'

Suddenly the producers had to write in a brother for Bret so that enough shows could be made to keep up with demand. Jack Kelly was chosen to play Bart a straight man who was more conservative than his brother, but just as unlikely to join a fight that he could possibly avoid. The two characters began alternating as leads on the show as they journeyed through small towns with odd names like Oblivion and Apocalypse. Kelly appeared in 75 episodes and Garner in 52.

Along the way, they associated with fellow card sharks like Dandy Jim Buckley (Efrem Zimbalist Jr.) and Gentleman Jack Darby (Richard Long). Samantha Crawford played by Diane Brewster, was a lovely female rogue who loved to challenge the Maverick brothers to see who could out-con the other.

The wise-cracking Mavericks both liked the ladies.

During its five year run the black and white show attained the number one spot in the ratings and audiences responded well to the mix of traditional Western adventure with good-natured humor; Bret in particular became a hero for many armchair cowboys. As a result, the writers increasingly began to play up the comedy elements, expanding the storylines to satirize other prime time programming and *Maverick* lampooned everything from *Gunsmoke* to *Dragnet*. The show also used actors known for other roles, like Edd 'Kookie' Byrnes from *77 Sunset Strip*, for cameo roles designed to make viewers' heads turn.

Critics found it difficult to explain the craze surrounding the show but many thought it was partly because the public were already growing fed up with traditional Westerns, and that there was a growing mass acceptance of the anti-hero.

Garner became dissatisfied with the series and he said later, 'After the first year, I didn't look at *Maverick*.' He went on, 'They slapped the series together and it was a case of sink or swim. The first three scripts were pretty straight; but I just couldn't take the character seriously. Nor could the director.'

The show continued to enjoy solid ratings through to the end of the 1950's, but hit a snag in 1960 when James Garner left the program over a contract dispute, 'As far as I'm concerned I'm all through at the studio. The reason I'm quitting is simple. They quit paying me. And that is a breach of contract. They said they weren't paying me because there were no more scripts for *Maverick*.' There had been a writer's strike going on in Hollywood, but Garner was quick to jump from the studio, saying, 'I'm ready to go on to other things.'

Still, he sued Warner Bros saying they had interfered with his right to work. In retaliation the studio wrote to everyone in the industry warning them that as far as they were concerned, he was still under contract to them and hiring him would be at their own peril. Kelly was also taken off contract and similar warnings were issued about him. Finally Garner and Jack Warner met head to head in court and Garner

won his suit. At the time he stated he wouldn't go back into television and wanted instead to work on movies, 'I loved Bret Maverick. But I had to think in terms of career. And *Maverick* wasn't going to last forever. I wanted to make pictures and I needed a certain amount of freedom to do it, but whenever a chance to do a picture came up, Warner's said, 'Absolutely not! You couldn't get me back in the saddle with a crane.' He later confessed that being under contract to Warners had been hard, 'I felt like a side of beef hung up in the refrigerator. From time to time they'd slice off a piece of me and bring it out on display'.'

It had not been a secret that Garner had been unhappy since the departure of Roy Huggins, who had left to head up TV production at 20th Century Fox, 'The show we did with Huggins was humor, genuine humor. The show they're doing now is comedy, slapstick.'

Later Garner invariably referred to *Maverick* as, 'That thing.' In fact it may simply have been that Garner was just tired of working on it, 'I don't think people have any idea how physically killing it is on a human being to be on screen every week in a one hour action series. I'm talking about a cumulative effect. When you do it for too many years, it'll get you. We have doubles, but you can use them only in long shots. So you've got to flop yourself on the ground here, and guys punch you and you get a little beat up there, and eventually you wind up comparing broken bones and torn muscles. I really felt like a plow horse who'd pulled the goddamn plow too long.'

To replace him, the producers introduced a new Maverick cousin, Beau.

Beau had been to London for his schooling and returned home, a 'proper English gentleman', to tend the family fortunes. Beau was played by Roger Moore, who starred in 15 episodes. The show later added another brother named Brent before finally ending its run in the summer of 1962. Robert Colbert played Brent Maverick.

Since closing, *Maverick* has continued to be a popular member of the cult television pantheon. Even today, it remains a favorite in syndication. Its enduring status as a beloved show also led to two short-lived follow-up series, *Young Maverick* and *Bret Maverick*, and a 1994 movie version of *Maverick* that featured original star James Garner alongside Mel Gibson and Jodie Foster. The remakes and follow-up prove that *Maverick*'s mixture of tumbleweeds and laughs was an enduring one indeed.

Later in life Garner mellowed somewhat toward the original series, 'I recall the original *Maverick* we ever filmed. It was a re-make of *Rocky Mountain*, an Errol Flynn movie; practically all of the first *Mavericks* were re-writes of old Warner Bros pictures. I even wore the coat and vest Flynn wore in *Rocky Mountain*, because they used stock footage from the movie for long shots, so I had to match my clothes to his. The first three episodes were directed by Budd Boetticher... He started injecting little bitty pieces of humor into the series almost immediately.'

Garner, Moore and Colbert remain active. Kelly died from a massive stroke on 7 November 1992, aged 65.

Moore also went on to international stardom as James Bond. Garner later scored another huge hit with *The Rockford Files*.

In 2001 he confessed to the *LA Times* that he preferred working to giving interviews, 'I get tired of talking about myself,' and he said about acting, 'When I was 50 I realized I might have a career here.'

Eighteen issues of *Maverick* comics were published between 1958 and 1962.

Eventually in 1977, despite all the bitterness he felt toward Warner Bros, Garner became involved in a new *Maverick* project although he emphasized he would have

no long-term involvement. He agreed to star in a two hour movie based on his old classic, 'But if that becomes the successful pilot for a fresh series, Warner Bros is going to have to find another star to roam the weekly range.'

In a Playboy interview in 1980 he commented, 'When I started *Maverick* there were about 17 Westerns on TV. I think it was the first pinprick in the balloon of TV Westerns, and when the series finished, so were TV Westerns. The same thing was true of *Rockford;* there were umpteen detective series when *The Rockford Files* first went on the air. How many detective series were left when it finished? ... I come in and scrape 'em up. I'm a killer of genres.'

# McCLOUD
## 16 September 1970

**THE** series of 90 minute color shows debuted on NBC on 16 September 1970 as part of the company's Mystery Movie franchise. The last episode aired on 28 August 1977, but some TV movies have been seen since then.

**Universal Television made the series. Stunts were by Bill Catching.**

Sam McCloud, played by Dennis Weaver, was a contemporary Deputy Marshal from Taos, New Mexico. When he is temporarily assigned to Manhattan's 27th Precinct, it is much to the dismay of Chief Peter B Clifford. McCloud chases crooks to the Big Apple and iconically rides a horse through the traffic filled streets.

McCloud takes most things into his own hands, reverting back to Western ways, and he often dragged Sergeant Joe Broadhurst, played by Terry Carter, into trouble with him.

Diane Muldaur was Sam's city girlfriend, Chris Coughlin. JD Cannon was the frustrated and harassed Chief.

Weaver won two Emmys for his portrayal of McCloud. During his time on the show, Weaver was elected president of the Screen Actor's Guild for several years. He died on 24 February 2006 following complications from cancer.

# THE MEN FROM SHILO
## 16 SEPTEMBER 1970

**TWENTY** four 90 minute episodes of the re-tooled The Virginian ran on NBC between 16 September 1970 and 8 September 1971.

James Drury was still around as the mysterious Virginian, sporting longer sideburns and Doug McClure was also back as Trampas; this time with a moustache.

The setting had moved forward in time to the early years of the 20th century and the latest owner of Shiloh Ranch, which lay 40 miles outside of Medicine Bow, Wyoming, was Colonel Alan MacKenzie, played by Stewart Granger. His manner, as a former Indian military academy member, was formal. He even brought his own batman, Parker, played by John McLiam, to the ranch.

Shiloh, which covered thousands of square miles of mountains, plains, tumbling waterfalls and multi-colored canyons, remained the wonderful backdrop to the conflict between those who embraced change and all that new development has to offer and those who wanted things to remain as they had always been. Classic difficulties of the time were still raised including water rights, rustlers and squatters, but the cowboy whose law was his six-gun was on the way out and gunfighters were the exception rather than the rule.

Lee Majors played Roy Tate, a ranch hand, en route from *The Big Valley* to a bionic body.

The feminine touch that had existed in *The Virginian* was sorely missing in this series.

Unwisely the producers on *The Men From Shiloh* adopted the formula of a rotating storyline and Trampas and the Virginian appeared in different storylines, each one made by a different producer. It led to a lack of continuity and Lee Majors was rarely given a chance to make an impression. Stewart Granger's storylines were unmemorable. The Granger character lacked warmth and he expressed his personal dissatisfaction with the series, 'I created the role myself and the episodes took ten days at a time to shoot. But I have to say again I did not enjoy doing the show. I hate doing TV. It's all rush and dash and you work too many hours. It is done too quickly, so there is no quality in a show.'

Granger's general dissatisfaction with the show included fellow cast members and he was often at odds with James Drury who could be as enigmatic as The Virginian himself. He was well known for his temperamental outbursts and he tended to be difficult in interviews and hated being photographed with other members of the cast.

It became obvious that *The Men From Shiloh* couldn't survive into a second season and the final episodes went unnoticed. In fact its failure to attract a dedicated audience had as much to do with the decline of the Western genre as with the quality of the show itself and, in many respects, this was the last of the great Westerns. Expectations for it had been high, perhaps too high, but viewers were disappointed and frustrated by the new format. Despite *The Men From Shiloh* attracting many of Hollywood's top stars as guests, time had run out by the end of the 1970–1 season.

Following the cancellation of *The Men From Shiloh*, Drury found work hard to come by. His reputation for being demanding on set worked against him and his only subsequent series was *Firehouse* in 1974. He worked on a *Virginian* TV movie which starred Bill Pullman in his own role.

He lives in Houston.

Doug McClure went on to star in the short-lived Western series *The Barbary Coast* with William Shatner, a series of Edgar Rice Burroughs fantasy movies filmed in England and the sitcom *Out of this World*. His last TV appearance was on an episode of *One West Waikiki* and he could be seen with a host of TV Western favorites in the big screen version of *Maverick*.

In a 1994 interview McClure expressed plans for the return of Trampas to TV, 'It's the turn of the century. A lot of it would unfold as you tell the story. Part of that would be that he's still a cowboy, a top hand, but the world has changed. There's a car now. There's flushing toilets. Things have changed and become industrial. That would make it interesting.'

Unfortunately McClure's premature death at the age of 59 from lung cancer on 4 February 1995 extinguished all hopes of ever seeing him as Trampas again except in reruns of *The Virginian* and *The Men From Shiloh*.

Granger died. Lee Majors lives in Florida.

# THE MONROES
## 7 SEPTEMBER 1966

**THE hour long, color show was filmed by Century Fox TV on location in Jackson Hole, Wyoming. It debuted on ABC on 7 September 1966 and ran for just 17 episodes before leaving the air on 30 August 1967.**

As the Monroe family is crossing a wild river on the way to Wyoming, a current sweeps the parents away to their deaths.

It is 1876 and 18-year-old Clayt and his 16-year-old sister, Kathy, are left to care for their three siblings. Michael Anderson Jr., was Clayt, Barbara Hershey was Kathy, Keith and Kevin Schultz played twin brothers and Tammy Locke was the little sister, Amy.

Wicked Major Mapoy, who ruled the valley that the Monroes finally settle in, does everything he can to get rid of the children.

Liam Sullivan was Major Mapoy. Ben Johnson starred as a friendly one-armed cowboy called Sleeve. James Westmoreland was one of Mapoy's men smitten with Kathy. Ron Sable starred as Dirty Jim, an Indian who attaches himself to the family.

Sullivan and Johnson have died.

Anderson Jr., Hershey and Soble are the only cast members still involved in the industry.

# MY FRIEND FLICKA
## 10 February 1956

**THE** series derived from the stories of Mary O'Hara and premiered on the CBS network on 10 February 1956. It left the air on 18 May 1958 after 39 episodes. Although filmed in color, CBS ran the show in black and white. When NBC reran it the next year, they showed it in color.

The half-hour, black and white show, produced by 20th Century Fox TV revolved around young Ken McLaughlin and his magnificent horse, Flicka. Set at the Goose Bar Ranch in Montana late in the 19th Century, Ken, played by young Canadian actor Johnny Washbrook, his mother Nell (Anita Louise) and father Rob (Gene Evans) struggled to ranch and deal with the problems of a rough land. The premise of the show was quietly unassuming and it praised family values and the ethic of hard work.

Anita Louise died in 1970 of a stroke. Evans died in 1998. Washbrook is no longer involved in the film industry and his whereabouts remain something of a

mystery after his family took him back to their native Toronto after the series folded.

*Gene Evans who played Rob in* My Friend Flicka, *died in 1998*

## TRIVIA

Flicka means 'little girl' in the Swedish language but the horse's real name was Wahama. She was a pure Arabian chestnut trained by Les Hilton. Her stunt double in the series was a quarterhorse-type gelding named Goldie.

# NAKIA
## 21 SEPTEMBER 1974

**THE** show, filmed in color, debuted on 21 September 1974 on ABC. It was produced by Charles Larson and was shot on location in Albuquerque and Indian Pueblos. There had been a made-for-TV movie of the same name that served as the pilot aired on 17 April 1974.

*Nakia* was an hour long contemporary western set in modern day New Mexico. Deputy Nakia Parker, a man of Indian heritage, refused to give up his ways or his Indian friends.

His boss was Sheriff Sam Jericho, played by Arthur Kennedy. Taylor Lacher starred as Deputy Hubbel Martin and John Tenorio was a young Indian, Half Cub.

Gloria DeHaven played Irene James, the office secretary.

Robert Forster starred as Nakia. He was honest and only made decisions based on the evidence to hand.

The show didn't do very well and ran against *The Carol Burnett Show* on CBS at 10.00 pm, and after 13 episodes the series was gone, its last episode airing on 28 December 1974.

Part of the problem stemmed from its Native American influence. Although Forster made a convincing Navajo, many of the guest-stars looked or acted nothing like their Native American characters. Add to that the fact that many of the plots relied on Nakia's native abilities (he was able to silently sneak up on someone while wearing his moccasins, for example) and it is no wonder that the series didn't last.

Arthur Kennedy died on 5 January 1990.

Robert Forster remains much in demand in Hollywood.

# NED BLESSING, THE STORY OF MY LIFE AND TIMES
## 18 AUGUST 1993

**THE hour long, color series was produced by CBS Television and it debuted on 18 August 1993. It ran for just six episodes before the plug was pulled due to the lack of audience. However the program was erratically aired and it simply never caught on.**

In this long forgotten but interesting show, Brad Johnson starred as gunfighter, Ned Blessing. In the cell of a small town jail an elderly Ned Blessing, having lived a long and tumultuous life, awaits a rendezvous with the hangman's noose. While waiting to pay for his misdeeds, he spends his last days writing an account of his exploits, good and bad.

Johnson is still active in the industry and later starred in *Soldier of Fortune*.

# THE NEW LAND
## 14 SEPTEMBER 1974

**THE hour long color series went on air on ABC on 14 September 1974. It managed only six episodes before leaving the schedule on 19 October 1974.**

This show concerned the hardships and triumphs of the Larsons, a Scandinavian immigrant family who settle in Solna, New Mexico in 1858.

The family was headed by Anna, played by Bonnie Bedelia and Christian, played by Scott Thomas. Kurt Russell starred as Bo, the eldest son and Todd Lookinland and Debbie Lytton played Tuliff and Annelisse.

# THE NEW ZORRO
## 5 JANUARY 1990

**THE** legendary Zorro shot back onto The Family Channel Network in this half hour color series. It debuted on 5 January 1990 and starred Duncan Regehr in the title role. The 22 shows per series were shot outside Madrid, Spain throughout the three seasons it aired.

Henry Darrow starred as Don Diego/Zorro's father, Don Alejandro. Patrice Camhi starred as Victoria, a tavern owner in Pueblo De Los Angeles around 1840. Only deaf mute, Felipe, knows Zorro's true identity. Cruel Alcade would give anything to find the secret out.

Juan Botta and Michael Tylo starred as Felipe and the Alcade respectively.

# NICHOLS

## 16 SEPTEMBER 1971

**THE hour long color show debuted on NBC on 16 September 1971. The company cut Nichols and the series finished after 26 episodes on 1 August 1972.**

James Garner had left the small screen to make movies after walking away from *Maverick* in the early 60's, swearing he would never return and lamenting the fact that he'd had no control of his work. By 1971 he was ready to change his mind, saying that the kind of movies he enjoyed working on such as *Support Your Local Sheriff* had become rarities in what was increasingly 'a pornographic bullpen.' Garner said, 'I got tired of reading scripts that repelled me. I turned down lots of them. Maybe I'm a prude.'

Prude or not, he'd been a hero to all the contract players in the industry by defying Warner studio boss, Jack Warner, and sitting out the remainder of his one year contract. He had believed he was right and had won his case, but hadn't worked for 12 months. Eventually he set up his Cherokee Production Company and confessed, 'I said I wouldn't return to TV unless I was broke or the business changed. I'm not broke. The business *has* changed.'

The arrangement Garner now struck with NBC suited him and the amount of money they offered him to choose any vehicle he liked was sufficient to tempt him back into the saddle. Executive producer, Meta Rosenberg, had assigned three writers to, 'come up with something.' One came up with a detective series, another a lawyer show, but eventually Rosenberg and Garner selected a winner, Frank Pierson who wrote the pre-World War One Western. Pierson went on to become the producer and director of *Nichols*.

Garner had more say in what went on, 'I own *Nichols*. I made a deal with NBC to deliver twenty four one-hour shows and they can run them twice and that's that.'

The star played a hesitant sheriff in the town of Nichols, Arizona in 1914, where he constantly ran up against the Ketchum clan, 'I'm very unwilling. I owe the town a lot of money and pay off my debt by working as sheriff. But I always end up owing them more than my salary. So they've got a sheriff for nothing.'

The early 20th century background was interesting for a Western series and automobiles and motor cycles were often used in the show. The sheriff himself rode a 1913 Harley Davidson. He didn't wear a gun and talked his way out of tricky situations.

Margot Kidder starred as Ruth, Garner's girlfriend, Neva Patterson played Ma Ketchum, Stuart Margolin and John Beck were her worthless sons.

Despite winning critical acclaim, *Nichols* unexpectedly failed to catch on with audiences. Producers considered that perhaps the character of Nichols was not clearly defined so they made some changes and moved the show from Thursday to Tuesday nights at 9.30 pm.

Garner himself said that he didn't believe in ratings, 'I felt the same way when I was doing *Maverick* and the ratings were up there consistently. It's an antiquated system. We all know it. That includes the network people. Yet we have to live by it. I'm surprised to see grown men acting according to what they disbelieve.

'I'm an actor and a producer. I make the best films I can. I don't worry over demographics. That's the word now! I'd throw this system out. You don't have to leave everything to such small samplings.'

Garner may have despised the rating system, but the changes had already begun on *Nichols* including changing the show's title to *James Garner as Nichols*, shifting the emphasis of his character and setting more of the adventures out of town, 'Situations were instigated by the people around me in the show. Now I'll be inaugurating more of them. I'll be less passive. Instead of reacting, I'll be more aggressive.'

The changes were not enough to save it. Once again Garner felt disillusioned with television, 'When you sign up, you go over to the property department and just pick out your ulcer.' He said, '*Nichols* was my favorite of all the shows, but it was five or ten years ahead of its time. Chevrolet, its sponsor, made a deal with NBC to get rid of it. I knew we got cancelled, so I decided to kill him off in the last episode.'

'I remember going to Detroit and showing Chevrolet the series and they were disappointed because it wasn't *Maverick*. Frankly *Nichols* was above their heads and above their intelligence. They just didn't understand it and so they walked away. They didn't wait to see whether or not it would be a clanker on the air. Which it was not.

'I think *Nichols* would have built up its audience and become stronger and stronger, but they really didn't give it a chance.'

# THE NINE LIVES OF ELFEGO BACA
## 1958

**THIS** action-filled family-oriented hour was produced for ABC. It also went into syndication. It was shot in black and white and later in color. Beginning in October of 1958, six episodes ran through the 1958–9 season and more followed the following year.

The story of a mild-mannered New Mexico lawman was one of several shows that ran under the *Walt Disney Presents* banner. It starred Robert Loggia as the real life Mexican lawman of Socorro County, New Mexico, Elfego Baca. Skip Homeier starred as Ross Mantee.

Lisa Montell, Nestor Paiva and Robert Simon also featured.

Baca was a living Western legend, plagued by the constant onslaught of young guns, all eager to prove their mettle by killing him to become the new fastest-gun in the West.

Location work was filmed Santa Fe and Cerrillos.

Loggia went on to find stardom in his next weekly TV assignment as a good-guy burglar in 1967's *T.H.E. Cat.* He has had a fitfully successful movie career as a leading man, but finally came into his own when he took off his toupee and became a

character actor, often in roles requiring quiet menace. As Richard Gere's bullying father, Loggia dominated the early scenes of *An Officer and a Gentleman* (1981), and was equally effective as the villain in *Curse of the Pink Panther* (1982). He also starred as mafia functionaries in *Scarface* (1983) and *Prizzi's Honor* (1985). He was nominated for an Oscar for his portrayal of a detective in *The Jagged Edge* (1985), but his most likeable screen character has been the toy manufacturer in *Big* (1988), the film in which he and Tom Hanks dance to the tune of 'Heart and Soul' on a gigantic keyboard.

Loggia also worked the television series *Mancuso, FBI* and starred as Grandpa Victor in *Malcolm in the Middle.*

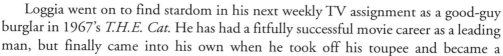

253

# NORTH AND SOUTH
## 1985

**THIS** 60 minute epic TV series was adapted from John Jakes' best selling novel and was broadcast on the NBC Network in 1985. Music was by Bill Conti. Cinematography was by Stevan Larner and it was directed by Richard T. Heffron.

The impressive cast of *North and South* included Patrick Swayze as Orry Main, James Read as George Hazard, Lesley-Anne Down, Wendy Kilbourne, Kirstie Alley, Jean Simmons, Terri Garber, Genie Francis, Philip Casnoff, Lewis Smith, John Stockwell, David Carradine, Inga Swenson, Jonathan Frakes, Wendy Fulton, Jim Metzler, Tony Frank, Erica Gimpel, William Ostrander, Andy Stahl, Georg Stanford Brown, Olivia Cole, Robert Mitchum, Hal Holbrook, Robert Guillaume, Morgan Fairchild, Johnny Cash, Gene Kelly, David Ogden Stiers, Forest Whitaker, Elizabeth Taylor.

The series outlined the friendship between the two boys, George Hazard and Orry Main, who meet at West Point. George is from a wealthy Pennsylvania steel family and Orry is from a Southern plantation where his family keep slaves. In the years leading up to the Civil War their friendship is tested as their families interact and hostilities between the North and South increase.

The first series, in particular, was a considerable success with audiences and critics. There is talk of doing another miniseries called *North and South: The Next Generation*. This miniseries would focus on the mid 20th century descendants of the Mains and Hazards as they deal with issues such as the Cold War, Civil Rights, the Kennedy Assassinations, Mowtown music, Beatlemania, Psycedelic Rock, the Vietnam War, Woodstock, and Watergate.

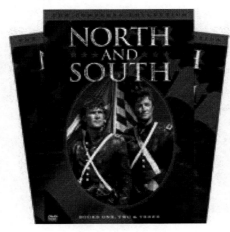

# NORTHWEST PASSAGE
## 14 September 1958

**MGM** TV made this half-hour color series. The show premiered on the NBC Network on 14 September 1958 and it unfortunately found itself up against shows like Maverick. Although it was quickly rescheduled it left the air after its 26 episode run on 8 September 1959.

Set during the French and Indian War of 1754–1759 the story takes place in what later became New York State. Major Robert Rogers had formed Roger's Rangers to explore the wilderness and to help search for a route across America by water, but the men found themselves in the middle of a major battle.

Rogers was an experienced explorer and Indian fighter, as was Marriner. Towne was a Harvard graduate from a wealthy family who became the mapmaker for the Rangers. Keith Larsen was Major Robert Rogers, Buddy Ebsen was Sergeant Hunk Marriner and Don Burnett was Ensign Langdon Towne. Philip Tonge was General Amherst.

Philip Towne died right after the show ended in 1959.

# THE OREGON TRAIL
## 21 September 1977

**THE** show was shot in color at an hour in length by Universal City Studios for NBC. Much of the location work was done in Flagstaff, Arizona. It debuted on NBC on 21 September 1977, but it was cancelled after six episodes and it went off the air on 26 October 1977. The remaining seven episodes were unaired by NBC although some of these were later spliced together to make TV movies.

Evan Thorpe, disillusioned with life in Illinois, decided to leave his farm to take his three children along the Oregon Trail so he could try his hand out West. They joined a wagon train headed for the Oregon Territories and Thorpe was soon elected wagon master. Along the way they faced Indian marauders, storms, con men, and plenty more.

Rod Taylor starred as Thorpe. Andrew Stevens played his son Andrew, Tony Becker was William, the youngest son and Gina Maria Smika played Rachel, his daughter. Charles Napier was the unfriendly scout, Luther Sprague and Darleen Carr was Thorpe's love interest, Margaret Devlin.

All cast members remain active in the industry with Stevens now a successful producer.

# THE OUTCASTS
## 23 September 1968

**THE violent series ran for 26 episodes from 23 September 1968 to 15 September 1969. Screen Gems produced the hour long colour show for ABC.**

*The Outcasts* was an excellent Western series starring Don Murray and Otis Young. Murray played Earl Corey, an ex-Confederate officer and former slave owner who had lost everything. He teamed up with newly released slave Jemal David, played by Young, and they became bounty hunters.

Produced during a time of racial unrest, *The Outcasts* depicted a situation in which blacks and whites could live together – but with an underlying and not-always-hidden hostility.

*The Outcasts* was probably most notable for being the first television Western with an African-American co-star. Its short run probably reflected the rapidly-changing US racial climate in the late 1960's more than the quality of the series itself.

Otis Young died of a stroke, aged 69, on 12 October 2001.

# OUTLAWS
## 28 December 1986

**THE hour long show was shot in color and debuted on CBS on 28 December 1986. It left the air on May 1987 when the audience failed to warm to it.**

*Outlaws* was a far-fetched sci-fi Western. Starting in 1899, Texas Sheriff John Grail was in pursuit of bank robber Harland Pike and his gang. A freak electrical storm transported them all to a contemporary Texas. Pike and Grail don't understand what has happened to them but had to reconcile their differences so they can adjust to their new environment. Together they opened the Double Eagle Detective Agency.

The show had a strong cast including Rod Taylor as Grail, William Lucking as Pike. Patrick Houser played Billy, a gang member, Charles Napier was Wolfson Larsen and Richard Rountree was Isiah 'Ice' McAdams. Christina Belford starred as Lieutenant Maggie Randall, who was their liaison officer at the Houston Police Department.

# THE OUTLAWS
## 29 September 1960

**THIS** hour long, black and white NBC series debuted on 29 September 1960 and left the air after 50 episodes on 13 September 1962. The show commanded the coveted 7.30–8.30 NBC Thursday night line-up following on the heels of such popular Western shows as Gunsmoke, The Life and Legend of Wyatt Earp, Have Gun, Will Travel, and Maverick.

*The Outlaws* looked at the struggle between the lawmen and outlaws in the Oklahoma Territory of the Old West during the 1890's. Each story was seen through the eyes of the outlaw being pursued through that episode and was shot in documentary style.

Veteran film heavy, Barton MacLane starred as Chief Marshal Frank Caine. Don Collier was Deputy Will Foreman and Jock Gaynor as Deputy Heck Martin. In a land full of land grabbers, train robbers, thieves and murderers, the local peace officer was hard-pressed to maintain any semblance of law and order.

More often than not, outlaws would strike and run, escaping into territory so remote that danger lurked around each corner. No ordinary town sheriff could have handled the devious badmen, and people like Bill Doolin, the Daltons, and Sam Bass eluded capture for many years.

What was needed was a drastic change in the Territorial judicial system, and President Grover Cleveland took action. He appointed Caine and two deputies. Since Guthrie was the Territorial capital at the time, it became the headquarters for the Office of the Marshal Service, a home base to tie all the stories together.

In the second season, Collier was promoted to Marshal and Slim Pickens as Slim and Bruce Yarnell as Deputy Marshal Chalk Breeson were added to the cast.

Throughout the series, there was a stream of outstanding guest stars including Jack Lord, Vic Morrow, Dean Stockwell, Leonard Nimoy, Gene Evans, Ray Walston,

Warren Oats, Simon Oakland, Jackie Coogan, James Coburn, Robert Culp, Steve Forrest, and William Shatner. Even little Johnny Washburn (*My Friend Flika*) had a starring role as a 12-year-old orphan in one of the episodes. Some of Hollywood's leading ladies also made appearances. Stars like Sue Ann Langdon, Pippa Scott, Anne Helm, Phyllis Thaxter, Jean Allison, Diane Foster, and Patricia Barry had prominent parts.

Barton MacLane died in 1969 of cancer, Slim Pickens in 1983 of a brain tumor, Bruce Yarnell died in 1973 in a plane crash and Jock Gaynor died in 1998.

Collier went on to work on *High Chaparral* and *The Young Riders*.

# OVERLAND TRAIL
## 7 FEBRUARY 1960

**SEVENTY** eight hour long black and white shows were made by Revue Productions for NBC and it debuted on 7 February 1960. Sadly only 17 episodes were made and it left the air on 11 September 1960.

*Overland Trail* concerned two men, Fred Kelly, played by William Bendix, a tough superintendent of a stage line, and his young assistant Frank 'Flip' Flippen, played by Doug McClure.

Together they were responsible for moving the stage line from Missouri, across the Rockies and on to California and the Pacific Ocean. Kelly was a crusty old soul, while Flip, who had been raised by Indians, had a more adventurous streak.

Bendix died in 1964 of pneumonia.

McClure died of lung cancer. He received his star on Hollywood's Walk of Fame two months before his premature death on 4 February 1995, aged just 59.

# PARADISE
## 27 OCTOBER 1988

**THIS** series debuted on 27 October 1988. It finished 56 episodes later on 10 May 1991. The shows were an hour long and filmed in color for CBS by David Jacobs and Lorimar Productions. The majority of filming took place on Disney Location Ranch in Placerita Canyon Newhall California, with additional scenes for episodes filmed at notable western locations such as Vasquez Rocks and other familiar locations.

Left to Right:

*Brian Lando*
*Lee Horsley*
*Sigrid Thornton*
*Michael Patrick Carter*
*Matthew Newmark*
*Jenny Beck*
and
*Dehl Berti*

Lee Horsley played gunfighter, Ethan Allen Cord. He plied his trade in the mining town Paradise in the 1890's but was unexpectedly landed with having to care for his dying sister's four children. He reluctantly accepts the responsibility and settles down on a ranch outside town. The series began with Cord being shot and waking up to find his niece and nephews tending him.

The town's citizens often called on his services to aid their defense against outlaws. Australian actress Sigrid Thornton played Amelia Lawson, Cord's love interest.

Cord's only friend was Indian Shaman, John Taylor, played by Dehl Berti. The four children were Jenny Beck as Claire, Matthew Newmark as Joesph, Brian Lando as Ben and Michael Patrick as George. James Crittendon was town Deputy Charlie.

A number of old Western stars appeared on the show including William Smith, Robert Fuller Jack Elam, Buck Taylor, Chuck Connors, Don Stroud, and Pernell Roberts. In a memorable two-part episode, Gene Barry and Hugh O'Brien recreated their 1950's television roles of legendary gunslingers Bat Masterson and Wyatt Earp.

The final episode of the series ended with Sheriff Cord sending his family out of town, while he prepared to meet his old arch enemy in one final gunfight to determine who was the fastest on the draw.

Dehl Berti died on 26 November 1991.

Horsley went on to star in *Hawkeye* and Thornton returned to Australia.

## TRIVIA

In the third and final season some changes were made to the series and a new opening sequence introduced its new name, *Guns of Paradise*, an apparent attempt to remind viewers that the program, despite its title, was a Western.

# PEACEMAKERS
## 30 JULY 2003

THE show which debuted on 30 July 2003, by Michael R. Joyce Productions, Inc. began with a two-hour pilot and was followed by a further eight episodes. Rick Ramage was the writer/executive producer and the director/co-executive producer was Larry Carroll.

The Western Frontier was fast disappearing with an encroaching civilization and the arrival of the industrial age in 1882 and nowhere was the clash of the old and new more evident than in law enforcement. With the advent of such innovations as fingerprinting and photography, modern police investigation was born.

*Peacemakers* was set in the frontier town of Silver City and the story revolves around the often contentious relationship between a grizzled, middle-aged Federal Marshall Jared Stone, played by Tom Berenger and his cocky young deputy, Larimer Finch played by Peter O'Meara. Finch was a British-born former Pinkerton agent from Chicago with a degree from Yale and a wagonload of forensic equipment. Stone on the other hand was a hard-bitten, set-in-his-ways federal marshal. Although Stone preferred to use tried-and-true methods in tracking down criminals, he begrudgingly acknowledged that Finch's newfangled techniques brought results. 'It's called a fingerprint,' explained Finch as he worked on a murder suspect with patronizing stuffiness.

Practically everyone who previewed the USA Network adventure series arrived at the same descriptive conclusion: 'CSI Goes West.'

Back in the mid 70's *Hec Ramsey* featured Richard Boone as an aging gunfighter who used 'modern' scientific methods in his job as deputy sheriff, much to the dismay of Rick Lenz, the young police chief who hired him. That series fared better than *Peacemakers*.

---

## TRIVIA

The show was nominated for a 2004 Canadian Society of Cinematographers Award for 'Best Cinematography in TV Drama'. It also won the 2004 'Bronze Wrangler' Western Heritage Award for 'Outstanding Factual or Fictional Drama'.

# PISTOLS 'N' PETTICOATS
## 17 SEPTEMBER 1966

**THE show was shot in color by Universal TV and debuted on CBS on 17 September 1966, running to 19 August 1967. Twenty six episodes were made together with a pilot which never aired.**

This half hour comedy series, created by George Tibbles, took place around the town of Wretched, Colorado and its main theme was the legend about sharp shooting Henrietta Hanks and her family.

> *'Here's the legend about the Hanks in* Pistols 'n Petticoats. *Henrietta can fire a gun with one hand mik'in the goat and hit a coyote on the run in* Pistols n Petticoats. *The story goes that gradma was the best at shootin' buttons off a wrestlers vest. Shootin' buttons off a wrestlers vest. Grandpa kept his gun in trim, nobody messed around with him. Nobody messed around with him. Chasin' bandits were fun for them from Bristol to Terra Haute. Everybody in the west would run from* Pistols n Petticoats. *That's the legend about the Hanks, just as she was wrote. They kept busy protecting banks in* Pistols n Petticoats.*'*

Ann Sheridan starred as Henrietta and Douglas V Fowley was Grandpa Hanks. Sheridan died of cancer of the oesophagus and liver aged 51 after filming only 21 episodes on 21 January 1967. She had been ill throughout filming and was evidently too sick to appear in some segments and she only had a couple of lines in others. The ones with less of Sheridan were not nearly as funny as the others and the series was doomed with her loss.

Ruth McDevitt was Grandma. Carole Wells was Lucy, the only Hanks who couldn't use a gun, Gary Vinson filled out the cast as Sheriff Sikes. Lon Chaney Jr., appeared as Chief Eagle Shadow.

Fowley, McDevitt and Vinson have all died.

## TRIVIA

Warner Bros billed Sheridan as the 'oomph' girl and she later became the inspiration for the brand of woman's house-slippers called 'Oomphies'.

# PONY EXPRESS
## 1959

**THIS half hour, black and white show was shot around Phoenix, Arizona. It aired on NBC through the autumn 1959.**

*Pony Express* starred Grant Sullivan as Division Agent, Brett Clark.

Don Dorrell played his assistant and friend, Donovan and veteran character actor, Earle Hodgins rounded out the cast as the horse tender.

The series dealt with the problems of running the Pony Express through dangerous country.

Hodgins died and neither Sullivan nor Dorrell remained active in the industry.

# THE QUEST
## 22 SEPTEMBER 1976

**THE hour long action packed show was shot in color by Columbia Pictures TV and debuted on NBC on 22 September 1976. Much of the location work was filmed in Tucson, Arizona. The series left the air on 29 December 1976.**

Morgan and Quentin Beaudine's quest was the search for their sister, Patricia, who had been captured by Cheyenne. After years of separation they joined forces and set out together to find her.

Kurt Russell starred as Morgan, who had been raised by Indians and Tim Matheson starred as his brother, Quentin, who had been educated in San Francisco.

| TRIVIA | TRIVIA |
|---|---|
| Matheson, along with partner Dan Grodnik, bought National Lampoon in 1989 when the magazine was facing financial decline. They were unable to reverse the decline and sold it in 1991. He has acted in over a hundred film and television projects and between 1999 and 2003 had a recurring role as Vice President John Hoynes on *The West Wing*. | Russell played pro baseball (2nd base, California Angels) until a torn shoulder muscle forced retirement in 1973. His friend, Ron Shelton wrote the Crash Davis role in *Bull Durham* (1988) for him but the studio insisted on Kevin Costner. His father is Bing Russell a former baseball player, who played the deputy sherriff on *Bonanza* for six years. |

# THE RANGE RIDER
## 1952

**GENE** Autry's Flying A Productions made this classic action filled TV series. It ran from the autumn 1952 until 1954. The total of 78 episodes could still be seen in syndication as late as 1965.

*The Range Rider* featured the exploits of the honest, principled and tough Range Rider and his boyish sidekick, Dick West. Jock Mahoney starred as The Range Rider and Dick Jones was his young friend. Dressed in a fringed buckskin shirt and a white Stetson, the Range Rider wore moccasins not boots.

Both lead characters romanced the ladies and punched the outlaws, and it was a very highly regarded show.

The Range Rider's horse was called Rawhide. Dick rode a steed called Lucky. The Theme song was 'Home on the Range'.

Mahoney died on 14 December 1989 from a stroke at the age of 70. Jones lives in Northridge, California, and remains a popular guest at film festivals. He provided the voice of Pinocchio in the Walt Disney cartoon feature film.

# RANGO

## 17 JANUARY 1967

**THIS** ABC comedy Western debuted at a half hour length, in color, on 17 January 1967 and left the air on 1 September 1967. Only 13 episodes were shot.

*Rango* starred Tim Conway as Rango Starr, an inept member of the Texas Rangers. To keep him out of trouble, he was posted to remote Deepwells Ranger Station, where, even though nothing had happened for 20 years, he was soon up to his neck in problems.

He worked with an Indian named Pink Cloud, played by Guy Marks. Norman Alden was Rango's exasperated captain, Ranger Horton.

Frankie Laine sang the show's theme song.

Dell published one Rango comic book.

Whilst the series wasn't successful Conway himself starred in a number of Disney films in this period and was frequently teamed with Don Knotts in movies like *The Apple Dumpling Gang*.

---

## TRIVIA

The name of Conway's character, Rango Starr, was a salute to Beatles drummer, Ringo Starr.

---

# RAWHIDE
## 9 JANUARY 1959

**THIS** major western TV series, originally to be titled, Cattle Drive, ran for seven years on CBS. The show debuted at an hour in length on 9 January 1959. Many of the 144 black and white episodes were written, directed and produced by Charles Marquis Warren before the series left the air on 4 January 1966.

*'This is the landscape of Rawhide, desert, forest, mountain and plains; it is intense heat, bitter cold, torrential rain, blinding dust. Men risking their lives, earning small reward – a life of challenge – Rawhide...'*

*Rawhide* was the saga of a group of cattle drovers and their weekly adventures, struggles and travails as they pushed a herd of cattle over 1,000 miles up the dusty Chisholm Trail from San Antonio, Texas to the rail head at Sedalia, Kansas City during the 1860's.

The trail boss and father figure, Gil Favor was played by Eric Fleming. The part had been based on Dunson, the role John Wayne played in *Red River*. His volatile ramrod was Rowdy Yates, played by a young Clint Eastwood, long before he found fame playing Dirty Harry. The two were often at odds with each other but always worked together for the good of the herd and the men. Rowdy always got the girl.

Each week, the drovers overcame natural disasters such as flood, drought, or human problems with the dangerous or odd characters they collected along the way as they struggled to deliver the cattle. Occasionally, the series had the crew reach their destination and deliver their herd, only to start up a new trail drive the next week.

Paul Brinegar starred as Wishbone, the cranky cook. CBS had asked producer, Charles Marquis Warren to be sure to put a comedy actor into the series and Brinegar had just finished working with Warren on *Cattle Empire*. Robert Cabal played Hey Soos Patines, the wrangler. He only appeared sporadically at first but his part grew later in the series. James Murdoch was Mushy Mushgrove, the cook's helper. Steve Raines was Jim Quince and Rocky Shahan was Joe Scarlett, two drovers. Sheb Wooley starred as Pete Nolan, the scout. Toothless was played by Bill Thompkins, Clay Forrester by Charles Gray, Jed Colby by John Ireland, Simon Blake by Raymond St. Jacques and Ian Cabot by David Watson. John Cole played Bailey and can also be seen in several episodes as an Indian or rustler.

Warren had worked previously on *Gunsmoke*, and had just finished work on a Joel McCrea movie, *Cattle Empire* when CBS approached him to see if he was interested in coming up with an answer to *Wagon Train* that would catch the public's imagination for their network.

This could have been a problem as Westerns already abounded on the networks, but Warren had enjoyed his work on *Cattle Empire* and felt he could produce an energy packed show centered on a cattle drive and using that film for its inspiration. He made a much grittier show than *Wagon Train* and it had an edge of realism about it because Warren made use of a diary written by George C. Duffield, who had himself worked the San Antonio to Sedalia trail. The diary remained an important feature of *Rawhide* during the seasons that Warren was with the series.

Warren also lifted ideas from Borden Chase's novel *The Chisholm Trail*. He created one of the most memorable lines in television history, 'Head 'em up, move 'em out.'

After a rocky start, when CBS pulled the plug on the show for some months, fearing there were already too many Westerns on TV, *Rawhide* was reinstated to become one of the most popular early Westerns.

Warren remained at *Rawhide's* helm for the first three seasons but his departure signaled many changes and much of the original hard authenticity was left behind. Endre Bohem, who had worked on the show for some years, was promoted to producer. He retained the actors but changed the writers and storylines.

The series ended abruptly soon after Eric Fleming drowned in a canoe accident while filming a movie in Peru.

Fleming had mysteriously left the show in 1964 to follow an impulse to travel, paint, sculpt and act from time to time. But there has been a continuing controversy about the real reasons for his departure and rumors abounded. Some accounts indicate he may have been fired for accepting a role in 1965's *The Glass Bottom Boat* while still under contract to CBS. Anyway in February 1966 he commented, 'I don't want to act any more. I'd like to become a teacher. I was never a great actor. I never expected to be. I'd like to settle down on the beach in Hawaii.'

He had been contracted with MGM-TV to film the two-part adventure series *High Jungle in Peru*. Whilst filming location shots on the Huallaga River on 28 September 1966, Fleming fell from a dug-out canoe after paddling it beyond the rapids. His body was lost in the turbulent water and was not recovered for three days. His remains were donated to the University of Peru for research purposes.

After his death, Eastwood took over as trail boss for the last 13 episodes of the final season. The series is often remembered as the vehicle which launched the career of Clint Eastwood.

Frankie Laine sang the show's popular theme song. Rocky Shahan, James Murdoch, Steve Raines and Paul Brinegar have died. Eastwood went on to international fame and fortune.

CBS continue to sell video and DVD of the show.

# THE REBEL

## 4 OCTOBER 1959

**THE REBEL** ran for three seasons on ABC, debuting on 4 October 1959 and going off air on 18 June 1961. Seventy six black and white episodes, 30 minutes in length were produced.

The half hour show was produced by Andrew J Fenady and starred Nick Adams as Johnny Yuma. Adams, Fenady, and director Irvin Kershner had formed a partnership, Fen-Ker-Ada to pitch *Young Johnny Yuma* (which became *The Rebel*) to Dick Powell at Four Star Television. When it was taken up it became one of the most intriguing Westerns on television and a real cult classic.

*The Rebel* told the story of an embittered young ex-Confederate soldier at the end of the Civil War. All the episodes centred on Johnny Yuma's search for peace. He roamed through the West of the 1860's, still wearing parts of his uniform, and writing his journal as he traveled from town to town. He had his own brand of law, and sometimes used his sawed-off, double-barreled shotgun to enforce it. He had high morals and principles and interjected himself into the plights of the citizens in an unofficial capacity, calling upon his ethics to uphold justice.

The casting of Nick Adams in the role of the angry young man was inspired and his own life was full of turmoil. He was a great admirer of John Wayne, and he frequently consulted the legendary actor, seeking his advice and support. He also read everything he could find on the Civil War and brought a breathtaking intensity to Yuma.

An interesting note to the series is that Elvis Presley was originally scheduled to sing the theme song but the producer preferred to use Johnny Cash instead. The song became a big hit for Cash and is still known as one of the best theme songs ever written for television.

Soon after the series ended Adams was discovered dead in his bedroom, fully dressed in a shirt, blue jeans and boots, his back propped against the wall. He had apparently taken a massive dose of the sedative paraldehyde combined with the tranquilizer Promazine. Paraldehyde was typically prescribed for alcoholics to control tremors and it is an irony that the drug had been prescribed by Dr. Andrew Adams, Nick's own brother. Adams had been suffering from the stress resulting from his waning career after the unexpected cancellation of *The Rebel*, divorce and a child custody battle. On 3 March 1968, Los Angeles County Coroner concluded, 'The mode of death is certified as accidental-suicidal and undetermined.'

Dell published three issues of *The Rebel* comic book.

# REDIGO
## 1963

**COLUMBIA produced this 13 week run for NBC and it aired through 1963. The show was written and produced by Andy White and directed by Leon Benson.**

*Redigo* was a short-lived half-hour spin-off of the more ambitious one-hour *Empire* in which Richard Egan played Jim Redigo, the foreman of the Garrett ranching empire. *Empire*, which also starred Terry Moore, Anne Seymour, Ryan O'Neal and Charles Bronson, lasted only one season (1962–3). In *Redigo*, the title character ran his own prosperous, albeit less grand, cattle ranch in 1960's New Mexico.

Along with Egan the regular cast included Elena Verdugo as Gerry, Roger Davis as Mike, Rudy Solari as Frank Martinez, Mina Martinez as Linda Martinez and Don Diamond as Arturo.

# THE RESTLESS GUN
## 23 September 1957

**THE half hour series debuted in black and white on NBC on 23 September 1957 and ran to 14 September 1959. Seventy seven episodes were produced by Revue Productions and Universal Studios Television.**

*The Restless Gun* was actually a better-than-average Western that boasted film star John Payne in his first foray into weekly television as its main attraction.

Payne played fast gun Vint Bonner, a man unable to settle down after the Civil War.

He was a quiet and serious man who would have been happy finding peaceful resolutions to his problems, but this was rarely possible as he roamed the violent West trying to help others. He often took employment as a hired gun and sometimes he acted as sheriff and officers of the law. His steed was called Scar.

Future stars, Chuck Connors, Dan Blocker and Michael Landon all got their early breaks on this show as guests. Blocker actually made his TV debut in an episode called *The Child* while James Coburn played his first major role in *Take Me Home*.

Payne died on 11 November 1989 of heart problems.

# THE RIFLEMAN
## 30 SEPTEMBER 1959

**THE half hour shows, filmed in black and white, debuted on ABC on 30 September 1959 and ran until 1 July 1963. The Rifleman was often placed in the top ten weekly ratings.**

This classic TV Western, and also one of the most successful, told the tale of New Mexico rancher Lucas McCain, a homesteader struggling to make ends meet while raising his young son, Mark, alone. As Lucas, Connors was one of TV's first single parents.

Lucas expertly used his trick rifle, a modified 44.40 Winchester with an enlarged trigger guard which cocked as it went into action. He was so adept with it that he could fire six rounds in 4/10ths of a second. He only needed to cock the rifle once, usually in a twirl, to fire 12 shots. With it, he had earned his reputation as 'The Rifleman.'

Six foot five, Chuck Connors starred as Lucas and Johnny Crawford played his son. In nearby North Fork the aging marshal, Micah Torrance, was brilliantly played by Hollywood character actor, Paul Fix. McCain often helped the marshal out. Micah was dedicated and honest, but a bit past his prime. Since there seemed to be a large number of baddies to control, he counted on McCain's lightning speed, sound judgement, and strong sense of fair play to help him keep the peace. There were two

---

## TRIVIA

Lucas rode Razor and Mark rode Blue Boy.
*The Rifleman* theme song was by Herschel Burke Gilbert.

---

ladies in the life of The Rifleman, Milly Scott, the store-owner, played by Joan Taylor and Patricia Blaie as Miss Lou Mallory.

Chuck Connors said, 'The Western is an escape from reality and you have to accept certain things in them. A Western may excite or bore you, but it's always relaxing. There's a value in that.'

Connors became highly marketable after his starring role in *The Rifleman*. His films in the 1960's included the title role in *Geronimo* in 1962, *Flipper*, and *Move Over, Darling* in 1963, *Synanon* in 1965 and *Ride Beyond Vengeance* in 1966. Connors also starred in the western series, *Branded* which was telecast from 1965 to 1966.

His career was still flourishing when he died from lung cancer on 10 November 1992, aged 71.

Johnny Crawford was one of the original Mouseketeers from the famous Walt Disney Mickey Mouse Club of 1955. He was nine years old when he became a Mouseketeer and went into *The Rifleman*. His older brother, Bobby Crawford, starred in his own western, *Laramie*, at the same time. *The Rifleman* launched Johnny's acting career and he appeared in over 250 television parts, 15 movies, and 12 plays. He also starred on the rodeo circuit for two years and cut a number of best-selling records. He had five hit singles and four albums in the Top 40, which launched a second career. Today, he has his own Los Angeles-based, 16-piece, 1920's style dance orchestra and plays to sell-out crowds.

He also remains active in the film industry. After Connors died he said, 'He was just my hero. He was very expressive and always concerned, but he was also tough as nails.'

Paul Fix died 14 October 1983.

# RIVERBOAT
## 13 SEPTEMBER 1959

**THE black and white series debuted on NBC on 13 September 1959 at an hour in length. Produced by Revue Productions, the series attracted many top star guests before leaving the air on 16 January 1961 after 44 episodes and a two year run. Most of the filming was done on the Universal back lot.**

This series was based on the Mississippi and Missouri rivers during the 1840s. Grey Holden played by Darren McGavin, was the captain of the riverboat, *The Enterprise*. Burt Reynolds starred as the pilot, Ben Frazier, in his first continuing role.

Other cast members included Jack Lambert as first mate Joshua, Michael McGreevey as Chip, the cabin boy and Dick Wessel as Carney, another loyal crew member. Noah Beery Jr., played Bill Blake and William D. Gordon was Travis.

Moth McGavin and Reynolds are still active in the film industry.

Noah Beery Jr., died in 1994 of cerebral thrombosis.

# THE ROAD WEST
## 12 SEPTEMBER 1966

**THE hour long show was produced in color by Universal Television Productions and it debuted on NBC on 12 September 1966. It ran for 29 episodes before departing on 28 August 1967.**

The series told the tale of pioneering widower Benjamin Pride who moved his family from their home, (which had been overrun by renegades after the Civil War), in Springfield, Ohio to the Kansas Territory.

Barry Sullivan starred as Pride, Andrew Prine was his son, Timothy, Brenda Scott was daughter Midge and Kelly Corcoran played youngster, Kip.

The principal cast also included Kathryn Hays as Elizabeth Reynolds, Ben's love interest, Glenn Corbett as Chance Reynolds, her brother and Charlie Seel as Grandpa Pride.

Barry Sullivan died aged 81 on 6 June 1994.

Glenn Corbett died in 1993 of lung cancer and Charles Seel died in 1980.

Kathyrn Hays has been playing Kim Hughes on *As The World Turns* since 1972!

# THE ROUGH RIDERS
## 2 OCTOBER 1958

**THE half hour show was filmed in black and white by ZIV Productions for ABC. It debuted on 2 October 1958 and ran for 39 episodes until leaving the air on 24 September 1959.**

The show told the story of three veteran soldiers of the Civil War, one rebel and two Yankees.

Captain Jim Flagg and Sergeant Buck Sinclair had fought in the Union Army while Lieutenant Cullen Kirby had been a Confederate. After the War the three joined together to head west to search for a new life. Naturally, they encountered many bad guys on the journey.

Kent Taylor starred as Flagg, Jan Merlin was Kirby and Peter Whitney was Sinclair.

Peter Whitney died in 1972 of a heart attack. Taylor died on 11 April 1987 at the Motion Picture Home in Calabasas.

Merlin lives in the Hollywood Hills.

# THE ROUNDERS
## 16 SEPTEMBER 1966

**THE half hour show was shot in color by MGM Television and it had its first airing for ABC on 16 September 1966. It went off air after just 17 episodes on 3 January 1967.**

This short lived TV adaptation of the 1965 movie of the same name (starring Henry Fonda and Glenn Ford) featured Ron Hays as Ben Jones and Patrick Wayne as Howdy Lewis, two fun-loving, women chasing cowboys in a modern West.

The pair never had any money and deeply in debt, found themselves working for unscrupulous ranch owner, Jim Ed Love, played by Chill Wills. They let off steam (and usually lost their pay) at the Longhorn Cafe, with the help of their girlfriends.

Amongst the cast Bobbie Jordan played Ada, Janis Hansen was Sally, Jason Wingreen was Shorty Dawes and Walker Edmiston starred as Regan. Wills died on 5 December 1978. Both Hays and Wayne remain active.

# THE ROY ROGERS SHOW
## 31 DECEMBER 1951

**THE** King of the Cowboys galloped onto the NBC Television Network along with his Queen of the West on 31 December 1951. There were 104 half hour black and white episodes produced by Roy Rogers Productions before the series left the air on 23 June 1957. The successful show went into syndication and survived until well into the 1960's.

*The Roy Rogers Show* was mostly kid's stuff and Gene Autry was Roy's main competitor in shows predating the more adult *Gunsmoke.*

Along with horses Trigger and Buttermilk, Bullet the dog, Pat Brady and Nellybelle the jeep, Roy Rogers and Dale Evans kept law and order in modern times around the town of Mineral City. They lived at the Double R Bar Ranch. Harry Lauter played Mayor Ralph Cotton.

Rogers had been one of the first movie stars to see the potential of TV and zealously guarded his show to ensure success. He sued the network to prohibit exhibition of his movies in competition with the TV show and won.

Trigger was stuffed when he died.

Roy Rogers, real name Leonard Franklin Slye, died on 6 July 1998 of congestive heart failure. Dale Evans died on 7 February 2001.

# SAGA OF ANDY BURNETT
## 2 OCTOBER 1957

**PRODUCED for ABC by Walt Disney Productions, the show debuted in October 1957 with an initial six-episode order.**

Jerome Courtland starred in the one hour series of specials as mountain man, Andy Burnett. The show was set in the early 19th Century as Burnett and his friends trekked from Pittsburgh to the Blackfoot Indian Territory in the Rockies. The stories were based on the novels by Stewart Edward White. Each episode was hosted by Walt Disney.

Jeff York starred as sidekick, Joe Crane, and Andrew Duggan as Jack Kelly and Slim Pickens as Bill Williams rounded out the cast.

Pickens, York and Duggan have all died. Courtland later starred in the 1959–60 series, *Tales of the Vikings* and went on to become a well respected director.

# SARA
## 13 FEBRUARY 1976

**THE hour long show, made in color, debuted on 13 February 1976, but was cancelled after 13 episodes and it left the air on 30 July 1976.**

*Sara* starred Brenda Vaccaro as Sara Yarnell, a strong-willed school teacher from Independence, Colorado in the 1870's. Instead of fighting bad guys she struggled against ignorance and prejudice.

Other cast members included Mariclare Costello as Jilia Bailey, Sara's best friend. Albert Stratton starred as Martin Pope, the editor of the local newspaper and Louise Latham played Sara's landlady, Martha Higgins.

All cast members are still active in films and TV and Vaccaro sometimes appears on Broadway.

# SATURDAY ROUNDUP
## 1951

**THIS 60 minute anthology series was shot in black and white and went out on NBC through 1951.**

Each episode featured adaptations of James Oliver Curwood's Western stories and starred Kermit Maynard, a stuntman who had often stood in for his brother Ken Maynard in 1930's Western movies. Kermit was also a former champion rodeo rider who had an impressive 'B' movie credit list himself. He was sometimes credited as Tex Maynard and often starred as the outlaw.

Maynard died on 16 January 1971 of a heart attack.

# SERGEANT PRESTON OF THE YUKON
## 29 SEPTEMBER 1955

THE series of half hour shows was based on a popular radio program and was shot in black and white and later, color. It debuted on 29 September 1955 on CBS. Seventy eight episodes were made at locations such as Mammoth Lake and Big Bear, California. Sergeant Preston went off air on 25 September 1958, but was seen in re runs for many years after.

*'I arrest you in the name of the Crown.'*

With his horse, Rex and his dog, Yukon King, Richard Simmons as Royal Canadian Mounted Police Sergeant Preston, patrolled the Yukon Territory of Alaska during the Gold Rush days, protecting prospectors and settlers alike.

The show was created by George W. Trendle who had also been responsible for *The Lone Ranger* and *The Green Hornet*, and his quality was to be seen throughout this show. Many exterior shots were used to give the show authentic visual appeal.

After the show concluded, Simmons revealed that the Sergeant had a first name, Frank, but it was never used during the show.

Richard Simmons died in 2003 of Alzheimer's disease.

# SHANE
## 10 SEPTEMBER 1966

ONLY 17 episodes of this hour long color show were filmed for ABC. It debuted on 10 September 1966 and ran until 31 December 1966.

David Carradine reprised the role made famous by Alan Ladd in the 1953 film of the same name. Shane was a gunfighter who took a job on the Starett Farm where the family faced conflict from cattleman Rufe Ryker who wanted to get rid of all the homesteads in the Wyoming valley.

Jill Ireland starred as Marian Starett, Christopher Shea played her young son, Joey, Bert Freed was Ryker and Tom Tully played Tom Starett, Marian's father-in-law.

Although the show was not successful Carradine went on to the highly acclaimed *Kung Fu* series a few years later.

# SHERIFF OF COCHISE
## 1955

**SHERIFF OF COCHISE** debuted in Fall 1955 and ran in 61 markets in America and Canada. Later in 1958 its title was changed to US Marshal and it ran for a further two years. 156 black and white episodes were made by Desilu Productions for National Telefilm Associates.

This syndicated series of half hour shows, set in contemporary Arizona, starred John Bromfield as Sheriff Frank Morgan who kept law and order in Cochise County.

High speed chases and fist fights, along with modern detective work were emphasized in the show that co-starred Stan Jones as Deputy Sheriff Olsen. James Griffith was Deputy Tom Ferguson.

Jones died in 1963.

# SHOTGUN SLADE
## 1959

**THERE** were 78 episodes of Shotgun Slade filmed for syndication by Revue Productions for the CBS Network, running from 1959 to 1961.

The unusual series starred Scott Brady as a detective who hired out to Wells Fargo Co., banks and insurance companies, or anyone else who needed his help.

His weapon of choice was a lethal shotgun.

Brady returned to films after the series closed, but died on 16 April 1985 in Los Angeles, California, USA from emphysema.

## TRIVIA

During his 1950's B-movie heyday, Bromfield headlined in a handful of mediocre sci-fis, melodramas and westerns. Studios often put him in skimpy outfits and swim suits to show off his fine physique. He retired from acting in 1960 shortly after ending his run as the US Marshal. He became a commercial fisherman. When *Sheriff of Cochise* first aired, the real sheriff of Cochise visited the set and made him an honorary deputy.

# SKY KING

## 1951

**THESE** half hour, black and white episodes aired first in 1951 on NBC, but the series finished its run on the CBS prime time schedule on 12 September 1954, (it could still be seen on ABC up to 1968). It was re-run in 1987 on CBN. The show had originally been made for radio in 1946 and it was such a huge success that it continued to run on air until 1956. Children could listen to hour long episodes and also see new segments on television.

A total of 136 episodes were filmed. The last 64 shot were destroyed in a New York film vault fire.

The popular children's Western was set in Arizona and told the tale of Schuyler (Sky) King and his niece, Penny who found plenty of trouble around their Flying Crown ranch.

They tracked down their enemies in their plane, The Songbird. From 1951 to 1956 a Cessna Bobcat T-50 was used as the Songbird, but in the episodes made through 1957 to end of the run a Cessna 310B was used.

Kirby Grant starred as Sky King and Gloria Winters was Penny.

Ron Hagerty played King's nephew, Clipper. Ewing Mitchell was the sheriff of the nearby town of Grover.

Kirby Grant stared in or was a supporting actor in 53 motion pictures. He was killed in a car crash in Florida on 3 October 1985 and Mitchell died of a stroke on 2 September 1988 in LaJolla.

# SPIN AND MARTY
## (THE ADVENTURES OF)
## (1955)

**THE** Adventures of Spin and Marty, the story of a group of boys working on a dude ranch, was a segment of the Mickey Mouse Club that first ran on the ABC Television Network in October, 1955. The half hour segments were shot in black and white.

Lawrence Edward Watkin wrote the book, *Marty Markham*, which came to the attention of Walt Disney and his Mickey Mouse Club producer, Bill Walsh. They decided to serialize it and early in the summer of 1955 work began on what would be Production 8209 at the Disney Studio. Jackson Gillis was brought in to write a screenplay.

Filming was done on location at the Golden Oak Ranch in Placerita Canyon. The ranch was located in a serene setting with a stream and rolling hills, and in fact, Walt Disney was so pleased with the ranch that he later purchased it and it is still used as a movie ranch by Disney and, on a rental basis, by other film companies.

Tim Considine was signed to play Spin and David Stollery to play Marty for salaries of $400 a week. Not bad going for two 14-year-old boys in 1955.

The budget for the serial was $513,480, but it came in $60,000 over budget. Much of that was due to the strike of the Screen Actors Guild midway through the shooting schedule. Filming began under director William Beaudine Sr., on 13 July 1955 and continued until September 3rd of the same year.

In the first serial Marty, a wealthy city boy, who had been raised without the companionship of children his own age, antagonized everyone by calling the Triple R a dirty old ranch when he arrives with his personal butler. Marty disliked the outdoors and made things as difficult as possible for his fellow ranchers. He was afraid of horses and harassed by the other boys at the ranch. Good-natured Spin tried to help him get accustomed to life on the Triple R. Marty eventually decided to stay and, with help from foreman, Bill, who doubled as camp counselor, conquered his fears and learned to ride Skyrocket. Preparations for a local rodeo with neighboring camp, North Fork, used up much of the energy at the ranch, but Spin and Marty always found time for diversions.

Besides Considine and Stollery, other cast members included Roy Barcroft as Colonel Logan, the proprietor of the Triple R, Harry Carey, Jr., as Bill Burnett, the foreman, J. Pat O'Malley as Perkins, Marty's butler, George Eldredge as the doctor, and included among the kids, Sammy Ogg (Joe), who had earlier done an *I Love Lucy* show with David Stollery, B.G. Norman (Ambitious), and Tim Hartnagel (Speckle). These cast members remained throughout the three seasons. Other leads included Lennie Geer as Ollie, the wrangler, and Sammee Tong as the cook. Unique among the Mickey Mouse Club serials, *Spin and Marty* ran to three seasons.

# STAGECOACH WEST
## 4 OCTOBER 1960

**THE hour long, black and white show was made by Four Star Productions for ABC and it debuted on 4 October 1960. It left the lineup on 26 September 1961 after 38 episodes. Much of the series was shot at Apacheland Movie Ranch in Arizona.**

Stagecoach West, the Timberland Stage Line bossed by Luke Perry and Simon Kane, ran from Tipton, Missouri to San Francisco in the 1860's. Perry was played by Wayne Rogers and Kane by Robert Bray. Richard Eyer completed the regular cast as David Kane, Simon's 12-year-old son. The cast was rounded out with regular, James Burke as Zeke Bonner.

There weren't many Westerns made that dealt with the stage drivers on the lines connecting a more civilized America with the Wild West, and this series was perhaps the best of those.

Perry and Kane owned the line and were also the drivers. They encountered all sorts of hooligans and outlaws along their route. Young Davy usually went along to keep them company.

Most of the stories in this series revolved around surly passengers, outlaws, hold-up men and bad weather. There was limited romance, but mostly the stories were about the determination of the two drivers to keep the stage running in spite of the encroaching railroad companies.

Some of the biggest names in Hollywood were guest stars including John Dehner, Jack Lord, Darren McGavin, Lee Van Cleef, DeForest Kelley, Cesar Romero, Barbara Luna, Warren Oates, Jack Elam, Dick York, and Denver Pyle.

They weren't enough to keep it in the ratings and ABC soon unceremoniously pulled the plug. Today, it is mostly remembered for its catchy theme song.

Robert Bray died 7 March 1983 of a heart attack.

Wayne Rogers would be best known for his role as Trapper John on *MASH*. James Burke died in 1968.

# STATE TROOPER
## 1956

**ONE hundred and four half-hour, black and white episodes of this show aired between 1956 and 1959.**

Rod Cameron starred as Nevada State Trooper, Rod Blake in this contemporary Western, shot on location in and around Virginia City. Blake used modern vehicles and horses to pursue criminals. Robert Burton played Blake's deputy.

Cameron died on 21 December 1983.

# STEVE DONOVAN, WESTERN MARSHAL
## 1952

**THE low-budget series was made by Lone Ranger producer, Jack Chertok, who filmed it at Hal Roach Studios. Thirty nine half hour, black and white episodes were distributed by NBC Films and were marketed three times; in 1952, 1955 and 1957, all under slightly different titles. The show finally ran on NBC from autumn 1958 after its first run in syndication from 1952–6 and its second in 1957.**

Douglas Kennedy starred as Steve Donovan. Eddy Waller played his deputy, Rusty Lee. The two were traveling marshals who brought law and order to the West in the late 19th century.

Kennedy died in 1973 of cancer and Waller in 1977 of a stroke.

Dell Publishing produced three highly prized issues of Steve Donovan comic books.

# STONEY BURKE
## 1 OCTOBER 1962

**EACH episode of Stoney Burke was shot in black and white. It debuted on ABC on 1 October 1962 and went off the air on 2 September 1963.**

The contemporary Western set on the rodeo circuit starred Jack Lord as bronc rider, Stoney Burke. Loner Burke traveled the West, moving from one rodeo to another hoping to win the big prize; The Golden Buckle. He tolerated few people with the exceptions of E. J. Stocker, played by Bruce Dern, Cody Bristol played by Robert Dowdell, Warren Oates as Ves Painter and Bill Hart as Red. As the show only lasted the one season, Stoney never did win the buckle.

Warren Oates died from a heart attack in 1982.

After this series Lord went on to major success in *Hawaii Five O*. He died of heart failure aged 77 in 1998.

# STORIES OF THE CENTURY
## 1954

**THIS** unusual half hour, black and white series was produced by Republic Studios TV Department and incorporated many official records and authentic reports into its scripts.

Real characters such as Billy the Kid, Belle Starr and Sam Bass crossed the path of South-western Railroad detective Matt Clark and his assistants through the 38 episodes. The unusual part of the show was that Clark's assistants were always women.

Jim Davis starred as Clark and his female assistant Margaret 'Jonesy' Jones was played by Kristine Miller. For a short time Mary Castle starred as Frankie Adams, another assistant.

It aired in syndication in 1954–5 and was one of the first syndicated TV shows to win a major Emmy – Best Western or Adventure Series for 1954!

Davis achieved his greatest fame as Jock Ewing on *Dallas*. He died on 26 April 1981.

# SUGARFOOT
## 17 SEPTEMBER 1957

**WARNER Bros produced 69 episodes of this show for ABC. The hour long series ran from 17 September 1957 until 3 July 1961.**

Laced with humor and full of action, *Sugarfoot* remained a top ratings winner for four years. It rotated haphazardly through the season with *Bronco* and *Cheyenne*, but *Sugarfoot* was always eagerly awaited by fans. During its first two seasons, it alternated with *Cheyenne*. When Clint Walker got into a dispute with Warner Brothers in 1958 and *Bronco* was born, it alternated with *Bronco* during its third year as part of the *Cheyenne Show*. During its fourth season, it alternated with both *Bronco* and *Cheyenne*.

Will Hutchins starred as Tom Brewster a tailor-made role, created for him by executive producer William T. Orr. This was one of the few times a series was made especially for an unknown star. Will Hutchins apparently reminded Orr of the late, great Will Rogers. Hutchins talked like Rogers and had the same lazy manner and personality.

Brewster was a kind-hearted young drifter, a correspondence law school student who traveled from town to town seeking employment. A 'sugarfoot' in Western terminology is not a flattering thing to be. It implies a person one step below tenderfoot; a greenhorn at everything. Tom Brewster apparently didn't mind that he was called a sugarfoot.

He was equally handy with his guns or fists when necessary, but preferred to use the letter of the law to make his point. Toting a stack of law books and with his aversion to violence, he shared Cheyenne's penchant for meddling in the affairs of others. But whereas Cheyenne usually dispatched conflicts with firepower, Tom preferred to replace gunplay with rhetoric. The series was more light-hearted than *Cheyenne*, but otherwise held close to the formula of the heroic loner.

Some excellent episodes were made where Sugarfoot's evil double, The Canary Kid, showed up. The episodes which featured both The Canary Kid and Tom Brewster are considered some of the finest in television history.

After *Sugarfoot*, Hutchins went on to success as Woody Banner in *Hey Landlord* and then as Dagwood Bumstead in *Blondie*, not to mention hundreds of other performances.

Will and his wife now live in Long Island, NY and are popular guests at film conventions.

There were six Dell comic books on *Sugarfoot*, and every one of them are big collector items averaging around $15 each in today's markets.

# THE SWAMP FOX
## OCTOBER 1959

**THE** series debuted on ABC during autumn 1959 and was shown under the Walt Disney Presents banner. Eight episodes were filmed and ran until January 1961.

Leslie Nielsen starred as one of America's first freedom fighters, Colonel Francis Marion, known as the Swamp Fox by his enemies, the British, in this hour long color series that was set during America's Revolutionary war. The show provided great adventure and a small dollop of history.

*'My name is Francis Marion. I fought the British Redcoats in '76. Hiding in the Carolina swamps by day, surprising them with swift strikes at night. They called me a tricky swamp fox. So, a Swamp Fox I became...'*

the Colonel called as he harassed British troops before disappearing back into the swamps around Charleston, Carolina.

This show was another attempt by Disney as part of Wonderful World of Color to recreate the success of Davy Crockett. They even gave the lead a foxtail for his hat.

Regular cast members included John Sutton as Colonel Tarleton, Joy Page as Mary Videau (First Season), Barbara Eiler as Mary Videau (Second Season), Myron Healey as Major Peter Horry, Jordan Whitfield as Oscar, J. Pat O'Malley as O'Reilly, Mary Field as Cathy Marion, Louise Beavers as Delia, Slim Pickens as Plunkett, Hal Stalmaster as Gwynn, Patrick Macnee as the British Captain, Tim Considine as 'Young' Gabe Marion, Dick Foran as Gabriel Marion and Henry Daniell as Colonel Townes. The cast was rounded out with appearances by Richard Erdman and Richard Farnsworth.

Many of the stars of this show went on to bigger and better things, particularly Nielsen himself and Patrick Macnee of course became the legendary English gent, John Steed in *The Avengers*.

# TALES OF THE TEXAS RANGERS
## 22 September 1955

**THIS half hour, black and white show debuted on 22 September 1955 and ran until 25 May 1959 on the ABC network. It was produced by Screen Gems Productions. Fifty two episodes were filmed.**

Willard Parker played Ranger Jace Pearson and Harry Lauter was Ranger Clay Morgan.

The unusual series alternated episodes with the historical period switching from the 1800's to the present day exploits of the Texas rangers. While it was always about the Texas Rangers, one week they might be corralling desperados in the 1850's; the next they would be hunting down criminals in the 1950's.

Lauter died on 30 October 1990, aged 76. Parker died in 1966 of heart failure. Joel McCrea had played Jace Pearson on the radio series.

# TALES OF WELLS FARGO
## 3 March 1957

**THE series aired on NBC from 3 March 1957 until September 1961 and was made by Overland Productions. It ran consistently high in the Nielson ratings. Overland Productions was owned by Dale Robertson and Nat Holt, and the company was eventually sold to MCA.**

Dale Robertson starred as trouble-shooter, Agent Jim Hardie in this series that ran for 265 episodes. He was the man the stage company sent for whenever there was trouble along the line. Steve McQueen and Michael Landon got some of their earliest exposure on the show.

When the production went to color the cast was expanded to include Jack Ging and William Demarest.

Robertson had made it his business to learn every aspect of film making, studying

*Dale Robertson*

for two years at the USC College of Cinema and for several years learning to edit film with famed Eimo Williams. He had even learned how to score a movie. He became president and principal owner of United Screen Artists until, in 1976, he returned to his home state of Oklahoma to establish the Haymaker Farm in Yukon, where he bred horses and, twice yearly produced the world's largest quarter horse sale, the 'Haymaker Sales'. He sold the farm in 1989 but still lives in a house on the land.

After *Tales of Wells Fargo* ended, Robertson worked on another Western series, *Iron Horse*. He also hosted and starred in some segments of *Death Valley Days* and guested on many top shows of the 80's including *Love Boat, Matt Houston, Dynasty* and *Dallas*.

William Demerest died in 1983 of cancer.

# THE TALL MAN
## 10 September 1960

**THE series was filmed in black and white and debuted on NBC on 10 September 1060. Revue Productions made 75 episodes and its run ended on 1 September 1962.**

This half hour series made a quasi hero out of Billy the Kid. Barry Sullivan starred as Sheriff Pat Garrett and Clu Gulager played Billy.

The Kid was a young gunslinger who hung around Lincoln, New Mexico, where Garrett was working, and the two were on friendly terms. Still Billy's criminal tendencies always leant an air of tension between them. This was yet another fictionalized telling of the story of Sheriff Pat Garrett and Billy the Kid (William H. Bonney) who shared an almost paternal relationship. Each man knew they were on opposite sides of the law and would one day collide. Garrett is called the Tall Man because of his honesty and integrity.

Sullivan died on 6 June 1994 of a respiratory ailment. Gulager still occasionally works in the industry.

# TATE
## 8 June 1960

**THE series was shot in black and white and debuted on NBC on 8 June 1960. Thirteen half hour episodes were made and it left the air after a four month run, on 28 September 1960.**

David Mclean starred as hard-hitting Tate, a gunfighter who only had one good arm. His left arm, now encased in black leather, had been injured during the Civil War. Tate travelled the country searching for work, hiring out his gun. Patricia Breslin starred as Jessica Jackson.

Robert Redford made two guest appearances on the show in the episodes, *The Bounty Hunter* and *Comanche Slips*.

David MacLean died in 1995 of lung cancer.

# TEMPLE HOUSTON
## 19 SEPTEMBER 1963

**THE** black and white series ran for one hour and premiered on 19 September 1963. It went off air on 10 September 1964. Twenty seven episodes were filmed.

In real life Temple Houston was the son of Sam Houston. Temple traveled the circuit courts in the Southwest in the 1880's. Elegantly tailored, he cut a fine figure as he employed his famous oratorical skills in court. Naturally, he was pretty handy with a gun too. Also following the circuit court was George Taggart, a US Marshal who was somewhat past his prime as a gunfighter.

The real life Temple Houston was a contemporary of both Billy the Kid and Bat Masterson and according to legend, engaged in gunfights with both of them. Jeffrey Hunter starred in the series as Temple and Jack Elam played Taggart.

Rounding out the cast were Frank Ferguson as Judge Gurney, Chubby Johnson as Concho, and Mary Wickes as Ida Goff.

Jeffrey Hunter died in 1969 of head trauma after a fall in his house.

Jack Elam has also died. Frank Ferguson died in 1978 of cancer, as did Mary Wickes in 1995. Chubby Johnson died in 1974.

# THE TEXAN
## 29 SEPTEMBER 1958

**CBS** aired the half-hour black and white show between 29 September 1958 and 12 September 1960. Desilu Productions made the series which attracted top guest stars.

When movie star Rory Calhoun signed up to star in a TV series, The Texan was guaranteed to be a good one. Calhoun played Bill Longley, a fast gun who helped people keep law and order after the Civil War as he travelled the West.

Rory (real name Francis Timothy McCown) died of emphysema and diabetes, aged 76, on 28 April 1999.

# TEXAS JOHN SLAUGHTER
## 1958

**THIS** hour long, black and white series was made by Walt Disney Productions for Walt Disney Presents about real life Westerner, Texas John Slaughter. Thirteen segments were shot. It was yet another attempt by Disney to recreate the success of Davy Crockett. ABC aired the show in the autumn of 1958.

Slaughter was a colorful character who helped clean up Tombstone. Tom Tryon was cast as Slaughter and Harry Carey Jr., was his sidekick, Ben Jenkins. Also in the regular cast were, Betty Lynn as Viola Slaughter, Brian Corcoran as Willie Slaughter, Annette Gorman as Addie, Onslow Stevens as General Miles, Pat Hogan as Geronimo and R. G. Armstrong as Billy Soto. Stafford Repp played Sheriff Hatch, Ross Martin was Cesario Lucero, Jim Beck starred as Burt Alvordi, and Norma Moore as Adeline Harris.

Tryon later became a successful author. He died in September 1991 of cancer. Harry Carey Jr., is still active in the industry.

Ross Martin, became Artemus Gordon in Wild Wild West, but died in 1981.

# TOMAHAWK
## 1957

**OMEGA** Productions (Montreal Studios) and Radio Canada made this rarely seen Western adventure series for CBC. It was distributed by Associated-British Pathé. The show was produced by Yves Bigras, written by John Lucarotti, Jean Desprez and Renée Normand and directed by Pierre Gauvreau. It aired through 1957–8 season. Location filming was done at Ile Perrot on the St Lawrence River.

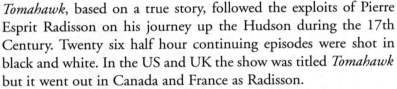

*Tomahawk*, based on a true story, followed the exploits of Pierre Esprit Radisson on his journey up the Hudson during the 17th Century. Twenty six half hour continuing episodes were shot in black and white. In the US and UK the show was titled *Tomahawk* but it went out in Canada and France as Radisson.

Jacques Godin starred as Pierre Esprit Radisson, René Caron played Medard Chouart, Sieur Des Groseilliers, (Radisson's brother-in-law and partner).

Raymond Royer played Onega (Radisson's Indian blood brother), Percy Rodriquez was the Iroqois Chieftain, Julien Bessette starred as Nahala (Radisson's Indian enemy), Jean Boisjoli was Mojida the Huron Chieftain, Francoise Faucher was Marguerite (Radisson's sister), Camille Ducharme was French Governor of 3 Rivers and William Robert Fournier the Dutch Governor of Fort Orange.

Godin also starred in the original live action 1965 children's TV series *Belle and Sebastian*, which told the mountain-based adventures of a young boy and his dog in a small village in the Pyrenees.

# TOMBSTONE TERRITORY
## 16 OCTOBER 1957

**THE half hour, black and white show, produced by Ziv TV, which debuted on ABC on 16 October 1957, ran for 91 episodes until 9 October 1959. After the show left the ABC schedule, new episodes were produced for syndication.**

This series was set in Tombstone in the booming 1880's and dealt with Sheriff Clay Hollister's efforts at keeping the peace along with his chief ally, Harris Claiborne. Claiborne was the editor of the newspaper, *The Tombstone Epitaph*.

Hollister was played by Pat Conway and Richard Eastham starred as Claiborne. Gilman Rankin was Deputy Charlie Riggs. Many of the stories that the show was based on were found in the real *Tombstone Epitaph*.

The series was filmed at locations including Bronson Canyon in Griffith Park, the Iverson Ranch in Chatsworth and the Melody Ranch.

*The Tombstone Territory* theme song, *Whistle Me Up A Memory* was penned by William M. Backer.

Richard Eastham was a singer-actor who starred on Broadway and sang with the St Louis Grand Opera while attending Washington University and successfully took over the male lead in South Pacific from the Italian opera singer Ezio Pinza. He was the narrator of *Tombstone Territory*. He later became a regular on *Wonder Woman* and *Falcon Crest* (his last TV role in 1882–3).

Pat Conway made several guest appearances on *Bonanza*, *Branded* and *Empire*. He died in 1981.

Gilman Rankin died in 1993.

# TRACKDOWN
## 4 OCTOBER 1957

**TRACKDOWN, produced by Vincent Fennelly for Four Star Productions, debuted on 4 October 1957 and ran 71 episodes, before leaving the air on 23 September 1959.**

Texas Ranger Hoby Gilman was played in this half hour, black and white series, based on actual Texas Ranger files, by Robert Culp. The show was produced by CBS with full co-operation from the Rangers. The cast also included Ellen Corby as Henrietta and Peter Leeds as Tenner Smith.

Gilman was a cool character Texas Ranger who patrolled during the 1870's and Culp, who often rode to the studio on a motorcycle, imbued Hoby with a hipness that was perhaps ahead of the time but which presaged the 60's yet to come.

As the show often used actual case files, it had the endorsement of the State of Texas. No other series was ever able to claim this.

Culp, who wrote some of the episodes, went on to star in *I Spy* with Bill Cosby.

The show's theme song, *Trackdown* was by William G. Loose, and John Seely. The Wanted: Dead or Alive character of Josh Randall, played by Steve McQueen, was introduced in this series.

Robert Culp and Steve McQueen raced motorcycles in New York together and it was Culp who encouraged McQueen to head for LA and he ended up in the series. They shared the same agent, Hilly Elkins.

When Vincent Fennelly was looking to cast for a new show, Elkins suggested McQueen. They decided to shoot the pilot as an episode of *Trackdown*, and Josh Ranall was introduced in the episode, *The Bounty Hunter*. McQueen and Culp also appeared together again in *The Brothers*.

# TRAVELS OF JAMIE MCPHEETERS
## 15 SEPTEMBER 1963

**MGM** Television produced the hour long show, which was filmed in black and white on their back lot, for ABC. The show debuted on 15 September 1963 and left the line up on 15 March 1964. Twenty six segments were made. Some of the episodes which starred Bronson have been edited into two-hour television movies.

The series, based on the novel by Robert Lewis Taylor, followed the adventures of the McPheeters, Doc Sardius and his son, Jamie on their westward journey toward California's Gold Fields in 1849. The show was unique as it was made from the 13-year-old's point of view.

A precocious Kurt Russell starred as Jamie and Dan O'Helihy played Sardius. Charles Bronson was Lync Murdock, the wagon master. Others who appeared in the series included James Westerfield, Sandy Kenyon and the Osmond brothers (Alan, Jay, Merrill and Wayne).

# 26 MEN
## 1957

**THE** action-packed show was shot in Arizona and was produced by veteran actor, Russell Hayden. Seventy eight half-hour episodes were made in 1957 and 1958 for syndication.

This was the story of the 26 Arizona Rangers who patrolled the Arizona Territory in the late 1800s.

Tris Coffin starred as Captain Tom Rynning and real life cowboy and quick-draw artist, Kelo Henderson co-starred as Ranger Clint Travis. Henderson had been raised on a ranch in Colorado and was an expert marksman. He taught many of the TV Western stars how to use their guns.

Tristram Coffin died in 1990 of lung cancer.

# TWO FACES WEST
## 1960

THIRTY nine black and white, half hour episodes were shot by Screen Gem Productions and in 1960 over 150 stations aired the show. It closed after one season in 1961.

*Two Faces West* was a syndicated series about twin brothers, Ben January, a doctor and Rick, a famous gunfighter.

Both roles were played by Charles Bateman.

The brothers had been separated as babies in an Indian raid but were later reunited in the town of Gunnison as men. They stayed together at the Gunnison Hotel owned by Julie Greer played by June Blair.

# UNION PACIFIC
## 1958

CALIFORNIA National Productions made 39 half hour, black and white episodes of this show for NBC TV in 1958. From 1961 it could be found on ABC.

Jeff Morrow starred as Bart McClelland, the railroad's district supervisor and Judson Pratt co-starred as Billy Kincaid, his right hand man and surveyor. Golden Nugget Saloon hostess, Georgia, was played by Susan Cummings. The Saloon was located in a railroad car that traveled with the train.

Nothing was allowed to stand in the way as the Union Pacific Railroad was pushed westward.

Jeff Morrow died in 1993.

# US BORDER PATROL
## 1959

THE 39 half hour, black and white episodes were made for the 1959–1960 season.

This was a contemporary Western concerned with the efforts of the *US Border Patrol* to stop crime along the US/Mexican border.

Chief Don Jagger, played by Richard Webb, dealt with illegal drugs, murder and smuggling.

Webb committed suicide.

# US MARSHAL
## 1958

**THE** Desilu crime/western production for First-Run Syndication was produced by John Auer. The half hour, black and white show went out during the 1958–1960 seasons.

*John Bromfield*
*and*
*James Griffith*

*US Marshal* derived from Sheriff of Cochise where Frank Morgan had jurisdiction over the state of Arizona. He had now assigned a new deputy, Tom Ferguson, to help out.

John Bromfield and James Griffith played the team and Robert Brubaker was Deputy Blake.

The theme to *US Marshal* was composed by Ray Ellis.

# THE VIRGINIAN
## 19 SEPTEMBER 1962

**THE show debuted on NBC on 19 September 1962. It ran for 225 episodes and eight years before leaving the air on 8 September 1971.**

'There's no type of acting that develops poise and grace like a television Western.'

Doug McClure

The show about the Shilo Ranch was the first 90 minute weekly Western and it was based in Wyoming around 1890. Charles Marquis Warren, fresh from his success on *Rawhide*, served as executive producer on the first 13 episodes, and was subsequently replaced by *Maverick* creator Roy Huggins and a host of producers including Frank Price, Joel Rogosin and Cy Chermak. The show had the most demanding production schedule in television history.

Taken from the Owen Wister novel, and four feature films, *The Virginian* starred James Drury as *the Virginian*, (and we never learned his real name.)

*The Virginian* was a man coping with change and trying to live his life according to a strict moral code. Drury had first appeared as *the Virginian* in an episode of the short-lived Screen Gems anthology *Decision*. The original 1958 half-hour pilot saw him fresh from the Civil War and veterinary school, arriving at the Shiloh Ranch in Medicine Bow, to help upgrade the owner's stock. With the half-hour format limiting character and story development, the pilot failed to sell.

Universal's TV subsidiary, Revue Productions, decided to give *The Virginian* another try. On 16 September 1962 James Drury made his second appearance only this time he was dressed in attire more suited to his role as the foreman of Shiloh Ranch.

Drury recalled the screen test that landed him the role for the second time. 'After the first test they wanted me to lose weight. This I did, went back for another test, the same thing happened and I went back a third time. There were about 75 actors all after the same role. The Friday before the Monday we started shooting the series, they informed me I'd be playing *The Virginian!*'

He was assisted by Trampas from the start and the two were the only characters to complete the run of the show.

The Shiloh Ranch changed hands several times but it was originally owned by Judge Henry Garth played by Lee J. Cobb. Roberta Shore starred as Betsy, the judge's adopted daughter, (she was the daughter of one of the judge's best friends and the woman they had both loved). Clu Gulager played Deputy (and later Sheriff) Emmett Ryker, a reformed gunfighter, and Pippa Scott was Molly Dodd, newspaper publisher, editor and reporter on *The Medicine Bow Banner* which she had inherited from her father. Gary Clarke and Randy Boone played Steve and Randy Benton, two ranch hands. Boone frequently sang on *The Virginian*. He also starred in Cimarron Strip.

Other regular cast members included Diane Roter as Jennifer Sommers, Judge Garth's orphaned niece (65–66), Sara Lane as Elizabeth Grainger, granddaughter to John and niece to Clay and Holly (66–70), Don Quine as Stacy Grainger, grandson to John and nephew to Clay and Holly (66–68), David Hartman as ranch hand David Sutton (68–69) and Tim Matheson as ranch hand Jim Horn (69–70). Floating cast members who appeared irregularly included ranch hands L. Q. Jones as Belden and Harper Flaherty as Harper, Ross Elliot as Sheriff Mark Abbott and John Bryant as Dr R. M. Spaulding.

The show also attracted a host of first-rate performers, including Bette Davis, Lee Marvin, Charles Bronson, George C. Scott and Brandon De Wilde. It also served as a training ground for up and coming talent such as Robert Redford, Peter Duel, Leonard Nimoy, Julie Sommars and Kurt Russell.

Lee J. Cobb spent his time on set observing the other actors and the work of the cinematographer, studying camera shots and light readings. He was a fine photographer himself and was often heard saying he would be just as happy behind a camera as in front of it.

Cobb was replaced by John Dehner as Morgan Starr. The Judge handed over control of the ranch following his appointment as territorial governor of Wyoming. Dehner only lasted one season however and he was replaced by Charles Bickford (John Grainger) as the new owner of Shiloh. Unfortunately his death in 1967 forced the producers to look for yet another replacement. John McIntire, who had successfully replaced the late Ward Bond on Wagon Train, was again asked to step into a part vacated by the death of an actor. He played John Grainger's brother, Clay and he introduced a wife to Shiloh, for the first time, in the form of real-life wife Jeannette Nolan as Holly Grainger. It was a departure from the standard widowed ranch owner character-type so beloved by a generation of TV Western producers.

The powers that be then decided it might be a good idea to change the name of the show to *Men From Shiloh* in 1970. It even got a new theme song written by Ennio Morricone which followed Percy Faith's distinctive theme which had triumphantly heralded the show's debut in 1962.

One of the strengths of the series had definitely been its ability to withstand the frequent departure of various cast members. Pippa Scott had been the first to depart in 1963 followed by Gary Clarke in 1964 (he resurfaced in the short-lived Western series *Hondo* in 1967), Roberta Shore left in 1965, following her wedding at Shiloh. She was moved out to Pennsylvania and Lee J. Cobb left in 1966. Like so many other stars of Western shows, Hollywood veteran, Cobb had complained about the daily grind of working on a TV series. Each segment was thrown together and filmed in eight days, with two shows often being shot back-to-back.

With his contract fulfilled, Cobb was eager to return to the relative leisurely pace of feature films.

And, in fact, many of the regulars were bored and McClure said, 'Even the horses knew the script. They'd come alive during our three or four lines of dialogue and then just drift off to sleep again.' He went on, 'I played Trampas so long I could anticipate the lines.'

In what was to be the last season, the Virginian and Trampas greeted the newest owner, Col. Alan MacKenzie (Stewart Granger), an Englishman. Lee Majors, fresh from Big Valley, also came over as Roy Tate.

An episode in the final season, *Holocaust* saw the ranch house burned to the ground, only to be rebuilt by the story's conclusion with *The Virginian*, Trampas and the Grainger's raising their glasses to a new beginning. An era in television history was nearing its conclusion, but the saga continued in a revamped form later that year.

James Drury and Doug McClure became something of a double-act through their joint success on *The Virginian*. In 1968 they both made cameo appearances on the pilot film of *It Takes A Thief*, followed by an appearance on *Rowan and Martin's Laugh-In*, both bemused by the antics of singer Tiny Tim. In 1983 they were reunited in an episode of *The Fall Guy* dressed as The Virginian and Trampas, but playing themselves, and in 1991 they appeared as Doug and Jim in *The Gambler – The Luck of the Draw*, with Kenny Rogers.

Doug McClure died in 1995 of lung cancer. During his days on *The Virginian* he had been the number one recipient of fan mail at Universal City Studios.

Lee J. Cobb died of a heart attack on 11 February 1976. During the 50's he had survived the communist witch-hunts; he said that his life had been shattered by the investigations and that he didn't know financial security until *The Virginian* came along, 'I never knew when I would be eating.'

Charles Bickford died in 1967, John McIntire in 1991, and Stewart Granger in 1993 of cancer.

Drury went into the oil industry before settling in Houston.

# WAGON TRAIN
## 18 SEPTEMBER 1957

**T**HE hour long, black and white show was made by Howard Christie for Revue Productions (the TV production arm of Universal Studios) and debuted on NBC TV on 18 September 1957. Wagon Train left the air on 1 September 1965.

Unlike most shows in the Western genre, *Wagon Train* always attracted big name guest stars in character studies, (including John Wayne who had made it a point never to appear on television as a character player). Each tale, titled around the story of a passenger, was told across the panorama of the American western expansion toward California in the post Civil War period.

Ward Bond and Robert Horton starred as ex-Union army major, and wagon master Seth Adams and the dashing, heroic scout Flint McCullough. Much was made in the early years of a long-running feud between Bond and Horton. Perhaps it was inevitable that the elder Bond who had been playing cowboys for years would have differences with the younger, professionally trained actor who had quickly stolen the show and Bond had a notorious reputation for being difficult to get along with.

Horton had made a point before the cameras even began rolling, of driving to St Joseph, the official starting point for the wagons, and heading toward Hollywood, via the historic route through Dodge City, Denver, Salt Lake City and Reno. He explained, 'The trip had a kind of romantic value for me. I'm a great one for poking around looking for plaques and cemetery inscriptions and it gave me a good, solid feel for the terrain *Wagon Train* will follow.' Naturally Bond was not the type of actor to feel his way into a role; he had spent most of his working life under the direction of John Ford, who wouldn't have appreciated an actor doing anything he hadn't specifically told him to do.

Their differences didn't seem to matter: on-screen, their chemistry worked beautifully.

Major Seth Adams (pretty much designed around Bond's own style) was burly and surly, a veteran of the Civil War and he ran his train bellowing all the way from St Joseph to Sacramento. He was a fair man. And the travelers looked to him to get them safely across the Territories toward their new futures. He was the kind of man people trusted. He had earned their respect.

And in much the same way that Horton was a constant thorn in Bond's side, so too, Flint McCullough aggravated the Major; and for pretty much the same reasons! McCullough was young, head strong and very nearly as stubborn as Major Adams. But whenever McCullough was late or the Major feared for him, you could always see the worry on the older man's face, even he if would never have dreamed of admitting to it.

McCullough was the hero and found plenty of danger along the trail. He was not a man to be messed with; he met trouble head on. Many of his difficulties revolved around women and as the train moved slowly westward he romanced Barbara Stanwyck, Linda Darnell, Rhonda Fleming, Felicia Farr, Susan Oliver and Nina Foch.

In Horton's capable hands, Flint McCullough became the thinking man's cowboy. He was educated, well-spoken and thoughtful without Horton ever having to sacrifice the toughness expected of a wagon train scout.

The program was often listed as one of the top five shows of the week.

The original cast included Frank McGrath as Wooster, the cook, and former stunt man, Terry Wilson as Bill Hawks, the right hand man.

*Wagon Train* survived many changes through its eight year run.

Ward Bond collapsed and died of a heart attack whilst taking a shower in a motel in Dallas on 5 November 1961. He had fallen behind the cubicle door and ambulance men had trouble getting to him.

John McIntire as Christopher Hale, assumed the job of wagon master and the absence of the major was never explained on the show.

In contrast to Major Adams, the new wagon master had a more relaxed management style. Gone was the bluster as Hale led with a steady hand. John McIntire's portrayal was of a man wise and fair, who rarely raised his voice to make his point understood.

Then, after five seasons of surveying the trail ahead, Robert Horton suddenly left the show to pursue a successful career in the musical theatre and through 1965 to be the sole star of TV's *A Man Called Shenandoah*.

Fresh from his success as Jess Harper in *Laramie*, Robert Fuller as Cooper Smith or 'Coop' took on the job of scout for the train, mounted on his willing horse, Gambler. Also added were Denny Miller as Duke Shannon and then Michael Burns as Barnaby West arrived in late 1963 heading west in search of his father.

Robert Fuller's scout was all rough and tumble. He never started fights, but he finished quite a few! Fuller was entirely believable in the role and viewers recognized

that this was a man to face the dangers ahead of the train unflinchingly. Coop was soon a favorite and Fuller brought with him to *Wagon Train* all of his *Laramie* fans.

*Wagon Train* switched networks in 1962 and although reports of the sums that changed hands for this vary, ABC did pay a huge amount to bring the show under their umbrella. For one season in 1963, they tried taking it to an hour and a half format and filming it in color. This was to compete with *The Virginian* (also from Revue). But when that experiment proved unsuccessful the show returned to its original one hour length. And worse, they returned to shooting in black and white which drove viewers to more modern shows and *Wagon Train* left the air, doomed by its own producers.

Robert Fuller went on to star in *Walker, Texas Ranger*.

Ward Bond was inducted into Hall of Great Western Performers by the National Cowboy and Western Heritage Museum on 21 April 2001.

John McIntire, born on 27 June 1907, passed away on 30 January 1991 of emphysema and cancer. He had been married to actress Jeanette Nolan from 1935 until the time of his death.

Robert Horton is retired and lives in California.

# WANTED — DEAD OR ALIVE
## 6 September 1958

**STEVE McQUEEN** had his first big hit in this show as bounty hunter, Josh Randall, starring in the CBS show which premiered on 6 September 1958 and ran to 29 March 1961.

Through the 94 episodes Randall used a custom-made .30-.40 caliber, sawn-off Winchester carbine; nicknamed the 'Mare's leg', which he wore on his side like a handgun and which could be fired with blazing speed. The gun became a legend in the annals of television Western lore and added to McQueen's anti-hero image and of the character Randall who was infused with a combination of mystery, alienation and detachment. It was McQueen's portrayal that really made this show stand out from the typical run-of-the-mill TV Western.

The character of Josh Randall had first been introduced to viewers in *Trackdown*, starring Robert Culp, in the episode called *The Bounty Hunter*, which aired on 7 March 1958. McQueen generated so much fan mail that Four Star Productions decided on a spin, using the *Trackdown* story in their new series, *Wanted: Dead or Alive*.

*Wanted: Dead or Alive* was set on the frontier of the 1880's when it was common for bounty hunters to make a living from the rewards offered for capturing criminals. Since bounty hunters were not hampered by the constraints that confronted lawmen, they always did pretty much as they pleased. Many of them acquired a reputation for bringing back the wanted man dead, which did not endear any of them to either the law or the town citizens. This antagonism didn't faze Josh Randall, who took it upon himself to apprehend anyone having a price on his head. In successive episodes, he would ride into a town, check out the wanted posters, and the hunt was on.

Over the course of the series, Randall came to be known by all as an honest man. He spoke few words, but was dignified and acted according to his own code of ethics. Lawmen from all over the Southwest and as far north as Wyoming, knew him. They often asked for his assistance in tracking down a particularly bad hombre that they had been unable to bring to justice.

Toward the end of the second season, Randall acquired a young sidekick named Jason Nichols, who mysteriously disappeared by the start of the third season. Wright King starred as Nichols.

This series drew some top names in Hollywood as guest stars including Michael Landon, DeForest Kelley, Nick Adams, Warren Oates, James Coburn, Victor Jory, Clu Gulager, Jay Silverheels, Lee Van Cleef, Dyan Cannon, John Carradine, Mary Tyler Moore, and Cloris Leachman.

McQueen died aged 50 from a rare form of cancer on 7 November 1980.

## TRIVIA

McQueen was nicknamed 'The King of Cool' and he was one of the biggest box-office draws of the 1960's and 1970's but was known to be combative with directors and producers; regardless, he was able to command large salaries and was always in high demand. After completing *Wanted-Dead or Alive* he went on to star in movies such as *The Magnificent Seven* (1960), *The Great Escape* (1963) and, of course, *Bullitt* (1968). He was an avid motorcycle and racecar enthusiast and whenever he had the opportunity to drive in a movie, he often did so himself, performing many of his own stunts.

# THE WESTERNER
## 30 SEPTEMBER 1960

**NBC** ran this Four Star Productions show between 30 September 1960 and 30 December 1960.

The series, starring Brian Keith as Dave Blassingame, was massively underrated, despite the help of acclaimed director Sam Peckinpah.

Uncompromisingly tough scripts saw the cowboy and his dog, Brown, roaming the West, going from job to job.

Keith committed suicide in 1998 and was a great loss to the industry.

# WHIPLASH
## 20 SEPTEMBER 1962

**THERE** were 34 episodes of the half hour, black and white show made on location between 20 September 1962 and 12 September 1963.

This was an Australian western starring American actor, Peter Graves as Chris Cobb. Set in the 1850's, the owner of Cobb & Company Stagecoach Lines, attempted to forge the first stagecoach line across the Australian Outback.

Anthony Wickert starred as Dan.

Graves had just finished working on *Fury* when he was signed for the more adult *Whiplash*. He went on to greater fame of course in *Mission Impossible*.

# WHISPERING SMITH
## 15 MAY 1961

**THE half hour, black and white shows were filmed in 1959, and were scheduled for the 1959–1960 fall season, but the production was jinxed and although 26 episodes were made only about half were ever shown before it quietly left the air on 18 September 1961.**

Audie Murphy made his only foray into a television series, based on the Alan Ladd movie of 1948, in this doomed show. Although it was plagued with all sorts of problems, *Whispering Smith* was a neat little Western set in Denver in 1870.

Murphy disliked the scripts, the way the show was made and the lack of promotion from the start; he much preferred working in movies. Murphy starred as Tom 'Whispering' Smith, a railroad detective, from 15 May 1961, even though production had first started in September 1959.

The entire premise of this show was based on the adventures of the first police detective to bring modern methods of analysis and tracing techniques to the practice of catching outlaws in the West. Actual cases from the files of the Denver Police Department provided the basis for each episode, and Whispering Smith and George Romack were the railroad investigators intent on protecting the railroad from fraud, robberies, and murder. Whilst this may have been standard private eye fare the setting for their escapades was relatively unique, and the show also featured some interesting guest stars including a young Robert Redford, Harry Carey Jr., Marie Windsor, a pre-Kildare Richard Chamberlain, Minerva Urecal and a pre-Gilligan Alan Hale Jr.

Guy Mitchell co-starred as right hand man Romack. Sam Buffington rounded out the cast as Police Chief John Richards. With only seven episodes in the can, co-star Guy Mitchell fell from a horse and broke his shoulder and Murphy, already less than impressed with television, was all for abandoning the project right from the start.

When the show finally appeared in the summer of 1961, the Senate Juvenile Delinquency committee filed charges that the show was too violent and it was panned. Mid way through production, Buffington committed suicide and had to be replaced.

Murphy was killed in a plane crash near Roanoke, Virginia on 28 May 1971. Being the most decorated American soldier of the Second World War, he was buried with full Military Honors at Arlington National Cemetery.

Guy Mitchell died in 1999.

# WICHITA TOWN
## 30 November 1959

**THE** half hour, black and white show only ran between 30 November 1959 and 30 September 1960 on NBC.

Set in the rowdy cow town, real life father and son, Joel and Jody McCrea played marshal and deputy in Wichita, Kansas Territory. Joel McCrea starred as Marshal Mike Dunbar and Jody McCrea played his deputy, Ben Matheson.

Dunbar had led a cattle drive to Wichita and decided to settle there. Matheson had been foreman at the Circle J Ranch.

Ex-gunfighter, Rico Rodriguez, played by Carlos Romero, was occasionally recruited to help out around the town. The main cast was rounded out by George N. Neise as Doctor Nat Wyndham, Bob Anderson as Aeneas MacLinahan and Robert Foulk as Joe Kingston. MacLinahan was the smithy and Kingston was a bartender.

Joel McCrea died on 20 October 1990 of pulmonary complications.

Foulk died and 1989 and Neise died in 1997 of cancer.

# WIDE COUNTRY
## 20 September 1962

**ONLY** 28 episodes were made of this hour long, black and white show that centered on the rodeo circuit. The series was made by Revue Production between 20 September 1962 and 12 September 1963. It was directed by **William Witney**.

Earl Holliman starred as Mitch Guthrie and Andrew Prine played his brother, Andy.

The two were rodeo cowboys on the traveling circuit. Mitch was a champion bronco rider who tried to keep his kid brother, Andy, from pursuing the same life.

Andrew Prine is probably best known for his Western/military roles in the early 60's and was a mainstay on *Gunsmoke*, but his best known work was his first starring role as James Keller in *The Miracle Worker*. Military roles followed in *The Devil's Brigade* and he also worked on various Western films including *Bandolero!* and *Chisum*.

# THE WILD WILD WEST
## 15 SEPTEMBER 1965

**THERE** were 104 hour long, black and white and color episodes produced for CBS TV which ran on Friday nights between 15 September 1965 and 7 September 1970. In its first season it won an Emmy Award Nomination for Ted Voightlander for *Individual Achievement in Cinematography* and the show came in 23rd in the season's ratings. The series was produced by Bruce Lansbury and created by Michael Garrison. Music was from Richard Markowitz.

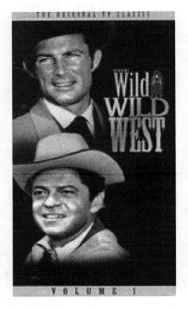

Part Western, part spy thriller and part SciFi, *The Wild Wild West* was a gadget filled action series set in the 1870s. It starred Robert Conrad as Secret Agent James T. West, a former Union soldier. Ross Martin was his partner, Artemus Gordon, a former con man and master of disguise and invention. Together, the two working in the Secret Service for President Ulysses S. Grant, fought various menaces aimed at the United States and the President, as well as investigating other Federal crimes.

The show rode on the post-James Bond spy craze of the 60's and featured all of the typical 'spy gimmicks' such as boot knives, miniature explosives and spike-firing grapple guns. It also featured a variety of criminal masterminds wielding high-tech items (for 1880) like robot squids, cyborgs, exo-skeletons, steam-powered giant puppets, earthquake machines, hallucinogenic drugs, shrinking potions, and the heroes rode to their assignments on a private train.

*The Wild Wild West* boasted many fight scenes and Conrad said, 'The fight sequences were carefully choreographed bar-room brawls that tended to last a significant amount of time on air. They were then repeated again in some other location a few minutes later.'

The major nemesis, diminutive Dr. Miguelito Loveless, was a master of gadgets. The show's producers and writers mixed all this with typical Western movie conventions, a nod to the old movie serials, and some modern-day styling. The odd and often quite mad, villains were at the heart of the show's success.

Conrad believed it was the violent fight scenes that led to the show being taken off air; he didn't think this was a bad thing as the stunts had caused many injuries. It was certainly not cancelled due to its ratings and had rather more to do with the President of CBS, Dr Frank Stanton, pledging to Congress to reduce television violence.

In 1979 CBS produced *The Wild Wild West Revisited*, a two hour television movie. James West is brought out of retirement in 1885 to reunite with Artemus Gordon (who had become an actor with the Deadwood Shakespearian Strolling Players!) to foil the plans of Miguelito Loveless Jr., the son of their old adversary.

In 1980 *More Wild Wild West* was produced by CBS. The two hour movie aired in two parts on the 7 and 8 October. Five years after their last reunion West and Gordon are again teamed to fight against Professor Albert Pardine 11, a madman who is out to defeat the world with his weapons of doom.

# WILDSIDE
## 21 MARCH 1985

THE show debuted on ABC on 21 March 1985 and left the air just one month later before all the filmed episodes had been shot. Walt Disney Productions made the hour long color series.

*Wildside* dealt with the exploits of five legendary gunfighters who were trying to live as ordinary citizens in Wildside County.

They were really a law enforcement unit attempting to keep the peace.

Bill Smith starred as Brodie Hollister, J. Eddie Peck was his son, Sutton and Howard Rollins Jr., played the explosives expert, Terry Funk was Prometheus and John Di Aquino was Vargas.

# THE WRANGLER
## 14 AUGUST 1960

JASON EVERS starred as the wrangler, Pitcairn, for a limited run between 14 August 1960 and 15 September 1960. The half hour show was shot on tape by NBC in black and white.

Pitcairn wandered the country searching for work as a bronc rider or ranch hand. He rode the 1880's Western frontier helping people. His sole companion was his horse, Sam.

Evers, a member of the Academy of Motion Picture Arts and Sciences, is perhaps best known for playing Dr. Bill Corter in the 1962 cult film *The Brain That Wouldn't Die* (1962). He made frequent guest appearances on shows such as *Matlock, The A Team, Murder, She Wrote, Knight Rider* and many others.

He died, aged 83, on 13 March 2005 in Los Angeles, California, of heart failure.

# YANCY DERRINGER
## 2 OCTOBER 1958

**THE** half hour, black and white series debuted on CBS on 2 October 1958 and ran for 38 episodes before going off air on 24 September 1959.

This Western was set in New Orleans just after the Civil War. Derringer, a ladie's man, was an ex-Confederate soldier who became a card shark and detective. He was also a Special Agent for John Colton, Civil Administrator for New Orleans. His constant companion was shotgun wielding Indian, Pahoo.

Yancy entertained himself at Madame Francine's Club where he played cards and watched out for trouble. He carried his derringer in his hat. Jock Mahoney played Yancy, X.Brands was Pahoo and Frances Bergen was Francine. Other regulars included Robert McCord and Fred Crone.

X.Brands died of cancer on 15 May 2000 and Mahoney on 14 December 1989 from a stroke.

---

## TRIVIA

In Pawnee Pahoo-Ka-Ta-Wah means 'wolf who stands in water'. In the series Pahoo carried a knife in his headdress.

---

# THE YELLOW ROSE
## 2 OCTOBER 1983

**THE one hour, color Western soap debuted on NBC on 2 October 1983. It lasted for just one season and left the air on 12 May 1984.**

The Yellow Rose was a 200,000 cattle ranch, run by the Champion family, in modern West Texas. The weekly stories featured constant struggles for money and power.

Laden with big names, Sam Elliott starred as Chance Mckenzie, a mysterious ex-convict, Cybill Shepherd was Colleen Champion, David Soul was Roy Champion, Edward Albert was Quisto Champion. The cast was well rounded by Susan Anspach as Grace, the housekeeper, Ken Curtis as Coryell and Noah Beery Jr., as Dillard. Will Sampson played John Strongheart, Michelle Bennett was L.C. Champion, Tom Schanley was Whit Champion, Jane Russell was Rose Hollister and Chuck Conners played Jeb Hollister.

Ken Curtis died on 27 April 1991.

Noah Beery Jr., died on 1 November 1994.

Chuck Connors died on 10 November 1992.

# YOUNG DAN'L BOONE
## 12 SEPTEMBER 1977

**EACH episode of the show was an hour long and was shot on location in Tennessee in color. It debuted on CBS on 12 September 1977. It was cancelled after four episodes on 4 October 1977.**

Rick Moses played Boone in this 20th Century Fox TV production.

In the show Boone explores Kentucky with an English boy named Peter and a runaway slave called Hawk. John Joseph Thomas played Peter and Ji-Tu Cumbuka, Hawk. Devon Ericson starred as Boone's love, Rebecca Bryan.

# YOUNG MAVERICK
## 28 November 1979

**AFTER** just seven hour long color episodes, the show which set out with such high hopes and debuted on 28 November 1979, went off air on 16 January 1980.

Ben Maverick, a cousin of Bret and son of Beauregard (Roger Moore), played by Charles Frank, was first introduced to viewers in a TV movie, *The New Maverick* which also starred James Garner and Jack Kelly. The ratings for the movie led to this spin off which also starred Frank's real wife, Susan Blanchard.

The show reprised the original *Maverick* series and was produced by Warner Bros. CBS-TV had bought the series for its mid-season schedule knowing that James Garner would not feature regularly as he was already tied into *The Rockford Files*. Originally it was going to be screened by ABC, where the pilot had been shot. But when their option ran out CBS agreed to make a new pilot.

Charles Frank enthused, 'I've never read scripts as good as these. The show is fun, well-written… and it's a Western.'

His character was similar to that of the original Bret; a con man, but now with a 'Lovely thorn in the side – a female counterpart who is essentially a better con artist than he is.'

Blanchard said of the character she played, 'She loves Ben, but you never think she sleeps with him. She is an old-fashioned, pure girl. She is very jealous of the other girls he gets involved with.'

When he had first been approached to play the part of Ben, Frank had been wary, 'I didn't want to be compared to Garner. But I had been working in a Western shooting in Arizona and seen how excited people there were to see a Western in production. I realized the popularity retained by that genre.'

John Dehner starred as the marshal who often tangled with Ben Maverick.

Whilst the producers had thought to lure in viewers with the name, 'Maverick', they also hoped that the audience wouldn't notice the new show didn't compare with the original. Although *Young Maverick* had no one on board with the flare of Roy Huggins, creator of the original, they did employ writers such as David Peckinpah (son of director Sam). Unfortunately Garner's charm simply couldn't be written into any script. And the critics panned the show saying that viewers were going to be bitterly disappointed… but probably not surprised.

Garner himself agreed in November 1980 to re-create Bret for yet another TV series, 'The writers are working on it now, so I'm not sure what they are going to do with it. I do know that Maverick is going to be 20 years older. This time I just sit there in my rocking chair… and let someone else do the work.'

# THE YOUNG REBELS
## 20 SEPTEMBER 1970

**SEVENTEEN hour-long color episodes were made for ABC and The Young Rebels first aired on 20 September 1970. It went off air on 3 January 1971.**

The show was set in 1777 during the American Revolution. It was the duty of the rebels to harass British troops behind their own lines.

Rick Ely starred as Jeremy Larkin, Hilarie Thompson was Elizabeth, Alex Henteloff played Henry and Lou Gossett Jr., starred as Isak Poole.

# YOUNG RIDERS
## 20 SEPTEMBER 1989

**THE hour-long show, shot in color around Mescal, first aired on 20 September 1989. It ran for three seasons on ABC before leaving the air on 23 July 1992. Sixty six episodes were made by MGM/ UA TV.**

Set in the days just before the advent of telegraph and just preceding the outbreak of the Civil War, this series presented a highly fictionalized account of a Pony Express way-station located in a ranch in Sweetwater, Wyoming Territory. The young riders are kids working for the Pony Express in 1860.

The riders did deliver some mail from time to time, but spent most of their time rescuing escaped slaves, protecting the innocent, and being nice to the Indians. Rumblings of the imminent Civil War allowed some moralizing on that issue, but they were generally righting any wrongs they encountered along the way. In the Third Season, the entire crew moved to Rock Creek, on the Nebraska-Kansas-Missouri border, which allowed for the introduction of more urban concerns.

The show initially aired with five male riders and one female rider, who disguised herself as a boy so she could work for the Pony Express. Anthony Zerbe was Teaspoon Hunter, the kid's trainer. Melissa Leo starred as the cook.

Ty Miller was The Kid, Josh Brolin was Young Jimmy Hickok, Stephen Baldwin was Bill Cody, Travis Fine played Ike, Don Franklin was Noah, Chris Pettier was Jesse James and Gregg Rainwater was Buck Cross. Yvonne Suhor was Lou. Clare Wren was Rachel Dunn who joined in the second season after Leo left. Don Collier starred as storekeeper, William Tompkins.

All three seasons saw *The Young Riders* in the top ten of the ratings, before ABC had the brainchild of moving it to the 'death pit' Saturday night timeslot from September 1990 – August 1991. With falling ratings, ABC then changed hours again to Saturday night from September 1991 – January 1992, but without any real success. In a desperate attempt to revive the show, ABC once again reverted back to Thursday nights from May 1992 – July 1992. It was too late. By moving it all around in their lineup, ABC executives succeeded in killing it.

# ZANE GREY THEATRE
## 5 OCTOBER 1956

**THIS** weekly half hour, black and white show, produced by Four Star Productions, ran on CBS for 145 episodes between 5 October 1956 and 20 September 1962.

The series attracted many top Hollywood stars. Each week a different actor played in a tale of the West, some indeed written by Zane Grey.

Dick Powell hosted and often starred in episodes.

Powell died on 2 January 1963.

# ZORRO
## 10 OCTOBER 1957

**THE half hour, black and white show ran for almost three years on ABC, debuting on 10 October 1957. After 114 episodes it left the line up on 24 September 1959.**

This Walt Disney series starred Guy Williams as Don Diego De La Vega or Zorro. Zorro rode out whenever he was needed to help the downtrodden folk of Pueblo De Los Angeles in 1820's Spanish California.

Captain Monastario is the brutal tyrant that Zorro rides against on his steed, Tornado. Britt Lomond starred as the Captain, Henry Calvin played Sergeant Garcia and Don Diamond played his private. George J. Lewis was Don Alejandro, Zorro's unsuspecting father.

Only Bernardo, the mute manservant, played by Gene Sheldon, knew Zorro's secret.

Williams died on 7 May 1989, aged 65, in Buenos Aires, where he had been living. Disney Studios released several episodes of Zorro on video.

# ZORRO AND SON
## 6 APRIL 1983

**THE half hour, colour show debuted on CBS on 6 April 1983 but after only nine episodes it was withdrawn on 1 June 1983.**

The comedy was based 25 years after Zorro first became famous and age has taken its toll on Don Diego after he had been injured.

Don Carlos, Diego's son is sent for, to help carry on the legend. Henry Darrow starred as Don Diego and Paul Regina played Carlos. Faithful manservant, Bernardo, was played by Bill Dana and the Commandant of Pueblo De Los Angeles, Paco Pici was played by Gregory Sierra.

Bumbling Sergeant Sepulveda was Richard Beauchamp.

# PART THREE

**The death of the television western**

# PART THREE: THE DEATH OF THE TELEVISION WESTERN

**THE** frontier may be dead and the great stars and directors associated with the genre long since departed and not replaced, but at least one hundred and ninety eight Western series were made specifically for television. Many of those old shows can stand the test of time and they have indeed become a cultural legacy to the world. The dusty old cowboys who populated them made us believe in heroes. They provided shelter through our own troubled times, they were entirely dependable and predictable; upright, straight-talking-and-shooting. They offered the simplest of answers to the complex problems we all faced through the Cold War era. They gave us codes and completely defined value systems to live by where we were bound together in our expectations. The white hat was worn by the good guy, the black hat by the bad; we anticipated a gun-fight showdown whenever two people came face to face on a deserted street; townsfolk represented family and community values; cattlemen were loners.

All the elements of the code, which included the spectacular scenery of wilderness and dramatic spread, were put together to tell morality tales and their success depended on the most basic human reactions to excitement, tension and resolution, violence, death, and examinations of physical and moral strength.

None were more aware of those defining elements than the early television producers who presented the Wild West at its most archetypal level, a place where good triumphed over evil and order was always wrestled from the teeth of chaos in under an hour. The television Western was a safe place to pass controversial and complex comment indirectly, and whilst the cowboy had already been repeatedly defined in literature, drama and the cinema, it was in the medium of television he found his ultimate spiritual home. Due to the special nature of the world created there, he came to stand at the centre of American popular art and culture and in adapting his form to television the producers assured themselves of a ready made mass audience.

In the heyday period of the 50's, the triumph of the television cowboy undoubtedly lay in the easy escapism he offered, but he was also a metaphoric victory for American goodness in the modern West. Pride in the achievements of Seth Adams in *Wagon Train* directly translated to the inhabitants of a contemporary United States. To accept such a preponderant number of Westerns on prime time TV in the 50's and 60's, viewers had to approve of the community being forged or defended in each episode and in this manner television's Western heroes became symbolic Cold Warriors. They showed how it was possible to win against treachery and that it was never necessary to co-exist with, or accept, evil. In those times of challenge, the television Western was relevant drama and the message was communicated most effectively, in the privacy of family living rooms.

Throughout the 1950's and 60's American households were snapping up their first television sets and in 1961 the average American household watched TV for five hours and 22 minutes a day. Television had become the principal form of entertainment and in 1963 over two thirds of the population was watching television Westerns, making them the dominant force in network programming.

In order to retain that lofty position, producers, writers and directors and stars had to strive to win and retain sponsors. They were vital and neither success nor failure was determined by the individual merit of a show but purely according to ratings and each sponsor was interested in just one thing; winning a high enough ranking to indicate a mass audience for its particular sales pitch. Every single Western **had** to appear at the top end of the charts or fall by the wayside.

As the television era moved into the more sophisticated 70's, Westerns were increasingly up against it and the number ranking in the Top 25 shows each season could be counted on one hand: *Gunsmoke, Bonanza, The Virginian* (under its new title *The Men from Shiloh*), and possibly *Little House on the Prairie*. New Westerns premiering in the 70's never caught on and, except *Little House on the Prairie* they all had very short runs.

Times had changed, cultural, economic, political and social attitudes had shifted. Americans no longer felt threatened by the gigantic post-war Russia and their attention was increasingly focused on fighting what they perceived as a lesser foe in South Easy Asia. The message of the Western was suddenly less relevant to them in the emerging circumstances. Younger audiences made demands for new, lighter scheduling – they were not interested in Western morality. Increasingly too, sponsors began losing interest in what appeared to be a dated, old-hat product.

Any time a genre fails so greatly to attract viewers or retain sponsors, it can be guaranteed that the television networks will cease considering any new series of the same type.

The boom of the 50's and 60's had seen an extraordinary number of Westerns produced; the networks had all been sodden with them and that sheer saturation is evident considering that, during the same period, only 25 series about private eyes and ten medical dramas aired. But still, of those Westerns made, few showed any originality or made any attempt to cash in on shifting tastes.

Around 20 of the Western series made from 1955 to 1975 were about gunslingers or drifters. Another 20 dealt with lawmen (sheriffs, US Marshals, Texas rangers, and so on), and ten with ranches or homesteads. The sameness of the shows made in that period is evident in the vast territory they left unexplored. Despite the popularity of medical dramas in the 60's, there have only been two Western shows with doctors as main characters (*Frontier Doctor* in 1958 and *Dr. Quinn Medicine Woman* in the 90's). Similarly, none took advantage of the traveling medicine shows so infamous all along the real frontier. Only three TV Westerns made between 1955 and 75 featured lawyers as their main characters and only two, newspaper editors. Just two focused on wagon trains (*Wagon Train* and *Overland Trail*) and another two on the cattle drive (*Rawhide* and the short lived 70's series *The Cowboys*).

Falling ratings were the direct factor forcing the gunslingers to begin hanging up their guns, but the causes of low ratings were both complex and devastating. Whilst the 70's witnessed a mini boom in the sprawling family sagas such as *Bonanza* the advertisers recognized that those shows missed out on up to 50 percent of a potential market and despite the early slump both producers and sponsors were quick to investigate opening up new avenues for their shows. *Bonanza* creator, David Dortort admitted, 'We do not have any moms built into our show – or for that matter, any women. We are, as it were, anti-momism.' By its themes and its characterizations the Western had always represented a modification of the lone-rider heroics but as the domestic Westerns took off, an interesting departure from convention had been *The Big Valley* starring Barbara Stanwyck as its leading character, a strong self-reliant female head of a pioneering family. This series saw the first introduction of a woman as an important figure, a character integral to Frontier life, but now a reflection of the awareness of sponsors and producers that women as domestic consumers were vital members of the viewing audience. For ten of its fourteen seasons, it rated among the Top Ten TV attractions and through 1964–67 it was the most watched series in America.

For a while the sponsors were satisfied with its swollen audience, but then, just as the mothers had started to tune in, more and more of the younger audience was turned off and the demographic-fixated advertisers knew the Westerns were still only attracting the white, wrinkly end of the market.

The Nielsen ratings for December 1967 revealed that no Westerns appeared in the Top Ten amongst children aged ten to eleven. Only *The Guns of Will Sonnet* ranked in the Top Ten of teenagers aged 12 to 17, albeit at the number one spot and *The High Chapparal* was the only Western appearing in the Top Ten for adults aged 18 to 34. If shows could no longer attract young adults the death of the genre was inevitable.

In a sign of desperation, young heart throbs were thrown at the shows and stars such as Clint Walker had to rip off his shirt in almost every episode in an attempt to attract more young female viewers. Still ratings declined.

If the rise of the television western had coincided with the Cold War, its fall might be seen as a direct correlation of America's foray into South East Asia. The Cold War had been reality, and like the innocent ranchers of countless Westerns who found their existence threatened by outlaws, unassuming Americans were compelled to defend themselves. It was easy then to see themselves at the centre of a noble cause. The Western myth portrayed lonely men riding off to take up arms in noble defense, and the myth fitted real life. The Western plot offered a perfect filter through which to view the Cold War.

But this was far from the case where the Vietnam conflict was concerned. The young soldiers fighting in Vietnam had been nurtured on the abundance of Westerns. This generation of warriors learned as children to define itself with reference to cowboy imagery. They had accepted the Western because its stories explained so much so easily and clearly.

But as the war in Vietnam progressed, costing America billions of dollars and almost 60,000 lives, many began to feel the price, when it resulted ultimately in defeat and no political advantage, too high. If the Western flourished because it mirrored popular thought through the Cold War, when that era ended, the unquestioning trust that characterized that time was left eroded and useless.

In the blending of legal, moral and political self-justification that had been the television Western, millions had watched the triumphs of their forefathers over the moral threats that they understood. They had witnessed a nation in the making; their country in its formative years. They had seen a clean world in which to start again, a land full of heroes who defended American belief systems.

But what began as a crusade for the achievement of fundamental legal rights in Vietnam soon degenerated into confusion and moral dilemma.

The formulaic framework of the Western did not fit the new litigious world. Many began looking at their world more closely and they decided that the bad guys were actually the good guys, and the good were bad. In South East Asia Americans lost their innocent, cowboy qualities. Noble self-sacrifice became a socially disquieting phenomenon. As American soldiers rode out to the rescue of the South Vietnamese, doubts about the justness of the cause grew at home. News broadcasters showed protest marches on the streets, drug use by the front-line troops, draft-card burners, clergymen protesting against the war, dislike of the allied South Vietnam troops and the killing of officers by the enlisted men in the field. This was not the stuff of television Westerns or cowboy heroes. Increasingly moral ambivalence and reformism led to a split from traditional Western judgements and a stunning re-evaluation in American thought clashed grotesquely with the certainties of the Old West and the value systems upheld by the heroes were no longer accepted by large components of the population.

Although there had been a critique of violence on TV, the nightly slaughter of the Vietnam War now seen nightly on TV saturated the American culture in violence. Somehow this all rendered the mayhem integral to the Western excessive and an increasing discomfort with the glorification of violence grew; the adult Western had brought a controversial dose of gore to prime time television and when Congress began holding hearings on the subject, network executives came under serious pressure to tone down the gunplay. Violence had always been a major component of adult Westerns. In *Gunsmoke* it had been promised every week in the view of Marshal Dillon striding out into the street to face and draw against his challenger. In *The Rifleman* Lucas McCain fired off a dozen rifle shots in rapid succession as the series was introduced. Paladin in *Have Gun-Will Travel* always pointed his gun directly at the TV viewer as the credits rolled. Many series exploited the use of firearms in their opening images and several shows revered deadly weapons, as in *The Life and Legend of Wyatt Earp*, which featured Earp's Buntline Special, a customized gun with a 16" barrel. Ballistic savagery permeated all Westerns and had grown from a view of the world where adult men moved through society with guns strapped on their hip and significantly, this emphasis had spurred gun sales in USA and by late 1958 weapons manufacturers were producing 10,000 Western-style guns every month in order to satisfy customer demand, although *Cisco Kid's* Duncan Renaldo pointed out in an interview in 1959, 'We shot in self defence, we shot the guns out of bandit's hands, but we didn't kill. We had action and entertainment, but not murder, gore or vengeance.'

Guy Madison of *Wild Bill Hickok* agreed, 'Few of us instilled violence for violence's sake' and Jock Mahoney, star of *Range Rider*, continued, 'We had some wing-ding fights where I'd completely demolish some stores and cabinets, but good always won out. That was the message of the TV Western.'

Increased gun sales or not, it seemed that the body count in many Westerns was proving to be a turn off that was reflected in declining viewing statistics. Television executives were sensitive to the public debate that had been hotting up and in fact as early as 1955 officials at NBC had formalized a set of rules to regulate excessive violence in their shows. Although they imposed a degree of self-censorship, network concern was heightened when the chairman of the Federal Communications Commission, Newton Minow, openly attacked the television Western as banal and violent; a discredit to the industry in the way it projected the American image abroad. On 9 May 1961 he condemned the sadism and murder and rebuked Westerns as a hindrance in the not-so-cold propaganda war with the Soviet bloc, 'What will the people of other countries think of us when they see our Western badmen and good men punching each other in the jaw in between the shooting?' He asked, 'What will the Latin American or African child learn from out great communications industry? We cannot permit television in its present form to be our voice overseas.'

The anti-violence groups jumped on the back of Minow's speech and increasingly brought pressure to bear against the producers who panicked and began to shy away from making Westerns.

James Arness commented in 1958, 'People like Westerns because they represent a time of freedom. A cowboy wasn't tied down to one place or to one woman. When he got mad he hauled off and slugged someone. When he drank he got good and drunk.' But by the mid 60's, *Gunsmoke* producer, John Mantley, felt compelled to start writing different story lines focussing on character rather than action. The real Dodge City had been awash with brutality and sex and Mantley bitterly regretted the softening process saying, 'The Western was a simplified re-enactment of the eternal struggle between good and evil in which good always triumphs and evil dies in the shootout.' Still he knew the only way to stay in business at all was to adapt; to ride with changing times.

In 1961 David Levy, NBC vice president in charge of TV programs said in a letter to John Champion, the producer of *Laramie*, 'I believe we should do everything possible to reduce shootouts, killings and unnecessary violence. I would also urge you to eliminate excessive drinking. I believe that on reflection and with greater creative effort on the part of writers and greater supervision on your part the stories on *Laramie* can be exactly as Western without subjecting you or us to justifiable criticism.'

In 1965 an interim report of the US Senate Juvenile Delinquency Subcommittee, chaired by Senator Thomas J. Dodd, came to the conclusion, 'It is clear that television, whose impact on the public mind is equal to or greater than that of any other medium, is a factor in molding the character, attitudes and behavior patterns of America's young people.' The violence permeating TV Westerns was already being singled out as a major contributor to juvenile delinquency, and a brutalizing reflection of a violence-prone society.

Of course there were plenty of other factors slowly strangling the life out of Westerns, and even as they had first settled into their weekly time slots, over-exploitation had been eroding the genre's early success. The glut and declining quality of Westerns from the late 50's onward meant there may have simply been just too many buckskin escapades clogging the channels. As a society given to commercial crazes, 30 years of cowboy drama had already satisfied much of the mass appetite for the genre and executives had been over-zealous in creating uncomfortable clichés; that, added to the newly enforced reduction in the elements of tension and gunplay, saw some shows become gimmicky and too far removed from the real West to stand any chance of prolonged success.

The altered programming practices of the seventies also gave rise to greater competition from the cop thriller, science fiction epics and sitcoms which were proving massively popular in the new era of Civil Rights movements, the ecology movement and the crusade for women's rights. New good guys and bad guys began to emerge. The Western also faced new foes as moral confusion grew in America.

Nationalistic interpretation in Westerns had been as selective as it was simple. The fate of the Native American in such programs had always been contradictory. In reality, the Americanization of the West had entailed the systematic subjugation of those who had lived in the wilderness. Native Americans had lost their freedom in the historic Western push and few Westerns had ever communicated that reality. There had also been other nation states with claims to parts of the frontier but the TV Western had consistently ignored them all. They were all-American; Caucasian, Anglo-Saxon and generally Protestant. Native Americans might be portrayed as noble anachronisms standing in the way of the white expansion or hostile savages; only very occasionally were they assimilated or accepted into the fight of white social dominance.

Such depictions had led to Indian rights groups protesting against the perpetuation of outdated racial stereotypes. In 1960 the Organization of Oklahoma Indian Tribes and the Association on American Indian Affairs criticized the networks for their distortions of Native Americans. They attacked series which showed Indians as drunken, cowardly outlaws, usually attacking wagon trains. In response the Oklahoma state legislature passed a resolution in 1960, condemning network television, 'There is no excuse for TV producers to ignore the harm that may be done the children of America by repetitious distortion of historical facts pertaining to the way of life of any race or creed, including the American Indian.'

As early as autumn 1967 the fate of Westerns was foreshadowed in the case of *Custer*, an ABC series based on the exploits of Lt. Col. George Armstrong Custer. Whatever expectations the network had for the show, *Custer* was outdated from its inception. Even before it went on air, Native American organizations assailed the program as detrimental to Indians and the spokesman for more than 24,000 Chippewa Indians said, 'The *Custer* series will stir up old animosities and revive Indian and cowboy fallacies we have been trying to live down.'

Among other races traditionally abused in the Western were Asians. In reality they had played a major role in building the West and Asian labor had been especially important in the construction of the railroad. In the TV West however Asians became cooks and experts in laundry, or criminals. In the seventies they became an increasingly powerful anti-cowboy lobby.

The television Western may have started out with everything going for it, but by the 70's it had become so irrelevant that it had all but disappeared, as it was slowly battered into an undignified submission.

Of course, powerful careers were on the line and television producers and executives weren't in a position to simply throw in the towel. Initially they didn't give up on what they thought could still be a good thing, after all the Western had been their lucrative bread and butter for many years. They fought every step of the way to retain the genre's relevance to as wide an audience as possible and although the end was in sight from the mid 60's onward, the television Western wasn't lost without a fight of epic proportion.

Through the late 60's TV Westerns had received a timely injection of hip in shows such as *The Wild Wild West*, a bond-style slice of spy-spoofery. The ranch saga *The High Chaparral* followed America's changing cultural climate by treating the Apache with dignity and respect and proved to be one of television's finest shows. The seventies might be a bleak time out on the range but other shows such as *Alias Smith and Jones* worked well for a time. And there were some interesting new twists added to the tired old stories. Some turned out to be top class shows such as *Hec Ramsey*, which was an attempt to compete with the modern cop shows and starred wonderful veteran actor Richard Boone. This show comfortably combined elements of the Western alongside the modern mystery thriller. It started out as one of the rotating elements of the umbrella series, *The NBC Mystery Movie*, and featured an ex-gunfighter turned deputy sheriff who used magnifying glasses, fingerprinting tools, scales and measuring tape rather than a gun. The show ran two years and was deemed a resounding success.

*Nichols* was another unusual, but less successful effort which took place at the end of the Old West and featured a very pacifistic hero, audience pleaser, James Garner in the title role.

Many of the last-gasp Westerns were extremely strange and some new shows fared better than others. *Kung Fu* rode in on the back of the popular martial arts craze with David Carradine as Kwai Chang Caine, a Buddhist monk born of Chinese and American parents. Caine of course was unique among Western heroes. Besides being Chinese, (as already noted, the only other Orientals featured in Westerns had been cooks and laundrymen), he did not use a gun, relying instead upon the martial art kung fu for self defence. The series' execution also differed greatly from other Western TV series as it used flashbacks to Caine's days as a pupil in the Shaolin Temple and action scenes were often filmed in quirky slow motion. Even with all its gimmicks, *Kung Fu* only ran two and a half seasons, though one of its directors, Jerry Thorpe, won the 1972–3 Emmy for Outstanding Directorial Achievement In Drama (Series) for the episode *An Eye for an Eye*.

Even with the 1972 appearance of Caine, the central character was still portrayed by a white actor. Bruce Lee had served as consultant to the show whilst it was in development, but when he applied for the lead role he was rejected out of hand; the producers told him they felt a Chinese actor would not be accepted as a hero by the American television audience. This was despite the fact that Lee was already an established international movie star.

Another factor in the death of the TV Western was probably the development of the television contract system in the Seventies. In the 50's and 60's the networks tended to buy series for one season and it was rare that a show was cancelled before that season was up; hence the vast majority of TV shows in the 50's and 60's ran at least one year. By the early 70's this had changed and the networks began cancelling series after only a few months or in some cases, weeks. Many series in the 70's only managed to last one month. Of course this was bound to be detrimental to series of any genre and many shows were cancelled before they had any chance to build up an audience, and it is significant that two of the 70's' biggest hits, *The Waltons* and *All in the Family,* were both on screen several months before winning respectable ratings. They were given the benefit of doubt. Historically, TV Westerns had always taken time to become hits. *Gunsmoke* and *Bonanza* were both on a full season apiece before they broke into the Top Twenty. Similarly, *The Virginian* had aired for two seasons before it cracked into the Top 25. Many of the Western TV shows cancelled after less than a year on the air (such as *Dirty Sally* and *Nichols*) may have turned out to be hits had they been allowed more time to find their following. As it was, many TV shows of the 70's probably went off the air before viewers even realized they were on.

All the Westerns of the seventies attempted to differ to some degree from their predecessors but when a series did repeat a theme from earlier shows (such as *The Cowboys* with the cattle drive and *Oregon Trail* with the wagon train), it was a theme which had not been over done by previous Westerns. Unfortunately this burst of originality came too late and admittedly many were poor quality, lack luster affairs anyway. When viewers had the choice of watching high quality sitcoms such as *All in the Family* and *M*A*S*H,* they found no reason to watch yet another Western with only average writing, direction and action and also a latent sense of desperation.

In 1971 long running *The Virginian* went off the air. In 1973, following the death of Dan Blocker and a schedule move to a new time, *Bonanza* was lost after its glorious 14 year run. One of its problems shared by all Western productions had been the spiraling production costs. Lorne Green had predicted in 1972, 'Maybe the show will end when it becomes uneconomic. All the costs have risen. It used to cost $90,000 to do a show. Now it's more like $200,000. There are 14 years of re-run property. Would adding a 15th year (at those costs) do very much?' (*LA Herald Examiner* 25 October 1972).

There could be no denying it; the television Western was in serious decline although 1974 saw the debut of *Little House on the Prairie*. Whether or not this show can be considered a real Western, it did prove immensely successful, and it gave the genre its last sniff of oxygen. The series ranked in the Top 25 shows for several years and lasted a decade.

In 1975 *Gunsmoke* finally fell after its phenomenal 20 year run and the 1975–6 season saw no new Western TV series for the first time since *The Lone Ranger* debuted in 1949. The 1976–7 saw the debut of two short lived Western series, *The Quest* featuring Kurt Russell as a white man raised among Native Americans and Tim Matheson as his San Francisco educated brother, searching for their lost sister. The series had the misfortune of being up against that season's smash hit, *Charlie's Angels*, and it disappeared after only three months.

*How the West Was Won* featured James Arness as Zeb Macahan, a rugged mountain man left in charge of his brother's four children. The series was vast in scope, and was filmed on location in Utah, Colorado, Arizona, and Southern California. It left the air after seven months. *Oregon Trail* vanished in a matter of weeks.

In the following seasons Westerns became rarities. For a mere few months in 1979, CBS aired *Young Maverick*, a spin off of *Maverick* centering on Ben Maverick, Beau's son and Bret's second cousin. A sequel to *Maverick, Bret Maverick* (featuring James Garner once more in the title role) aired on NBC through much of the 80–81 season.

Throughout the 50's and deep into the 70's, no one would have dreamed that the television Western was destined to end up a victim of its own success; lying defeated by its massed enemies. The United States of the post Bicentennial era was no longer the land the Western had celebrated and America was not the place it had once been.

Set in the past where history could be manipulated to serve contemporary purposes, it had been filled with symbolic action relating to the popular mentality of society. The genre may not have been intended as calculated indoctrination, nor historical reconstruction, but tales of the Old West were meaningful secularized

American myths that served their particular public at that moment and TV Westerns undoubtedly flourished because they meshed with the widely accepted social and political views of the times in which they existed.

There is really no reason why the Western should be any less appropriate to today's audiences than for those of the 50's, 60's and 70's. Romantically and optimistically the genre's ability to define America's mythic heritage suggests that even in contemporary terms the Western was an unlikely candidate for cultural oblivion. In the 1970's scholars believed the Western was indestructible and would survive on many different levels. It provided both an escape and a challenge. Did the emergence of technology, with an emphasis on specialization, social control and power wielded by elitists, effectively destroy the Western? Did the individualist hero, using physical strength and moral courage to rescue innocents inevitably give way to corporate champions, professional heroes who acted for money in a technocratic society where mass production and consumption suppressed individuality in favor of the mass market? The prowess of the professional hero depends more on technical strength than strength of character. Increasingly the Westerner was replaced by the secret agent and the demographic shift from rural to urban foreshadowed the demise of the Western. An urban age demanded an urban hero; and the secret agent, an insider-outsider, was the updated gunfighter with added urbanity and cosmopolitanism thrown in for good measure. Who could believe in the dusty, low-budget West anymore when the heads of studios were searching for the massive financial successes of *Star Wars*?

Social thought in America had changed whilst the Western failed to make the suitable transition. And television programs in America can only survive if they win a mass audience and substantial fortunes. An audience of a few million is not enough. Programs that attract a mass audience are retained and those which don't pull in enough viewers are terminated.

However, the failure of the genre in recent times begs the question, has it temporarily passed out of favor or has the theme of the Western ceased to be relevant to Americans? Was it undermined, overexposed, or was it destroyed by more profound shifts in audience attitude? If it is dead as an art form, what does that imply for the moral and ideological messages traditionally communicated through the genre?

# POSTSCRIPT

'The Western belongs to every nation. We have no proprietary rights. I don't know of any country that isn't intimately familiar with the Western.'

Lee J. Cobb, 1970.

*Monument Valley, Arizona*

A genre in which description and dialogue are lean, and the landscape spectacular, is well suited to a visual medium. Western movies, usually filmed in desolate corners of California, Arizona, Utah, Colorado or Wyoming, made the landscape not just a vivid backdrop but a character in the movie.

'I can't help but long for a real return to the Western. Westerns are true Americana. They tell of the struggles of our ancestors… the story of the West is inspiring and terrible, idealistic and bloody, sublime and atrocious. It emphasizes this country's best and worst characteristics. The good parts of the story inspire us. The bad parts warn us of what we have to do to make things better. Even though many Westerns have only a light connection to the true history of the West, I believe exposure to these motion pictures can stimulate kids to learn more about what their forefathers endured to make the United States one nation, from sea to shining sea. I wish the kids of today knew more about the early pioneers and what they went through. Western films and television programs can help to induce this rich, colorful history, and I am heartened every time I see that a new Western has been made.'

Clayton Moore

**THE** last few years has seen the arrival of first *Deadwood* and then Spielberg's epic, *Into the West*. Either could be taken as an attempt to revive the Western genre on television but may simply be a vague salute to past glories and certainly neither can be seen as a Western in the most traditional sense.

In 1987 J. Fred MacDonald wrote the TV Western's obituary in his book, *Who Shot the Sheriff?* Declaring that it was 'no longer relevant or tasteful.' He noted the irony that 'The generation [baby boomers] that once made the Western the most prolific form of TV programming has lived to see a rare occurrence in American popular culture: the death of genre.' Indeed, between 1970 and 1988, fewer than 28 new Westerns in total were introduced as regular network series. MacDonald believed that, with the exception of the early 1980's of made-for-TV movies, the thunder of the Western had been silenced in prime time forever.

Even so, after the publication of his book, the TV Western did have at least one more moment of glory with the adaptation of Larry McMurtry's epic Western novel, *Lonesome Dove*, which became the television event of the 1988–9 season. The highest rated miniseries in five years, *Lonesome Dove* documented the final days of a life-long partnership between two characters who represent distinctly different models of manhood: Woodrow Call and Augustus 'Gus' McCrae. Call enacted the strong, silent tradition of the western hero. Like John Wayne's characters in *Red River* (Tom Dunson) and *The Searchers* (Ethan Edwards), Call was a powerful, tireless, generally humorless leader who outwardly feared no enemy, though his rugged individualism drove him toward the misery of self-imposed isolation. Call was masterfully portrayed by Tommy Lee Jones – but it was Robert Duval's performance as McCrae that stole the show. Where Call's outlook was utilitarian, Gus's was romantic. In some ways, Gus resembled the funny, spirited side-kicks of Westerns past: Andy Devine in *Stagecoach*, Walter Brennan in *Red River*, Pat Brady in *The Roy Rogers Show,* or Dennis Weaver and Ken Curtis in *Gunsmoke*. But in *Lonesome Dove*, the eccentric sidekick achieved equal status with the strong silent hero – and as a counter-point to Call, Gus rewrote the meaning of the Western hero, going a long way toward explaining why *Lonesome Dove* attracted a mammoth audience in which women viewers actually outnumbered the men. For a story in a genre that has traditionally been written almost exclusively by men for men, this was a major accomplishment and a ratings winner.

At the conclusion of the film Call was approached by a young newspaper reporter from San Antonio. An agent of the expanding civilization that Call has spent a lifetime loathing and serving, the reporter presses Call for an interview, 'They say you are a man of vision.'

Call replies, 'A man of vision, you say? Yes, a hell of a vision.' The words spoke of his disillusionment with the dream of Montana as a 'Cattleman's Paradise'; a vision that had inspired the tragic trail drive. They also put the full stop to the great last stand of the cowboy on the small screen. 'Hell of a vision' takes on profound connotations as an epitaph, a fitting epitaph for the television Western.

Socially relevant and humanistic Westerns like *Gunsmoke* and *Bonanza*, had succeeded because they had boasted stunning casts and crew and supportive networks behind them, which had allowed them time to build the audience, but networks seldom go out on a limb today; there is too much to lose and they no longer have that luxury of time or finance. There may have been some hope in recent surveys that indicated viewers would enjoy seeing more television Westerns. The success of *Lonesome Dove, Paradise* and *The Young Riders*, together with the popularity of *Dr Quinn, Medicine Woman*, indicated that there was still a potential audience out there. Perhaps all that is needed now is that magical mix of timing, talent and finance coming together in one place.

It would require a miraculous recovery to regain any relevance as a popular diversion; the very qualities of the Western seem no longer acceptable to the mass audience. Its mystique and symbolism, once questioned, left its messages incongruent with contemporary social reality and its stories unwelcome, its politics controversial and problematic.

The mythic resonance of the television Western had transcended its commercial vitality; which meant that people continued making them, sometimes even in defiance of commercial demand. Those old shows touched something deep and vital, which is why they have still never been quite finished off. America's gift to the world will continue to make brief, colorful, flourishing appearances, and will be both powerful and compelling.

Although from the 1980's onward there have been a number of stuttering and short-lived efforts to recapture the Old West it has been the more unusual series that have proved there might still be a future for the television Western. Of these, more than any other, the arrival of HBO's *Deadwood* has attracted sustained attention and with its success the networks should be scrambling to imitate it; so far, however, nothing much has happened. Whilst it has caught the imagination of a dedicated cult audience, many others find it too profane and uncomfortable. Generally, the Western is still seen as old hat, geared toward an older audience than most of the networks are looking to pursue. While *Lonesome Dove* still stands as one of the great achievements of the last 20 years, the Western itself has pretty much gone the way of the old-school variety/comedy show. Not long ago, USA Network aired a Western-mystery hybrid, *Peacemakers* – sort of a frontier *CSI* – but canceled it after its promising start because the audience profile was simply too old. *Deadwood* is a more immediate attempt to revitalize the genre with its rugged, deglamorized settings, its gallery of complex and fascinating characters and its self-consciously profane tone.

*Deadwood* was created by *NYPD Blue's* David Milch. It is interesting that HBO, Milch and many others instrumentally associated with the production hasten to stress, perhaps for reasons of commercial caution, how un-Western *Deadwood* really is, because in reality the program has its boots as deeply stuck in the genre as any John Wayne cowboy ever did.

Now with *Deadwood* comes not only the first new hit TV Western in years, but also what the producers claim is one of the most authentic portraits ever of life in an Old West gold mining town. Everything certainly looks right, but Milch has created a West designed to shock and draw modern viewers. Novelist Pete Dexter wrote a book in the mid-1980's called *Deadwood*. It featured Calamity Jane and Wild Bill Hickok, along with Al Swearengen, owner of the Gem Theater; Seth Bullock, a hardware store owner, and his partner Sol Star; all are featured in *Deadwood*. In Dexter's original text there is little cursing.

Dexter, who has no connection to the series, says he did a lot of research for his novel and spent time in the Black Hills. He never came across the use of that much profanity. 'It seems to me it's condescending to the viewer to think that throwing those kinds of words often makes a style point.'

Mary Kopko, director of the Adams Museum in the real town of Deadwood, won't confirm the use of profanity but points out that a law was passed making profanity illegal in 1878, which suggests that it was used to excess in the town.

But Dexter says, 'The idea a law was passed doesn't mean it was an everyday occurrence. If the FCC passes a law against people ripping off Janet Jackson's top, it's not because that happened all the time, but because it happened once.'

Other historians say it's more a matter of degree. Rick Slatta, author of several books on cowboys including *The Mythical West: An Encyclopedia of Legend, Lore, and Popular Culture* (ABC–CLIO), says that *Bonanza's* portrait of cowboys was 'sanitized to the nth degree.'

But he says *Deadwood* has gone to the other extreme. 'Cowboy and frontier types; these were vulgar people. I think HBO, in typical Hollywood fashion, has taken some social element and exaggerated it 100-fold.'

The high-blown oratory and purposeful deceit is classic *Deadwood*, in a television Western that has rescued the genre from a half century of irrelevance by re-imagining itself as a savage, grotesquely comic business parable.

*Deadwood's* creator smashes the museum relic that was the Western in order to bring the genre back to life. The series is more interested in settlers than gunfighters. There are no strong, silent types. He argues that real frontiersmen shot their mouths off before taking to guns. And everybody cursed to prove they were unafraid, that they belonged and, finally, as an expression of joy at having escaped the bounds of civilization back east.

Neither is the 1876 mining town saga a soothing pastoral. Forget about craggy South Dakota bluffs and rolling plains; we don't even see much sky here. The land exists for gold miners to exploit, while the town survives by exploiting gold miners. Perhaps the series works so well for modern audiences because it is an urban western. Every character is defined by their job.

Despite the successes and failures of Deadwood, the Western genre has certainly not suddenly sprung back to its former schedule position with television producers. The costs involved in making a Western have proved to be the limiting factor; a consideration that Steven Spielberg seemed hardly to notice when he decided which project to turn his hand to next.

Proclaimed as TNT network's 'most ambitious original production,' DreamWorks Television Productions teamed with the network to present an epic tale of the American West. Executive producer Spielberg hoped to show what the building of the West was like in his 12 hour miniseries, *Into The West*, which follows two multi-generational families, one settlers and the other Native American. They each tell the story of the development of the West from their own point of view.

This begins with intrepid young Eastern wanderer, Jacob Wheeler heading west to explore the land with Jedediah Smith, one of the West's famous mountain men. He became infatuated with the Indian tribe he came across and eventually married one of them.

The only sympathetic white characters Spielberg introduced during this story were the ones that love and appreciate the Indians. The story felt somewhat unbalanced in the telling and the only historical references save the building of the Trans Continental railroad, are those dealing directly with the various Indian wars. Both the war with Mexico and the Civil War are treated as entirely incidental to the narrative.

But the biggest problem with this effort is the portrayal of the Indians themselves. The real history of Native Americans is rich with inter tribal war, faltering and fluctuating alliances, suspicion and hatreds of each other that goes back hundreds of years before the first European set foot upon the New World.

Of course, America's claims to 'life, liberty and the pursuit of happiness' for all men was never extended to the Native Americans just as it was withheld from women and many other minorities.

All in all the complexity of the era is undermined in this project which portrayed the Native Americans as homogeneously as any 1930's Western movie did, though biased in the Indians favor instead of the favor of the triumphant cowboy. It is a shame that Spielberg wasted an opportunity to show us something we had never seen before on film but instead chose to portray just another politically correct and substance free amalgam of our history.

It also left us nowhere near answering the question we started out with, 'Where Have All the Cowboys Gone?'

Television continues to provide us with plenty of documentary scheduling about the Wild West, really good material too, investigating the old legends in depth, and from time to time a great television Western movie rears its head. But it does, sadly, look as though we have all ridden into the sunset as far as the Western goes. Shows that were too expensive to make, too many television executives demanding instant audiences, too many viewers demanding too much instant gratification, too many outdated moralities in a changed world, too much political correctness, too much competition...

... maybe it is time to bury the Western with its boots on...

... but let's never forget the glory that was the television Western

# SOURCES

Louis B Mayer Library at American Film Institute Special Collections

Television Genres – (The Open University 2003)

*The Movie Book of the Western* – edited by Ian Cameron and Douglas Pye (Studio Vista, 1996)

*I was the Masked Man* – Clayton Moore with Frank Thompson (Taylor Publishing, 1998)

*Tall in the Saddle* – Peggy Thomson & Saeko Usukawa (Chronicle Books 1998)

*Cowboy How Hollywood Invented The Wild West* – Holly George-Warren (Readers Digest, 2002)

*The Crowded Prairie* – Michael Coyne (IB Tauris, 1997)

*The Davy Crockett Craze* – Paul F. Anderson (R & G Productions, 1996)

Margaret Herrick Library National Film Information Service

*Television Westerns Episode Guide 1949–1996* – Harris M. Lentz iii. (McFarland & Company, May 1997)

*The Great Cowboy Stars of Movies and Television* – Lee Miller (Arlington House, 1979)

*James Arness: An Autobiography* by, James E. Wise Jr. (McFarland & Company September, 2001)

*TV: the most popular art* – Horace Newcomb (Anchor Press; [1st ed.] edition 1974)

*The Western From Silents to the Seventies* – Fenin and Everson (Penguin (Non-Classics); Rev. ed edition, 31 March 1977).

*Television Westerns: Major and Minor Series, 1946–1978* – Richard West (McFarland & Company, December 1987)

*Saturday Morning TV* (Hardcover) – Gary H. Grossman (Random House Value Publishing, 12 December 1988)

*Hollywood Cinema* – Richard Maltby (Oxford, UK 2003)

*Who Shot the Sheriff? The Rise and Fall of the Television Western* – J. Fred MacDonald (Praeger Publishers, 9 December 1986)

*Bonanza, A viewers Guide to the TV legend*, by David Greenland (R & G Productions, 1997).

# FURTHER READING

Barabas, SuzAnne and Gabor Barabas. Gunsmoke: *A Complete History and Analysis of the Legendary Broadcast Series with a Comprehensive Episode-By-Episode Guide to Both the Radio and Television Programs.* Jefferson, North Carolina: McFarland, 1990.

Gordon, S. *Gunsmoke's Chester.* Look (New York), 12 September 1961.

Jackson, Ronald. *Classic TV Westerns: A Pictorial History.* Seacaucus, New Jersey: Carol, 1994.

MacDonald, J. Fred. *Who Shot The Sheriff: The Rise And Fall Of The Television Western.* New York: Praeger, 1987.

Marsden, Michael T. and Jack Nachbar. *The Modern Popular Western: Radio, Television, Film and Print.* In, *A Literary History of the American West. Sponsored by The Western Literature Association. Fort Worth, Texas*: Texas Christian University Press, 1987.

Morhaim, Joe. *Why Gunsmoke's Amanda Blake, James Arness Won't Kiss.* TV Guide (Radnor, Pennsylvania), 15 March 1958.

Peel, John. *Gunsmoke Years: The Behind-The-Scenes Story: Exclusive Interviews with the Writers and Directors: A Complete Guide to Every Episode Aired: The Longest Running Network Television Drama Ever!.* Las Vegas, Nevada: Pioneer, 1989.

West, Richard. *Television Westerns: Major And Minor Series, 1946–1978.* Jefferson, North Carolina: McFarland, 1987.

Whitney, Dwight. *Why Gunsmoke Keeps Blazing.* TV Guide (Radnor, Pennsylvania), 6 December 1958.

*What's Gunsmoke's Secret?* TV Guide (Radnor, Pennsylvania), 22 August 1970.

Yoggy, Gary A. *Riding the Video Range: The Rise and Fall of the Western on Television.* Jefferson, North Carolina: McFarland, 1994.

# INDEX

Also by C. McGivern

*John Wayne; A Giant Shadow*
*The Lost Films of John Wayne*


And coming soon


*The John Wayne Centenary*
*Watching the Detectives*
*Claire Trevor; Hollywood Queen of the 'Bs'*